Child Development 0–8

Child Development 0–8

A Journey through the Early Years

Maria Robinson

Open University Press

Open University Press
McGraw-Hill Education
McGraw-Hill House
Shoppenhangers Road
Maidenhead
Berkshire
England
SL6 2QL

email: enquiries@openup.co.uk
world wide web: www.openup.co.uk

and Two Penn Plaza, New York, NY 10121–2289, USA

First published 2008
Reprinted 2008

A catalogue record of this book is available from the British Library

ISBN–10: 0335220975 (pb) 0335220983 (hb)
ISBN–13: 9780335220977 (pb) 9780335220984 (hb)

Library of Congress Cataloguing-in-Publication Data
CIP data applied for

Typeset by YHT Ltd, London
Printed by Bell and Bain Ltd., Glasgow
www.bell-bain.co.uk

The McGraw·Hill Companies

I not only use all the brains I have, but all that I can borrow.

(Woodrow Wilson)[1]

Contents

Foreword

During 20 years involvement in early years work, I have observed that many parents/carers and practitioners seem to intuitively grasp that a child's emotional world view, understanding of their experiences and ability to learn are closely linked. In addition, they also understand that children need to have direct experiences through reciprocal interactions with supportive and sensitive carers together with opportunities for play and exploration, in order to absorb the properties of their environment and transform these into an understanding of themselves and the people and objects around them. Adults observe that development takes place over time, that there are key shifts in development which occur at broadly similar time intervals and that infants and young children need to imitate and practice prior to gaining a new skill.

However, in my experience as a health visitor, teacher and lecturer to a range of professions as well as parents and foster carers/adopters, I have noted that not many texts pull together the detailed and in-depth information from different disciplines *and* the observable, time-related, developmental shifts taking place in the first years of life. Among all this, there is the reality, vulnerability and neediness of an infant or young child trying to make sense of the world in which they find themselves.

Personal experience and professional practice has taught me that in order to understand the individual child, understanding developmental processes is not something 'divorced' from real practice but an essential part of it. Therefore this book is not about any particular theory or theorist but rather an accumulation of many hours (years!) of observation and research into a range of developmental topics. Ultimately, there are two aims for this book: one is to bring together what seem to be the shifts and changes within the early years – the patterns and threads of the web of development – and the second is to share my understanding about what it can mean to be a growing child.

Acknowledgements

I would like to express my sincere thanks to friends and colleagues Julie Beams, Stephanie Davydaitis and Rosemary Gibbins for their valuable suggestions and support when struggling with the weight of information, the editors for their constant patience, advice and support through the odd crisis, to wonderful friends who put up with the dramas and to all those named (and unnamed) researchers whose work has underpinned this book. Finally, but certainly not least, to my husband Stuart for his unstinting support – especially at hair-tearing moments – and to our two dogs, Max and Toby, for keeping me sane!

1   Introduction

One of my earliest memories is being in the middle of our local market and screaming and crying at being told it was now 'time to go home'. I had been taken out for the afternoon by a friend of my adoptive mother and the poor woman had to cope with a child who was behaving very 'badly'. It was many years later when a series of coincidences led to access of my adoption papers that I gained insight into my behaviour. My earliest years had been marked by many changes of carer and/or dwelling and one of the methods used was to take me out for the afternoon and then 'going home' meant not the place (and sometimes not the people) that I had left earlier. As a child of around 4 years – not long adopted – the possibility of yet another move must have terrified me. What the adult made of my behaviour I will never know. I can only remember my flailing self, the concrete floor of the market, the hand and arm of the adult and a dim, peripheral awareness of stalls full of fruit and vegetables and an all pervading feeling of anguish.

What is interesting in thinking about this incident is to consider what the adult may have made of my behaviour – how did my mother's friend perceive me? Would she have thought I was 'out of control', 'spoilt', would she have felt able to 'manage' me or would I have frightened/dismayed her? On the other hand, perhaps if she had some understanding of my background, she may still have felt helpless, anxious or even angry, but may have also felt some degree of empathy and desire to comfort. In other words, what an adult needed to know in order to respond to such behaviour with insight and empathy would be the following:

- knowledge of my history
- the level to which I was able to understand my own emotions – and manage them – that is, my developmental or 'maturational' level
- what meaning the context or particular situation might have for me
- recognition of the adult's crucial role in being able to 'contain' my feelings

These factors would have supported the adult in making sense of what I was doing as it would have helped her see the situation from my point of view – which is what all adults who care for and work with children fundamentally need to do, that is, to try to assess the child's view of the world as it is perceived by them.

Sharing information about how the power and passion of feelings and the developing levels of maturation in the triad of brain, body and mind influences the behaviour of very young children has become something of a deeply personal campaign through teaching and writing. It is not just because studying development (especially about emotions) has gradually helped me understand something of the prejudices, fears and anxieties that have influenced both my professional work and relationships. It is also because I have learned that such feelings can sometimes get in the way of any of us achieving a sense of inner contentment and can colour the way in which we view other people and, crucially, the children we care for and work with. Knowing about our early years helps us not only to understand children whether as a parent/carer, early years practitioner, health visitor, child minder, social worker or anyone in the allied professions that come across children – but it also widens and deepens our knowledge about ourselves, which in turn, frequently leads to greater understanding of the child. It is therefore, in my view, essential knowledge for anyone with more than passing contact with children. Furthermore, far from being a topic that is 'dry as dust' with endless discussions about theorists, it is a subject that reflects the nature of development itself – dynamic, changing, exciting and challenging.

However, 'getting to grips' with a topic which is so universally pertinent brings with it a raft of responsibilities. It is safe to say that the wealth of research on brain development, attachment, thinking and learning does point to these early years being important in setting the foundations of our ongoing behaviour throughout life. This does not mean, of course, that our early experiences set our personalities and behavioural style in a 'frozen' state without the opportunity for change or further development. Thankfully, we always have opportunities for insight and change. We can continue to learn new skills, abilities and ways of behaving at any age with the opportunities for life experiences (which may even be initially very negative) to deepen our understanding, compassion and empathy over time (as well as perhaps learning to hang-glide and snowboard!) Nevertheless, it is also true that the impact of early experiences resonate at some level within us throughout life. What can change is our ability to understand the 'why' and 'what', which brings me full circle to the importance of understanding these early years and taking on board, as a society, what that means.

The crucial point is what we, as adults – whether in our professional and/or personal lives – do to children matters. This is not about 'parent blaming' – a concept which sadly often seems to sabotage discussion about the impact of the early years. Recognizing the importance of these years, the crucial adult role and the resonance of early experiences does not and should not mean 'finger pointing' at parents. Instead, such recognition could (and should!) imbue being a parent with the proper respect and status that such a responsible undertaking requires. It should also mean acknowledging that a style of parenting frequently reflects the parents' own history so what they do and how they do it will either repeat or contradict what they experienced. Knowledge about the emotional underpinning of being a parent would seem to be a very useful topic for pre-natal classes by supporting parents in recognizing, understanding and perhaps even forgiving some of the very mixed feelings they may have about their child, both when born and as he/she grows older. These ideas also apply to practitioners because any role that involves such close relationships with children will also activate individual ideas and expectations about children, bringing to the surface emotions the adult may not fully understand.

From the child's point of view, such knowledge in their adult carers encourages parents and/or professionals to have realistic expectations so that they do not ascribe motives, ideas and levels of behaviour that are way beyond the child's abilities. A classic and simple example is the expectation of very young children to 'share' and 'take turns'. The child who grabs or pushes in is sometimes labelled as being 'naughty' when the reality may be that the child has not reached the stage of maturity when they can learn to wait or understand that giving something to someone or taking turns does not mean giving something up for ever or never having a turn. It also means that the adult may take into account the circumstances surrounding the child's life, what experiences they may already have had, and may assess their behaviour in light of the child's ability to manage these experiences and any strategies they may have developed to cope. Such strategies of course will be profoundly influenced by the child's level of development at the time their experiences occurred, and whether they were 'acute' or 'chronic' in their manifestations. The child will do what they can with the 'tools' they have available and with children their 'toolbox' is very small.

So, what is it all about?

Human development is about anticipation, attainment and assessment. That is, what is going to happen, what is happening and to what level – something we all think about from time to time. For the parent, while (hopefully) enjoying the current achievements of their baby, they may also be anticipating when the child is able to do the next expected skill or ability. For example, a child's first step is a huge 'milestone' both for parents and child. For a child, unable to reflect yet on their inner world, the emphasis may be on becoming 'bigger' or older – ready for 'big school'. As an older child, we wonder about the changes invoked by puberty and later as an adult we may think about what may lie ahead for us in middle and old age. Outer physical and/or biological changes seem to provide a sense of continuity in the day-to-day progression of life as the years pass. Our inner lives change too, both in response to experience and in terms of developmental maturation. As children we do not think the same way as adults – literally so, as functional magnetic resonance imaging (fMRI) scans can demonstrate. Our understanding of our experiences shifts and changes over time in ways that are just as monumental as when we take our first step. Before we can think about the world and our experience, we have to first get to know it. We need to be able to have certain basic concepts in place, have ways of communicating and understand the differences between all the different types of experiences we encounter. This means that we must have some solid 'markers' to help us to make sense of all the information we encounter, such as the permanence of objects, stable categories of different objects and, crucially, people whom we can trust and whose behaviour we can anticipate.

These emotional and physical 'markers' provide fascinating questions such as, how do we learn that an object, viewed from different angles and in different positions, is the same object or that someone or something we cannot see at a particular moment still exists? We expect the faces of the people we know to remain constant. We trust that when we walk out of a room, the furniture will not disappear or move about.[1] We 'know' that a building we see from the side and which is on our left, is the same building if we turn round and approach it so that the building is now on our right. However, a telling example that we do indeed learn such 'truths' is given by Temple Grandin – a professor of animal management, who also has autism. In the above scenario, she would have to retrace her steps to view the building from the original viewpoint in order to 'check out' her understanding. For humans (and indeed for many primates and other animals), facial expression and eye gaze provides a great deal of information about feelings, interest and levels of involvement and curiosity – but how do we learn this in the first place? How do we humans share our understanding of happiness, sadness, fear or anger? What I have noticed is that while such feelings can be expressed in many different ways, there are nevertheless boundaries to such expressions, which are not only culturally or socially influenced but also appear to have an innate boundary which allows us to understand the particular emotion without too much confusion. The behaviour of someone expressing great sadness, even if accompanied by strong gesture and loud vocals, is as accurately assessed as being overwhelmed with grief as someone who is standing quietly with only tears or repeated swallowing and/or a trembling lip. We 'know' what emotions are and we also ascribe particular types of thoughts, inner feelings and styles of behaviour to these emotions and so they are familiar and recognizable when we encounter them.

To turn again to the environment, we recognize 'animals' and that there are groups or types of animals. We know about trees and that they are different from bushes and birds. We name, know and perceive colours in our world and we have a range of sensory experiences, including knowledge about our body parts (and can point to them), what position we are in (standing, sitting, lying, walking forwards) and where we are in relation to any other people whom we may be with and the objects surrounding us. What is even more fascinating is that not only are we aware of our physical position relative to what is in our environment, but also their relationship to where we are – in other words, our understanding of spatial relationships.

The full realization that all this 'world knowledge' has to be learned comes from the studies by researchers such as Damasio, Sachs and Rama-chandran of people with brain/body trauma and the strange phenomena that such trauma can induce. This includes not recognizing faces or parts of the body belonging to the self, difficulty in remembering the sequence required to make a cup of tea, getting dressed, or knowing where one's mouth is in order to eat.

Of course, we are not only physical beings but, as indicated above, we are beings who feel and react with a rich inner world composed of a mixture of our physiological state – our general internal feelings of calm or anxiety, fear or pleasure accompanied by the (usually) unconscious workings of our bodily organs and limbs – and the sense of who we are as an individual. Closely linked to all this is our own particular view of the world and the people within it as generally accepting or rejecting, and our behavioural style will reflect the sum of all the different influences pertaining to this inner world. Mirroring the slow growth of our skills and abilities in the physical and sensory domain, our inner world-view also develops over time based on our experiences, especially our interactions with our caregivers and particularly in the early months and years allied with our memory of all these experiences.

Where do we start?

The whole premise of this book is a journey through the early years – but a journey which instead of being simply in one direction will seem rather like a maze with many twists and turns as we examine the brain, the senses, how we learn, begin to think, how we feel and gradually construct the realization of being a 'me' with a 'you' as well. When we look at all these different bits of information (travelling in one direction and then another) and put them all together, we will see that there is a coherent 'shape' and that development is not a set of separate domains (physical, social and emotional, language and learning) but an integrated whole. That is not easily identified when reading literature on development which is not specific to the early years. A truly holistic view of development linking research findings to phases in the life span appears to be limited. For example, there are texts devoted to emotions (Damasio (1999, 2003) and Sroufe (1995)); to emotional regulation and neuroscience (Le Doux (1998, 2002), Panksepp (1998) and Schore, (1994)); to psychoanalysis and neuroscience (Kaplan-Solms and Solms (2000), Solms and Turnbull (2002)); to language and/or cognition (Sherry (2000), Springer, and Deutsch (1998) and Butterworth (1999)); and emotions, intelligence and philosophy (Nussbaum (2001)). Apart from Schore (1994) and Panksepp (1998), the latter whose particular interest is in human and animal emotions and the place of evolution in human development, the links that can be made between early development and the theoretical approaches and research findings from adult work expressed in these texts are not often explicit. However, by understanding this progress in an integrated way, the relevance of delay, dysfunction or superior progress in any individual aspect of development and/or behaviour can then be assessed from a wider perspective. However, there is a sea change occurring especially in the areas of neuroscience and education. For example, Blakemore and Frith (2005).

A 'holistic' view of development does find support in the Birth to Three Matters Framework (DfES, 2002), soon to be integrated in England with the Curriculum Guidance for the Foundation Stage (DfEE/QCA, 2000) into the Early Years Foundation Stage (DfES 2006/7) which covers from birth to 5 years. The Birth to Three Framework has its emphasis on seeing development as an integrated progression of slowly accumulating complexity in skills and abilities. The very terminology used to describe the different aspects of development, that is, a healthy child, a skilful communicator, a competent learner and a strong child, moves away from the neat 'packages' of development which have been used so often in the past.

Running through this book are the threads of my own views of what constitutes development and I have shamelessly borrowed the terminology of the Birth to Three Matters Framework to describe these threads, and have therefore identified four aspects to development and the components that seem to go with them.[2] Paradoxically, while wanting development to be thought about and reflected upon 'holistically' and emphasizing that practitioners and carers must approach understanding children in this way, we need to examine these areas separately in order to bring more sharply into focus how they link together (Table 1.1).

All of these aspects and components require a combination of genetic inheritance – both familial and human species specific – and experience. Futhermore, there are additional processes which seem to be part of the human experience which support growth and change including not only close social interactions and identification with others, but also imitation, curiosity and play/pretence, all of which appear to have an essential role in the way in which human children acquire and organize their experiences, which I discuss in other chapters.

It is apparent to me that development has a time trajectory. Certain time frames seem to be closely linked with very particular changes in different

Table 1.1   Aspects and components of development

Brain function	Sensory integration	Emotions/ feelings	Thought and communication	Physical development
Level of integrity of brain organization linked to both genetic and experiential factors	The level of functioning of each sensory system	Awareness of feelings and the sense of a feeling of self	The capacity to frame experience into internal imagery/internal 'language'	Awareness of the bodily self and allied spatial awareness
Level of integrity of the communication mechanisms within the brain	The commonalities and differences between the sensory systems in the processing of information	Ability to recognize emotions in self and others	The capacity for communication, its use and expression via facial expression, body language and spoken (or sign) language	Capacity for movement, both gross and fine motor
The health and functioning of the structures of the brain	The rate of maturation of each sensory system	Ability to express or contain emotions within social and cultural frameworks	Understanding of expression and gesture in others	Physical growth and change over time and rates of maturation
Specificity or otherwise of roles and functions within the brain	Impact of sensory systems on the formation of a sense of bodily and psychological 'self'	Type and quality of interactions including attachment formation	The presence (or not) of 'innate' knowledge	Level of integrity of reflexes, balance and coordination
The rate of maturation of different brain areas	Impact of sensory perceptions and thereby internal reactions to day-to-day experience	Ability to manage emotional reactions/ feelings to daily experience	The capacity for imitation, play and imagination in learning	

aspects of development, for example, a cluster of growing complexity in skills and abilities between 7 and 12 months of age. All species need the passage of chronological time to develop, but humans, higher primates and some other mammals such as elephants and dolphins seem to need much longer periods to acquire the skills and understanding they need to function within their particular world because of their specific complexities. However, what seems to be true for many species is that time provides a framework in which aspects of development can optimally take place and which if 'missed' may not lead necessarily to the lack of attainment of a skill but possibly a diminishing of its potential. While our biological clocks provide the prompts for sleep/wake and feeding, it is interesting to speculate whether a similar mechanism prompts the transition from one phase of development to the next, that is, from crawling to standing by oneself – providing that the relevant experience is available.[3] As individuals, we also follow a 'personal' timetable[4] as well as the 'global' timetable for the acquisition of human skills so that, within this general time frame, as children and adults we can exhibit wide variations in our capabilities – I still cannot tie my shoelaces!

Time in this developmental context, however, means both linear (or chronological) time, whereby the brain appears to have some intrinsic maturational timetable, and 'timing', whereby the impact of the type and quality of experience encountered by an infant and young child may vary in different ways dependent on the particular phase of maturation that might be occurring within the brain. For example, some emotional trauma may influence a child's ability to take advantage of play experiences within the context of the child's current abilities. Therefore, I suggest that linear time and development are intrinsically bound together. Hadders-Algra and Forssberg, (2002) highlight the importance of time in neural development in their discussion on motor systems. They identify 'phylogenetic' skills, which seem to occur across cultures at approximately the same ages, such as crawling, pointing, walking and talking, and which were reasonably thought to be due to the 'orderly genetic sequence' which resulted in the formation of general developmental rules. The concept of 'developmental milestones' for example grew out of these ideas.

While the idea of development being 'linear' or 'stage-like' appears to be currently reviewed (Schore, 1994; Fischer, 2005), nevertheless there is a substantial body of research and general observation which identifies periods of significant change. Examples of noted 'shifts' in development are given in Table 1.2.[5] This table also suggests a 'logic' of maturation within a broad chronological time frame from birth to puberty, a 'putting in place' of the requirements for the child to become an adult and take their place in the world.

The information that I have drawn from several sources indicates there is an overall consensus that 2–3 months, 8–12 months, 14–18 months and 2–3 years are periods incorporating significant change. These findings echo the general usage of these timings in the assessment of children's abilities and in supporting awareness of the different needs of children as they mature. In addition, positron-emission tomography (PET) and magnetic resonance imaging (MRI) are providing support both for the existence of broadly specialized areas in the brain for different functions and that children and adults may use different areas for the same task reinforcing a role for brain maturation (Johnson, 2001).[11] Consideration of a particular child's individual skills and abilities can legitimately be assessed against a range of acquired skills within broadly accepted time frames, which appear to tie in with research on surges in brain activity – thereby providing some support for the timing of brain maturation overall.

Although less quantifiably measurable, there appear to be similar distinct phases in the development of understanding of the physical environment, including such concepts as number. We also develop what are sometimes termed 'executive functions', that is, 'the ability to maintain an appropriate problem-solving set for attainment of a future goal' which includes 'planning, impulse control, inhibition of prepotent but irrelevant responses, set maintenance, organized search and flexibility of thought and action (Ozonoff et al., 1991: 1083). Generally we also possess the capacity to share understanding of emotions both in recognition of how others might be feeling and thinking, that is, while not being able to actually 'read' another's mind, we can and do infer intentions and beliefs. The latter is usually referred to as a 'theory of mind' (Leslie, 1987). However, in order to have a theory of mind, we need to be able to represent our own mental state and this, I believe, follows a sequence whereby there has to be both experience and identification of the 'me' as a 'me', recognizing feelings in the context of action which we experience and carry out. We do this before having the 'psychic space' to recognize that the feelings we have are also shared by others. For example, during the second year of life, there is increasing awareness of another's feelings and what we like or want may be different to what someone else might like or want (Gopnik et al., 1999).

While our bodies are changing, it is also true that changes are happening within the brain and these changes appear increasingly to correspond with both the type and complexity of skills and aptitudes including emotional and behavioural management over time. Johnston (1995) points out that the immature brain does not just differ structurally from the adult brain, but also contains temporary structures which 'regress post-natally' perhaps explaining the prominence and then quiescence of some very early skills. He does not give any examples but the 'stepping' reflex comes to mind, which was thought to disappear after a few months 'post-natally' but may persist in a different format, for example, in the patterns of kicking which in themselves appear to provide the basic rhythms for walking (Spelke and Newport, 1998).

Table 1.2 Examples of developmental shifts

Source	Area of study	General findings and timescales
International Foundation for Music Research (Hodges, 2002)	Musicality from birth to five years	Birth to 1 year: 'Newborns 1 to 5 days old have demonstrated an ability to discriminate differences in frequency – onset of cooing and purposeful vocal sounds is around 15–16 weeks Five-month old babies have shown sensitivity to melodic contour and rhythmic changes. Six-month old babies have been successful in matching specific pitches 1–1.5 years: Movement to music through rocking, marching, rolling, and attending intently are more pronounced 1.5–2.5 years: This is a period of spontaneous song, that is, improvised 2.5–3 years: Recognition and imitation of popular tunes or nursery rhymes 3–4 years: Child can now reproduce a whole song. However, pitch is variable! 5 years: The child is now able to sing an entire song in the same key
Barrett and Morgan (1995)	Mastery and motivation	Phase 1 0–8/9 months – infants show some awareness of contingency between their actions and outcomes, prefer to control events, prefer looking at novel stimuli important developmental shift around 8/9 months – leading to phase 2 Phase 2 8/9–17/22 months – increasing self-evaluation and awareness of standards for appearance and behaviour, increasing awareness of others and ability to 'undertake several steps in sequence while keeping a goal in mind', (think of how you make tea – you will have a sequence of steps to achieve your cup of tea – a child will gradually understand the sequence of actions to achieve what they want) Phase 3 17/22 months–32/36 months – learning more about persisting and achieving
Sroufe (1995)	Emotional development	0–1 month Built-in protection 1–3 months Orientation to external world 3–6 months Positive affect 7–9 months Active participation 12–18 months Practising period 18–24 months Emergence of self-concept

Source	Area of study	General findings and timescales
National Network for Child Care (Labensohn, 1972)	Speech	6–8 months Babbling 18–24 months Identifiable words and early 'crude' sentences 36–60 months Mastery of rules of language
Gopnick et al. (1999)	Speech	6–12 months Babbling/organization of sounds 12 months Sounds to words 18–24 months Putting words together
Lipton and Spelke (2003)	Number	Numerosity discrimination increases between 6 and 9 months
Damasio (1999)	Development of self	Proto-self, 0–2 months approximately Core-self, approximately 2–18 months Autobiographical self, 18 months[6]
Erikson (1950)	Psychosocial development	Birth to 12 months Trust versus mistrust 2–3 years Autonomy versus shame/doubt 4–5 years initiative versus guilt[7]
Piaget (2002)	Cognition	Birth to 18 months sensorimotor[8] Reflexive stage (0–2 months): simple reflex activity such as grasping, sucking. Primary circular reactions (2–4 months): reflexive behaviours occur in stereotyped repetition such as opening and closing fingers repetitively Secondary circular reactions (4–8 months): repetition of change actions to reproduce interesting consequences such as kicking one's feet to move a mobile suspended over the crib Coordination of secondary reactions (8–12 months): responses become coordinated into more complex sequences. Actions take on an 'intentional' character such as the infant reaches behind a screen to obtain a hidden object Tertiary circular reactions (12–18 months): discovery of new ways to produce the same consequence or obtain the same goal such as the infant may pull a pillow toward him in an attempt to get a toy resting on it

Source	Area of study	General findings and timescales
Nielson (2003)	Object concept	Invention of new means through mental combination (18–24 months): evidence of an internal representational system Symbolizing the problem-solving sequence before actually responding. Deferred imitation Birth to 4–8 months, (objects within reach) integration of information about objects, sound, feel, position, learning different ways of manipulating objects, associating qualities of different objects, showing preferences 6–15 months, learning to use objects for a purpose, learning names of objects (over time). Towards end of this period, begins to learn a sequence with objects, that objects can be separated, joined and inserted into another
Moore (1990)	Mark making/ drawing	14–18 months (approximately) 'scribbles' 24–32 months, more skilful 'whirls, lines and zigzags' 3 years+, 'labelling' of drawings, 'tadpole' people emerge 48 months to 60 months +, more sophisticated 'person' with trunk and limbs
Stern (1985)	Emotions/ interpersonal relationships	Identifies the following as 'epochs of great change': 0–2 months, 2–3 months; 9–12 months; 15–18 months
Schore (1994)	Emotions, neuroscience and the self	12 months, major shift in cognitive, motor and affective spheres[9] 15–18 months, symbolic representation[10] 14–18 months, emergence of shame and doubt
Atkinson (2000)	Vision	0–3 months, sub-cortical orientating 3 months, cortical control eye/head movements 5/6 months, integration with manual action in near space 12 months, visual control locomotion 18–24 months, automation of visuo/motor programmes to run in parallel

It is important to recognize that emotions as well as language, cognitive skills, movement and control over bodily functions are also 'interactive' with brain maturation. For example, babies are able to display facial, vocal and bodily signs of contentment and distress, which over the first year become more recognizable as similar in display to some corresponding adult emotions (Soussigan and Schaal, (2005). More sophisticated emotions such as embarrassment and shame are thought to enter the emotional stage at around 14 months, tying in with the beginnings of a sense of 'ownership' both of body awareness, represented through the strong feelings evoked in children of this age by the ideas of 'me' and 'mine'.[12] Schore (1994) provides evidence to suggest that this transition also reflects a change in the dominance of the two hemispheres in the brain, which gradually move from right to left in the early years, once language becomes the primary form of communication, culminating in left-sided dominance for most people at around 5–7 years.

Another time-related aspect of development which emerges is the apparent existence of so called 'sensitive' periods for development which have been given support by research studies in both animals and humans, particularly on the visual system, speech and emotional development – especially the formation of healthy 'secure' attachments. The delayed developmental progress of children in Romanian orphanages where stimulation and opportunity for exploration, expression of emotion and play was profoundly limited provides a poignant example of the powerful role of appropriate, timely experience. Once these children were given appropriate stimulation, skills in all areas of development such as the ability to form attachments, walk and use of language did occur – but the later this happened the less secure or skilful the end result, reinforcing the idea of 'sensitive periods' in this developmental time frame. A further example of how brain maturation may be linked to developing skills is the finding that before 10 months of age, the majority of infants perform poorly on cognitive tasks which require knowledge of object permanence and delayed recall. By the time infants reach 12 months they are able to perform such tasks, including the recall of recently experienced events. Schore (1994) quotes many studies including that of Diamond and Doar (1989), which revealed evidence of a major maturational change in the prefrontal cortex at 10–12 months, which would correspond with the shift in abilities around this time. Johnston's (1995) short but richly informative paper notes how the proliferation in synapses during this period also appears to promote changes in the organization of neurotransmitters and their receptors, which again may give some clue as to the processes underpinning the great changes which occur in infants and young children within this two-year period. These chemical responses reflect and are responsive to environmental stimulation. The reality of the sheer volume of activity at this time is demonstrated by the cerebral glucose metabolic rate, which is about twice adult levels at 2 years of age. In

Schore's (1994: 12) exhaustive references he quotes many studies indicating that the 'vast majority of the development of axons, dendrites and synaptic connections that underlie all behaviour is known to take place in early and late human infancy'.

To summarize, development in the early years of life is marked by a number of transitions in skills and abilities which grow in complexity – providing that the type of experiences the child has are appropriate and timely. Why the type and quality of experiences and especially the role that adults play are so crucial will become clearer as we begin our journey. This starts in Chapter 2 with the amazing and wonderful brain as it seems increasingly unrealistic to consider 'development' in these early years without reference to, and understanding of, how our brain develops and matures over time and so the chapter deals with the brain, structure and functions. Chapter 3 looks at the senses and face-processing as these are the building blocks of how we begin to sort out our experiences. Chapters 2 and 3 are perhaps, the most 'technical' of all the chapters because they set out the context for all development and behaviour. In combination, the brain and the senses provide the theatre in which the information from the external world is played out. The child's social, emotional and cultural environment provides the stage for the child's manifestations of that internal world – with the 'audience', that is, carers and practitioners, not only providing the prompts and props but also being the interactive participants in the same drama. Realistically, these two chapters can only provide a sample of the information available but I hope to encourage further reading.

Chapter 4 looks at the beginnings of development. Chapters 5 and 6 reflect something of 'aspects and components' outlined in the soon to be amalgamated Birth to Three Matters Framework and the Foundation Stage Guidance,[13] that is, emotional and social well-being in Chapter 5 and becoming a 'competent learner' in Chapter 6. Chapter 7 looks in more detail at the role of play and imagining while Chapter 8 considers the role of the adult. The final chapter provides a resumé of skills and abilities between the ages of 5 and 8 years, an overview of development together with some concluding thoughts about the developmental journey. In the Appendix there are detailed charts of the gradual changes in development from birth to 8 years which I hope will prove helpful in providing a picture of the abilities a child generally has within the broad timescales given.

2 Laying the foundations: brain works

The huge surge in neuroscience research from around 1990 together with the ability to watch the brain 'at work' through sophisticated imagery has led to greater (but far from complete!) understanding of how the brain works. Most crucially however, it has highlighted the rate of brain growth in the early years and the way experience physically shapes the brain. In order to understand development/behaviour we need to have a good grasp of how our brains fundamentally work. In this chapter, the brain's structure, maturation, function, aspects of hemispheric laterality and potential gender differences are discussed.

Before we move on, I want to enlarge and clarify a point that was touched on in Chapter 1. I believe that the period or phases when shifts in skills and abilities take place are times of particular vulnerability and sensitivity influencing the possible trajectories of physical/sensory and psychological growth. My reasons for this are as follows. Research appears to highlight an overall similarity in the way that sensory information is managed and organized. Both in functional organization and general architecture, for example, separation of information, integration, patterns, feedback loops, columns, and so on, there appears to be a common 'design' no matter what the developmental area or how complex the information routes. For example, Lewis and Maurer (2005) have identified multiple sensitive periods in human visual development. The key message from their findings, in my view, is that periods of sensitivity, vulnerability and 'repair' are variable within the development of vision *dependent on the particular area*, for example, acuity, global motion and peripheral vision. In other words, there is not a sensitive period for 'vision' per se, but different sensitive periods for the individual components of vision. I suggest that this principle holds for all aspects of development, that is, that the different components that make up individual aspects of development may have individual 'sensitive' periods which may also have varying timescales. Indeed, there is a hint of this in language development whereby semantics appears to be unaffected by age of learning and experience but phonology and syntax appear to be much more vulnerable (Blakemore and Frith, 2005). This leads to the implications of the influence of experience on what may be the 'sensitive periods' for such different skills and abilities as being able to 'mind read', to manage our emotions, to form attachments, as well as for sensory, movement and cognitive learning. It may also imply that there are not only periods of sensitivity/vulnerability, but also periods where intervention is at its most timely in all the developmental areas.

The journey begins . . .

Any information which works towards answering any questions about how we grow and change is fluid, as research continually presents new insights into how we mature and develop. Understanding our developmental journey from infancy into adulthood is a dynamic process as new information acts like turns of a kaleidoscope – the pieces of knowledge shift to form a different pattern or awareness. Two examples: firstly, it is not so long ago that many people believed that newborn babies could not see; Secondly, the following quoted by Karen (1994) from an interview with Sandra Scarr in the 7 November issue of the *Washington Post* in 1987 regarding day care. Asked what would be the best period for parents to take time off to be with their children, Scarr recommended the end of the first year and any time in the second year as before that children's 'brains are Jell-O and their memories akin to those of decorticate rodents'. Times have changed!

There is a fundamental question that we can ask at this point:

- What 'equipment' does the human infant have at its disposal to make its first discoveries of the world?

First and foremost we have a brain and a body which encompass our sensory systems, and these form the foundation and building blocks for infants as they construct meaning from the plethora of information coming from their environment.

An understanding, of how our brain works is not an exotic addition to understanding human development, but instead the frame on which such understanding rests. No emotion, sensation, thought or behaviour is possible without the machinery of the brain. The complex workings between neurons, chemicals and electrical impulses result in what we experience as our conscious 'living' selves. Of course, the brain is also responsible for the existence of our unconscious worlds – those hidden emotions, the quiet workings of the muscles, nerves and blood, the constant interplay between metabolism, heart rate and breathing, and their response to our experiences. As Lewis-Williams and Pearce (2005) point out, the human mind (and therefore the brain) contains universals of consciousness – a search for belonging, to understand the meaning of life and death, and a quest to understand human nature itself –

thereby bringing us neatly to a starting point for development and a number of questions. For example:

- How do our brains work?
- Does the brain 'develop' and mature?
- Does this maturation link with the emergence of skills and abilities?
- Are all our brains the same?
- How is experience organized in the brain?
- Does gender have an effect on the workings of the brain?

This chapter looks at some possible answers to these questions in the light of current knowledge.[1]

Background

How the brain develops and carries out its tasks has been hotly debated in the past, especially between those who believed in areas devoted to highly specific tasks and those who believed that information processing was spread throughout the brain and involved both hemispheres. What emerges is that in many ways, both 'camps' are right. There are parts of the brain which appear to have primary functions for movement, language, the senses, thought and emotions but, at the same time, other areas throughout the brain are involved in putting together the complete picture of incoming information, organizing it and providing a response. Goldberg (2001) proposes the way that the brain processes information as being 'gradiental', that is, processing is localized *and* more global, serial *and* parallel. In his view, disruption in one part need not necessarily mean a loss of a particular function but more a difference in the outcome of the process and its manifestations. In addition, the outcome of any disruption will also be dependent on the following:

- the particular source of the experience
- timing in the developmental life span

Dysfunction in development therefore, whether organic, caused by trauma or negative, persistent experience, could lead to different behavioural/visible outcomes dependent on what, where, how and especially when the disruption has occurred.

Fox et al. (1994) identified three models that can be used to investigate 'the effects of different environmental events on brain development and organization'. These are:

- the 'insult' model, which ultimately believes that once damage is done to the brain, of whatever kind, then the brain cannot modify its functions in any way
- the 'environmental' model, which fundamentally views the brain as 'infinitely plastic'
- the third model (their own approach), which views brain development and organization as involving both genetically coded programmes and the influence of the environment

Other researchers such as Changaux (2002) and Cabeza and Nyberg (2000) also suggest different approaches to how the brain interprets information, the latter basing their views on brain imaging studies of cognitive functions. They suggest there are three approaches:

- *The local approach* relates to the consideration of the role of brain regions to the processes in cognition, emotion and bodily responses to experience.
- *The global approach* spreads the interpretation out further to consider how these regions interact.
- *The 'network' approach* pushes the boundaries out still further to consider how these various systems dynamically interact with experience and with each other, forming an integrated feedback system ultimately influencing expressed behaviour.

Changaux also reminds us that in considering how the brain works, we must also consider our evolutionary history and the fact that the brain contains very ancient structures as well as more 'recent' additions. This may be especially pertinent in our rapidly changing world. We have evolved over millennia, but current social and technological change appears to be taking place in timescales of decades. In reality our brains may still be expecting a mammoth around the corner or, rather, emerging from behind a tree!

Panksepp and Panksepp (2000) also forcefully point out that our evolutionary history shared with mammals (and other species) resonates in the ancient structures in the brain. They remind us that the basic emotional systems in our brain are extremely old and the timing of the 'foetal development of (human) brain systems seems to parallel the historical pattern of their phylogenetic origin'.[2] They also insist that we cannot understand behaviour without taking into account that our humanity is rooted in our shared mammalian biology.

Barkow et al. (1995), Corballis (2002), Allman (2000), Mithen (2005) and Lewis-Williams and Pearce (2005) all remind us, too, of the evolutionary and biological roots of, for example, vocal language, vision, communication, socialization and the care of infants, and that we can only understand some of the roots of why we do what we do by taking these into account.

What about genes and the nature/nurture debate?

What ties in with this 'remembrance of things past' is to bring into the picture the role of our genetic make-up. Every cell in our body contains the genetic code transmitted from our parents packed in 23 pairs of chromosomes.[3] The genes are the units of deoxyribonucleic acid (DNA) function and each cell contains that part of the genetic code which deals with the particular part of the body. For example, muscle cells only use the DNA that specifies the muscle system and so on. What is fascinating is that the actual number of structural genes in a human is approximately 38,000 although there are about 3 billion base pairs. The human brain contains around 100 billion neurons with each neuron having the ability to connect with many thousands of others. This disparity between gene information and the capacity for neural interchange implies that the interplay between genes, experience and neural activity is much more complex and subtle than the unfortunate media interpretations of specific genes indicating specific behaviours. What seems to be happening is that we share both numbers of genes and the processes instigated by these genes across species – showing nature at its most parsi- monious, that is, using a small number of 'building blocks' but which interact in increasingly sophisticated and complex ways as we climb the evolutionary ladder.[4] Allman says:

> One of the more remarkable recent discoveries is that the genes that control head and brain formation in fruit flies are very closely related to the genes that control the formation of the more anterior parts of the brain in mammals ... These genes regulate the formation of the cerebral cortex and thus the most progressive part of the mammalian brain is controlled by genes with very ancient antecedents going back at least half a billion years.
>
> (Allman, 2000: 57)

Bouchard (1995) proposes a mix of both genetic influences and envir- onment, highlighting that the influence of each can also vary. For example, he states that in his view the environment is more important than genetics in the first year of life and adds: 'Overall these studies suggest that there is genetic influence on change for some personality traits between adolescence and adulthood but that the amount is modest with most change attributable to idiosyncratic environmental factors' (Bouchard, 1995: 98). He also suggests that in the first year *environmental factors are the primary factors in individual differences*, but goes on to state that, in his view, between 1 and 6 years of age developmental changes are more subject to genetic influences. For example, when discussing intelligence as measured by intelligence quotient (IQ) scales, he states that a common genetic factor (although unfortunately he does not say which one) which exists in the first year, continues to affect IQ but less so, over time. However, he adds that new genetic factors appear to emerge with ongoing but diminishing influence between 2 and 4 years. The implication here may be that such genetic influences are the source of the 'timing' of dramatic, cross-cultural changes in development during this period, for example, the broad acquisition of spoken language, changes in self-awareness, awareness of others' 'desires' and feelings, bodily functions and the type and quality of play.

Sroufe (1995) points out, however, that from a developmental point of view, behaviour is not simply the interaction of genes and environment, but genes, environment and the history of adaptation up to that point. I would add 'brain processes', including those echoes that have persisted throughout countless generations of humans – and possibly fruit flies! What we also need to remember is that the action of genes is not a one-way system. Environmental experience can also activate genes. A wonderful example from the animal kingdom is given by Quartz and Sejnowski (2002). They tell of the female prairie vole who only reaches puberty 'once exposed to a chemical signal from the urine of an unrelated male' (Quartz and Sejnowski, 2002: 45). They also inform us that 'visual experience turns on genes for the development of the visual part of the brain, turning off genes that keep it immature' (Quartz and Sejnowski, 2002: 45). These findings reinforce the notion that, while genetic codes programme for the formation of brain structures, environmental influences modify the expression of such formation and ultimately the type, quality and quantity of the connections within the brain. The mathematician Ian Stewart (1998) also reminds us that genes are only a part of the picture, with physical, chemical and mathematical processes all combining to make human physiology work – let alone the influences of experience and the environment. Fisher (2006) describes genes as neither specifying behaviours nor cognitive processes but providing different functions, such as acting as regulators, signalling various molecules, receptors and so on that all interact in highly complex networks.

Our development, therefore, relies not only on a genetic code but on both experience-expectant (that is, a normally 'expected event' such as crawling) and experience-dependent (that is, use) learning (Black and Greenough, 1986). Finally, Lerner (1998) stresses the view that it is the *relationship* between the components of development that are the causes of development and not the various components themselves – rather reflecting an integrated or holistic view of development. The nature/nurture debate somehow seems redundant as each profoundly influences the other and neither is the 'winner' in this contest. Alan Schore, in a video on attachment formation and brain development (Bowlby, n.d.), describes the influence of nature/nurture as '100 per cent/100 per cent'!

What do we currently know about the brain?

Over the past few years research into the brain via fMRI, MRI scans and PET imaging has allowed us to look in more detail directly at the living brain. While the amount of information available can be vast, complex and sometimes contradictory, nevertheless there is some reassurance to be found via this new and increasingly sophisticated technology. Many of the findings reinforce what researchers and practitioners have felt intuitively when thinking about development and behaviour. For example, an article in *Nature* (Cavanagh, 2005) describes research showing that the amygdala, which is a structure in the brain that is responsive to emotion, especially fear, activates when presented with a blurry fearful face faster than a sharply detailed face. This illustrated that even somewhat 'coarse' fear-related information is processed extremely quickly. This supports not only LeDoux's (1998, 2002) work on fear pathways in the brain – his 'quick and dirty' routes but also what many people experience, that is, that we are particularly alert to danger. This finding is particularly pertinent when we come to consider emotional well-being in Chapter 5.

However, understanding brain structure and function is not the whole picture because there is the brain's crucial relationship with the body, movement and the senses. The senses and our awareness of movement and the ability to position ourselves in space constitute a fundamental part of getting to know ourselves and finding out about our environment as well as forming a crucial part of understanding how information is organized. This will be covered in the next chapter which will also include an overview on faces, as processing faces and facial expression provides one of the key 'markers' for our development – a point which is revisited both later in this chapter and in others.

However, the next section is going to provide some possible answers to a very big question – how do our brains work?

Brain: structure, growth and functions

The brain is waking and with it the mind is returning. It is as if the Milky Way entered upon some cosmic dance. Swiftly the head-mass becomes an enchanted loom, where millions of flashing shuttles weave a dissolving pattern, always a meaningful pattern, though never an abiding one: A shifting harmony of sub patterns.

(Sir Charles Sherrington, quoted in Panksepp, 1998: 81)

Looking at a brain, with its wrinkly walnut appearance and rather 'sludgy'[5] texture, it is difficult to imagine the magic and beauty of its workings. It has visibly distinct regions that, according to Greenfield (1997), fold and intertwine according to some fundamental plan that is not yet fully understood. The basic plan, however, seems to be the same for both humans and vertebrates, even though the actual appearance and relative importance of the individual brain structures may be very different. Our brains have two distinct hemispheres, which sit on top of and around the brain stem – which tapers down into the spinal cord. The brain stem has two main functions. It acts partly as a 'relay station' of information with outputs spread widely across the brain both to and from the hemispheres and cerebellum. It also contains the sites of vital bodily functions such as breathing, arousal and attention, and the control of bodily temperature. It is the most primitive[6] part of the central nervous system and yet is the one most vital to life – damage here is usually rapidly fatal.

At the back of the brain stem, there is the 'cerebellum' meaning 'little brain' which looks somewhat like a cauliflower. While the cerebellum is indeed much smaller than the 'cerebrum' (the overall name for the two hemispheres), it nevertheless contains more neurons (or brain cells)[7] than the two hemispheres put together (Bear et al., 1996: Detlef and Sultan, 2002). Recent research on the cerebellum is pointing to complex and wide-ranging functions in addition to its long-established association with motor development and control, which can be exampled by a superficially very simple test – simply touch your nose with a finger. This seems so easy but people with damage to the cerebellum cannot do it.[8]

If we watch a very young child in the game of 'heads and noses, knees and toes', we can observe how difficult it is for the child to touch each part required accurately because pointing to different parts of the body illustrates not only the need for the child to understand the whereabouts of body parts but also that they can point in a *self*-referent way. It is interesting that a child's ability to point smoothly and quickly to different parts of the body improves over time and links with understanding of a self/body and language as well as movement. The child is often able to actively point earlier (around 8 months) but pointing to a part of the body seems to require a different 'loop' of skills and comes later.

The role of the cerebellum has also been implicated in the aetiology of autism. Research by Hashimoto et al. (1995), using brain imaging studies, and Bauman and Kemper (1994) both indicated a smaller size in the cerebellum compared with controls (and in the brain stem generally), while even earlier studies such as that of Hallett et al. (1993) in their studies of locomotion of autistic adults found a clinical picture, which suggested 'a disturbance of the cerebellum'. However, the cerebellum is also now thought to be involved in the ability to 'attend' and, indeed, being able to touch your nose requires a degree of close attention – as does touching any part of the body, as shown above. In addition, Townsend and Courchesne's (1994), Courchesne et al., 1994) study of people with problems in attention found that subjects with damage to the parietal lobe of the brain and cerebellar dysfunction were particularly affected in their ability to focus and/or change attention.

Diamond (2000) provides a strong case for the links between movement and learning, as she notes that both the front part of the brain (the frontal cortex) and the cerebellum have protracted maturational timescales. She also notes that there are strong connections between parts of the cerebellum and parts of the very front of the brain (the prefrontal cortex) with similar cognitive outcomes to trauma to both these areas. This finding is supported by related studies, such as, that of Gross-Tsur et al. (2006) and which I return to in Chapter 6. Neural imaging also indicates related activity on some tasks. The idea of these links seems intuitively to make sense, as babies make their discoveries through movement and sensory experiences.

Our two hemispheres generally mirror each other, although function can and does vary between the left and right hemispheres and differences are discussed in more detail later on. Each hemisphere is joined to the other by three connections,[9] of which the major one is the corpus callosum and it is via this structure that much of the communication between hemispheres is transmitted.

The surface of each hemisphere is covered by the cortex which is composed of six layers or sheets of neurons which are arranged in columns that cut across all the layers. These layers 'grow' from the bottom up, so the deepest layer is layer 1 and the topmost one, layer 6. This columnar organization of cells means that connections between the neurons can go up and down between layers and deep into the hidden structures of the brain as well as within layers. The surface of the brain is slightly different for all of us and the most identifiable features are grooves (or furrows) and ridges – sulci and gyri respectively – which give the brain its well-known wrinkled appearance but, more importantly, have characteristics unique to each of us and which bear the imprint of our experience – and which very recent research is beginning to indicate may also bear a relationship to the progress of development of the skull in the foetal period.[10]

The lobes that the more prominent grooves help to identify are the:

- frontal lobe
- parietal lobe
- occipital lobe
- temporal lobe

Most texts on the brain agree that certain major functions have been generally ascribed for each lobe *in adults* and these are as follows:

- Frontal appears to deal with the most abstract and complex of brain functions, for example, thinking, planning and conceptualizing, and in the conscious 'appreciation' of emotion.
- Parietal appears to be mainly involved with movement, orientation, calculation and certain types of recognition, somatic sensation and body image.
- Occipital is mostly taken up with visual processing areas.
- Temporal mainly deals with hearing, language, comprehension, sound and some aspects of memory and emotion.

I must emphasise that the research studies illustrate these functions mainly as identified in the adult brain and it is important to recognize, as Paterson et al. (2006) point out, that infants, young children and adolescents may involve different parts of the brain as well as broadly linking with those identified during activities also tested on adults.[11] Maturation is discussed later in this chapter and this will support the general ideas that the brain's processing functions mature via experience associated with a chronological, probably genetically encoded, unfolding of function and steady growth. Children's brains are growing and pathways are getting sorted out.

Some crucial structures

There are two significant areas associated with language, and these are Broca's area and Wernicke's area. The former is in the left frontal cortex while the latter is in the posterior part of the left temporal lobe, and the two areas are connected by a bundle of nerve fibres. Broca's area is associated with the process of speaking in general and researchers have further subdivided this area into regions which are involved in very specific parts of language production, such as mouth movements. Wernicke's area deals more with understanding speech and is linked with short-term memory function. There are matched areas in the right hemisphere which deal with the tone, pitch and emotional cadence of language.

Also deep inside the temporal lobes on the medial side is the hippocampus, which is vital for memory, spatial navigation and playing a part in emotional processing. Adjoining the hippocampus to the front and side is the olfactory cortex. Smell, incidentally, is the only sensory system with direct access to the brain – hence the power of smell in memory. These two structures are found in all invertebrates but the rest of the cortex is only found in mammals. It is this 'remainder' that has expanded so greatly over the course of evolution – particularly in humans, which is why it is so commonly referred to as the 'neocortex'. However, I will simply use the term 'cortex'.[12]

Other crucial structures to be mentioned here are the thalamus and hypothalamus. The thalamus has an essential role in that it appears to be the 'relay station' for sensory information from the eyes, ears and skin to and from the cortex – apart from smell as we saw above. It also may play another role in the way in which different cortical areas emerge during foetal development. Work done by Schlagger and O'Leary of the Salk Institute, quoted in Bear et al. (1996: 492), demonstrated that it may be information relayed through the thalamus that specifies the foetal formation of different areas in the cortex. This pre-natal role, if proved, would link very logically with the role taken by the thalamus post natally.

The hypothalamus lies just below the front end of the thalamus and is much smaller. The pituitary gland is attached to the hypothalamus and is generally referred to as the 'master gland' as it releases hormones that control other hormones. However, the hypothalamus itself regulates what the pituitary does – both directly through neural connections and via hormones – and so is a kind of 'master of the master gland' (Pinel and Edwards, 1998). The hypothalamus, incidentally, has a key role in the regulation of stress[13] which is an increasingly emerging 'hot topic' over issues regarding very young children in day care (see Ahnert et al., 2004; Biddulph, 2006; Gerhardt, 2005).[14] When one considers the intimate connection with the thalamus and the pituitary, one can begin to see how sensory information can influence bodily reactions and therefore feeling 'states' as well as the more abstract concepts such as emotional meaning.

A sidestep to emotions

Lying deep within the brain under the cortex and within the temporal lobe is the amygdala, which as mentioned earlier seems intimately connected with emotion, especially fear and anxiety, which in my view has particular significance.[15] It is an integral part of what is commonly termed the 'limbic system', itself identified with the experiencing of emotion. This system according to Carter (2000) also includes the hypothalamus, the thalamus and the hippocampus. All these structures have complex and dense connections with the cortex. LeDoux (1998), however, warns of the loose use of the term 'limbic system' when considering the aetiology of emotions. His main concern is that the limbic system has become too closely identified as the seat of emotions, whereas he believes that other areas of the brain are also involved and that the limbic system itself is also involved in cognition as well as emotions. LeDoux (1998) also makes the very interesting suggestion that different emotions may have different brain systems devoted to them because he notes that while seeing and hearing are both sensory functions, they each seem to have their own neural systems. Damasio's (2003; Damasio et al., 2000) work also identifies other structures, apart from the limbic system, to be involved in emotions. Echoing Le Doux, Damasio also notes different patterns of activation between these structures dependent on the type of emotion involved – which, incidentally, may also support the idea that different emotions may have different 'sensitive periods' as well as different 'emergent' times.

What is very important for us to note is that information from all the sensory systems feeds into the amygdala, particularly into one of the three areas into which it is divided. The senses all have a different pattern of connections and so it does seem that it is the amygdala that pulls all the information together. Damasio (2003: 60) summarizes it as follows: 'the amygdala is an important interface between visually and auditory competent stimuli and the triggering of emotions' and seems to respond to both consciously and unconsciously perceived stimuli.

Gallese (2001: 35) also noted that 'neurons responding to complex biological visual stimuli such as walking or climbing were reported also in the amygdala' linking some level of emotional processing, movement and observation. A further illustration of the convergence of findings identifying specific structures as involved with feelings comes from Trevarthen et al. (1999: 65) who describe the reticular system in the brain stem[16] as the Intrinsic Motive Formation because of its significance as the 'generator of initiatives and flexible responses of the body in its awareness of the world'.[17] Such findings in sub-cortical regions of the brain (and therefore older in evolutionary terms and earlier maturing), point to areas in the brain supportive of emotional processing and provide part of the evidence linking sensory information, the development of processing 'circuits' and, ultimately, individual responses.

The building blocks of the brain: neurons, glial cells and their interactions

Many of the fundamental pieces of knowledge that emerge as influencing our understanding of development concern the cells that make up the brain – the *neurons* – and how they connect with one another together with what aspects of neuronal growth impact on the ability within each human being to function. One of the main differences between neurons and other bodily cells is that neurons directly communicate with each other and are designed to do so, and it is these processes that contribute to the 'fine-tuning' that allows for the differences between individual brains within the basic overall architecture.

There are two main groups of cells in the brain – the neurons and glia. We are born with most of the neurons we will need – about 100 billion – but the glia outnumber the neurons by about 10 to 1! However, it is the neurons, which are mainly responsible for the vast majority of information processing in the brain. The main role that the glial cells appear to have is that of nourishing and insulating the neurons. However, a clue that they may have a function beyond what is currently apparent lies in the findings that rats reared in 'enriched'[18] environments appear to possess more glial cells per neuron than rats reared in more impoverished surroundings. Schousboe and Waagepetersen (2002) also provide some insight into the work of glial cells as they consider that far from being somewhat 'passive' in their nurturing, particular glial cells (the astrocytes) that surround the neurons have a highly dynamic role in the uptake of glucose in the brain, and glucose is the main brain 'fuel'. The brain's use of glucose is very high in the early years of life because the brain grows at such a rapid rate, and it may well be that the glial cells are especially important in these early years.

The basic neuron consists of three main parts – the cell body itself, which like all other bodily cells is the 'housekeeper', storing genetic material, making proteins and any other substances essential for the cells survival. The neuron differs from all other cell bodies because of two other structures, the dendrites and the axon (Figure 2.1). These form the basis of the neuron's ability to communicate. Basically, the dendrites are 'receivers' and the axon is the 'output' channel. It is axons which carry information to other cells and they can vary enormously in length (even several feet) depending on function. While most neurons have only one axon, these single axons can have many branches, so one neuron can send messages to many other neurons. The 'receivers' – the dendrites – also have structures on them ('spines') which play a key function in organizing incoming information. The importance of the spines has been demonstrated in startling fashion by two studies in Oslo and New York reported by Alex Dominguez (2002) of the Associated Press.[19] In the Norwegian study

> the researchers clipped the highly sensitive whiskers of mice and watched changes in the part of the brain that receives signals from the whiskers (that is, the dendrites). Two to four days after clipping, the number of spines created or lost in that area increased significantly, indicating new synapses (connections) were being created and others destroyed.
>
> (Dominguez, 2002: 1)

In a separate study, also in mice, researchers at the New York University School of Medicine found that such spines can be long lived, especially in adult mice. The findings suggest some spines can last an entire lifetime, but

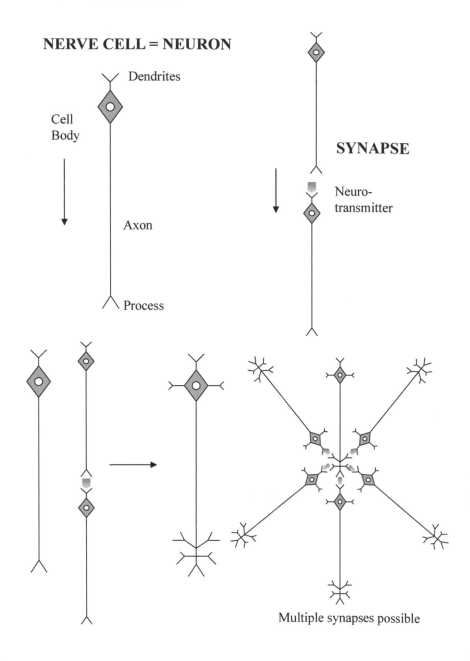

Figure 2.1   Schematic diagram showing brain neuron and connections (courtesy of Dr Danya Glaser, Great Ormond Street Hospital, London, England)

the New York University researchers said 'they also found evidence of changes in the shape of individual spines' dependent on changes in the environment/ experience. Confusingly, dendrites not only receive messages but can also send information to each other, which influences the ultimate 'message' that the neuron then sends to other cells. Neurons can also differ depending on which layer of the cortex they are in and the type and number of connectors they have, but all nevertheless follow the same basic structure, creating extensive patterns both with close neighbours and with neurons more distant.

Mirror neurons

The initially accidental discovery in the cortex of the macaque monkey by Gallese (1999, 2001; Gallese et al., 1996) and then by others such as Rizzolatti et al. (1996, 2002) of 'mirror neurons' was a breakthrough in considering the neural basis for imitation. These neurons were sensitive to the monkey observing an action using hand or paw and fired in the same way as if the monkey was doing the action. A paper subtitled ' "Monkey see, monkey do" ' (Carey, 1996) described these neurons in detail. The crucial point is that these neurons did *not* react if a tool was used for the same action or if the hand/paw did not come into contact with the object, but were specific to animal/human paw/hand activity on an object. What Gallese also found was that there were differences between these neurons in that some responded to specific actions such as grasping but another set responded more generally towards different actions which might be achieving the same goal. Gallese (2001: 34) saw the existence of mirror neurons as a component in supporting the 'relational nature of action' between 'agent' and 'observer' and felt that 'agency' was a 'key issue for understanding intersubjectivity and for explaining how individuals can interpret their social world'.

Similar mirror neurons have been found in the human cortex, which respond to both visual and motor sensory input. Brain imaging studies illustrating this activity included the superior temporal sulcus, the parietal cortex and Broca's (language) area. There also exist another type of visual/motor 'grasping related neurons', termed 'canonical neurons', which react to grasping, holding and manipulating objects – not to action observation but to the object.[20] These neurons potentially play a very important part in underpinning imitation and their dysfunction may also play a part in the difficulty that children with autism have with imitation, a topic which crops up in subsequent chapters.

An intriguing implication for imitation and its links with development is the potential for self-imitation via actual mirrors. For example, a baby, who does not yet recognize itself as itself in a mirror, nevertheless recognizes 'another' infant. If the baby picks up a brick, mouths and throws it, the child may notice the image doing likewise. If, as is speculated via the research, mirror neurons are activated when observing a hand action, this self-imitation may also serve to provide the infant with bodily and visual feedback, further supporting the child in developing motor skills and hand/eye coordination as well as, perhaps, serving towards the development of self-recognition.

How neurons 'talk' to each other

The way in which neurons communicate is via electrical impulse and chemical messenger. The information within the cell travels via a biologically instigated impulse action in contrast to a classic physical conduction of electricity such as when we switch on a light. This impulse is termed 'the action potential' and it is the strength and persistence of this impulse which determines (along with other factors) whether the information message ultimately is 'weak' or 'strong'. Most of the neurons in our central nervous system receive many signals both electrical and chemical, and this information is put together to form a single, one-way action potential. This is happening every moment that we are alive, whatever we are doing. However, the real magic of the neuron occurs in how this 'action potential' is transmitted across the tiny space termed the 'synapse' between the axon terminals and the dendrites. At the end of the axon, there sit little storage units full of chemicals. Once the action potential reaches these terminals, the chemicals get released and then these drift across the synapse to meet the dendrites of the targeted neuron (LeDoux, 2002). This causes an electrical response in the receiving spines which, in its turn, will eventually be released to another neuron only if an action potential is generated in the axon of this second neuron.

To summarize, the method of transmission from neuron to neuron is almost always electrical–chemical–electrical, a wonderfully simple formula which covers an extraordinary complexity. Neurotransmitters are the necessary links between neurons but their effects vary, depending on what is happening both to and within the person at any one time and what their particular role is. Different neurotransmitters have different functions. This variation gives some insight into why the same occurrence can lead ultimately to different reactions in individuals and why different drugs have different effects, as often they interfere with this complex interplay between the chemical messengers.

Myelination

There is a process of maturation not only of the brain but within the brain. The brain grows not only by the neurons themselves getting larger and making connections, but also by another very special process. A particular type of glia, the oligodendroglia, provide a layer of fat insulation around the axon – exactly like insulating electrical appliances. These layers wrap around the axon and cover it, allowing much more efficient transmission of the electrical signals along it. This process is called *myelination* and an unmyelinated axon transmits a much 'fuzzier' signal, which has implications for the quality and speed of processing. An interesting perspective on processing sensory information comes via personal correspondence with a person with 'high functioning autism'. This person described their way of dealing with sensory information as follows:

> The pipes are too small for the river to fit in. I can't process/intake/put out enough data to cope with reality and the demands of other humans. There is a ridiculous limit (compared to regular people) on what I can take in, turn around, and put out in terms of data bits to relate to my environment. I 'have to' concentrate on small bits of things or I am buried in stuff I can't understand or relate to or manipulate.

This is from someone in their middle fifties and I suggest that babies and very young children with the variable rate of myelination in their brains, also find that it takes time for them to 'turn around' information received into an experience they can manage and act upon. Remember that the myelination process takes place over time and at different rates in different areas of the brain (see Table 2.1 in the maturation summary section, for further information). All this provides reasons for careful reflection by adult carers on the type, quality and quantity of experiences they provide.

What also promotes differences in reactions to experience is the link between brain maturation and age. For example, a study by Johnston (1995) found that synapses are produced in greater than adult numbers in the first two years and that specific glutamate receptors which play a very important part in the transmission of messages were generally in a more receptive state and for longer periods than in adults. This potentially means that in the first two years of life, the neurons themselves are literally more open to experience – the downside being that brain function is also potentially more vulnerable to all types of adversity, including under- and over-stimulation. An example is from a study by Filippi et al. (2002) of children with developmental delay aged both under and over 2 years of age. They found that the children older than 2 had changes in specific neurotransmitter ratios in particular brain structures compared to controls. The children under 2 years did not show these changes, potentially illustrating that developmental delay may have an accumulative effect over time leading to the alteration in the neuro-transmitter ratios. Finally, full myelination of all the structures of the brain continues into the second decade and potentially into the early twenties.

Pruning

What researchers have noticed is that while the number of synapses any one neuron is capable of receiving is enormous, it is not endless and this capacity to create new connections appears to peak in early development and then declines with age. For example, the visual cortical neurons in the infant have one and a half times as many synapses as do the neurons in adults. In one species of monkey, a particularly sharp decline in synaptic activity has been observed during 'adolescence'.

Nature has its own way of sorting out the enormous number of con-nections between neurons so that we do not become 'overloaded' and enabling familiar situations to create similar patterns – a brain version of cutting a pattern for itself to fit the action. Synaptic connections surge when something new is learned and then, as the pattern becomes more refined and well known, superfluous connections are 'pruned'. This process of connec-tions and pruning goes on continuously while we learn new skills. A good example is when the baby is learning to walk. At first, when balance, coor-dination, speed, direction, and so on are all being sorted out, the activity within and between the relevant brain areas will be immense as connections are busily made. As the action of walking gradually becomes more skilful, some of the connections will not be needed and so they will be pruned off and a pattern for the child's particular style of walking will have been made. From this, it can be seen how logical it is that the main surges of brain activity occur in the early years and adolescence because it is during these times that new skills are being learned at a much faster pace across the developmental spectrum. As we get older, we do indeed learn new skills, new facts and gain new insights, but these are more a continuing refinement of the fundamental knowledge we have acquired in the early years. Like the brain, we build on what is already in existence and our early development brings together our genetic inheritance, our evolutionary 'hardware' and the influence of our daily experience. However, such processes do not stop in the early years but continue throughout the life span and we continue to make connections between neurons dependent on life experiences.

A further point is that pruning appears to be particularly severe following a large surge in synaptic activity, and interesting studies quoted by Locke

(1995) suggests that this process of connection and atrophy, may indeed have to do with periods of brain 'reorganization' which appear to occur at times of major transitions in development. For example, Locke noted that face and voice recognition appear to follow a general pattern of peaks and troughs of performance but there was a 'dip' between the ages of 10 and 13 years (broadly) which improved again at around age 14. It may very well be that times of major shifts in physical and/or psychological development, such as, the ability to walk or puberty, may either enhance, cause to plateau and even perhaps regress other aspects of development temporarily. This is another of the reasons I feel such phases may be times of particular vulnerability in both physical and psychological health. These ideas of shifts, plateaus and regression/discontinuities also fit in with Fischer's (2005) views on brain processing, which he sees as cycles of development combined with 'power spurts' in brain activity which occur not only in the early years but between the ages of 5–7 and 10–13 years. The latter corresponds with puberty and could suggest that the 'dip' in face/voice recognition is a consequence of the surge required for physical growth and emotional ups and downs!

Implications of brain pattern formation

Knowledge that the brain appears to work by forming patterns or loops of connections brings to mind that the emphasis often placed on routine and repetition in the lives of a very young child appears to logically support this process of 'wiring' and 'pruning'. Commonly encountered experiences may help the brain to 'sort out' the plethora of incoming information and will create a familiar 'wiring' environment based on the child's physical (including sensory), social, emotional and cultural environment – mediated naturally by the carers involved with the child. In turn this may increasingly help the child make sense of their environment – (and, of course, themselves) as experience can be 'checked out' by the brain as something familiar. A comparison can be made with 'social referencing' for example, whereby a child notes the parent's reaction to an unfamiliar person or object thus providing a 'yardstick' on which the child can process the novel occurrence.

This may help to understand why a persistently chaotic environment whether physically, emotionally, psychologically or any combination, especially for children, can impact on their ability to 'manage' both emotions and behaviour. In the early years our developing brains are unable to filter out as effectively the information bombarding them because of the immaturity of the processing systems in some areas. Therefore without such familiarity of experience on which to frame other experiences we would be constantly engaged in 'managing' our environment and our behaviour. The importance of this is indicated in our daily lives as we act in ways which, while varying according to context, nevertheless retain a familiar individual pattern. For quite a few of us, I would guess the familiar is almost essential for us to feel a sense of equilibrium and safety. Our brains are 'wired' to cope with what we know so that we do not have to be aware of our emotions and our behaviour from one moment to the next while retaining the capacity to deal with new information. This is because while neural connections may be pruned, the remaining connections can show increasing complexity. As LeDoux (2002) points out, new connections formed by experience are not entirely 'new entities' but are added to existing connections. However, as Kandel (2006) suggests, the real question is how these neural systems become complex cognitive and behavioural functions and how awareness and consciousness may in turn reorganize what is happening within the brain.

Our brains follow roughly the same basic processing patterns but it is experience that causes the different branches on the connectors between our neurons that allow for individuality, and from that individuality arises our responses to our environment based on both 'old' connections formed early in life and new modifications formed as we develop. This helps towards answering the question, are all our brains the same? The answer is both yes and no!

Maturation

Another crucial aspect of brain development already touched on is that the neurons with their axons and dendrites develop within a time frame. As Schore (1994: 13) points out 'different regions of the infant's nervous system mature at different periods ... and that different neurological systems may underlie different sensitive periods'. He goes on to quote studies, which indicate that 'even the individual layers of different areas in each cerebral lobe have their own developmental rate' (Schore, 1994: 13). In particular, the maturation of the pre-frontal cortex is essentially postnatal. The neurons grow axons and dendrites in this area in the first year of infancy and maturation continues into the first 'few years of life, making interconnections which are affected by environmental stimuli during the critical period and then become largely permanent' (Schore, 1994: 13). When we think about the way in which skills and abilities develop at various times, we need to consider what is happening regarding the process of myelination in the brain and the rate at which our brains are actually growing. Areas that seem to show the greatest increase in this process correspond broadly with increasing complexity and sophistication of function. For example, larger left than right white-matter (that is, myelinated axons) volume has been found in an area concerned with tracking changes of sound input in the adult human brain. A caveat is, however, that once an axon is myelinated, it is less 'inclined' to make new connections – giving a physiological reason for why 'old habits die hard'.

Different parts of the brain also do not mature 'all of a piece' but at variable rates and when thinking about a child's capabilities we need to consider how efficient their processing of particular types of sensory/emotional information might be. We also need to remember that time or timing does play a part in how the brain works – timing of the messages that move our limbs for example makes a difference in how coordinated or not we are (and, of course, the neurons, neurotransmitters and the connections between them all play a part).

A note about head size/circumference

Those of you who have had your own children or who have had experience of babies will know that alongside developmental checks, the baby's head circumference is measured too. This is because the rate at which our heads grow to accommodate the growing brain appears to happen within a particular range. A health visitor or paediatric nurse could show you the charts. Of course, head circumference per se needs to be looked at alongside the general 'build' of the baby, as some babies just have large or small heads (as do adults). However, significant growth or lack of growth in head circumference can indicate a problem. For example, a finding highlighted by Courchesne et al (2003) noted that a high proportion of the children with autism studied appeared to have a smaller than normal head size at birth followed by a faster than normal head growth spurt so that at between 6 and 14 months of age, the autistic children's head circumferences 'were substantially larger than normal children's' – a finding that persisted through to the ages of 3–4 years. There also appeared to be a link between the severity of the autism and the fastest abnormal growth rates. Growth rates generally are linked to how the brain is growing which includes the size of growth in neurons (grey matter) and 'white matter' which is the myelinated axons. While the brain's size increases fourfold between birth and around 5–6 years, the brain continues to 'reorganize' itself via the pattern-making connections built up on experience. Between the ages of 3–6 years the most rapid growth takes place in the frontal lobe areas but from around age 6 to puberty, the spurt in growth of grey matter shifts to the temporal and parietal lobes followed by a big spurt just as puberty starts in the frontal lobes again. This spurt then has a period of substantial pruning from the mid-teens to the mid-twenties (Giedd et al., 1999) indicating a time when types of experience and potential for interventions for those adolescents having problems may be optimal – echoing those times of change in babies and younger children.

Maturation summary

I have put together Table 2.1 to provide a brief overview of some of the reviews and/or key studies which examined brain growth via autopsy or, the more recent brain imaging techniques as well as the more traditional EEG studies, glucose uptake and blood volume studies to illustrate the variations in brain maturation.

While primate studies show similar developmental rates in all the different brain regions, the variation in human brain maturation may reflect the more complex range of human versus primate functioning. However, it is also true that the study of brain maturation is ongoing and there is much that is not known. However, Gur (2005) in a review of brain maturation studies suggests three generally accepted findings:

1. There is a 'large variability in the rate of maturation among brain regions'.
2. 'People are not biologically prepared to exercise mature frontal lobe control until they reach adulthood.'
3. The main index of maturation is the rate of myelination.[23]

Benes et al's (1994) findings (Table 2.1) also supported a generalized view that young girls appear to attain emotional maturity (as assessed by 'age appropriate achievement in language skills, reading and overall behaviour at school') before young boys as the myelin staining in the particular areas studied showed significantly greater amounts in young girls as compared to young boys of the same age. This led them to wonder whether the much higher incidence of childhood psychopathology in boys could also be related to this slower rate of myelination. Such findings also potentially reflect the different 'timetable' for male as opposed to female development, which may have its roots in the different requirements for different roles throughout our long evolutionary history. In addition, the second point has huge implications for the expectations we may have for teenage behaviour and how we deal with their problems. As adults, it may well be that we have reneged on our responsibilities to the young in our quest to provide them with a 'voice', independence and freedoms for which they may not be ready.

Two hemispheres – one mind?

One of the many fascinating and mysterious aspects of being human is the existence of symmetry and asymmetry in our bodies and brains. We have two eyes, two arms, two legs, two ears, one nose and one mouth but when we

Table 2.1 Brain maturation

Researcher/source	Findings
Diamond and Doar (1989) Schore (1994)[21]	Major maturational change in the pre-frontal cortex at 10–12 months Cerebral glucose metabolic rate, which is about twice adult levels at 2 years of age The period between 7 and 15 months appears to be critical for the myelination/maturation of rapidly developing limbic and cortical association areas
Observer Magazine (Carlowe, 2002)	Around the age of 8 months, the frontal cortex begins to actively organize in areas associated with personality and emotions while those areas associated with more abstract thoughts occurs around the age of 12 years
Thompson et al. (2000) study of a small number of 'normal' children aged 3–15 years across time spans of up to four years (MRI scans)	Rostro-caudal wave of growth in the corpus callosum Between the ages of 3 and 6 years a striking growth rate in the frontal circuits of the corpus callosum, which sustain mental vigilance and regulate the planning of new actions In children aged 6–15 years, highest growth rates in 'temporo-parietal systems, which are functionally specialized for language and for understanding spatial relations
Bartzokis et al. (2001) studied frontal and temporal lobe volumes in males between the ages of 19 and 76 years	Grey matter reached maximum volume 'at approximately 12 years in the frontal lobes but not until age 16 years in the temporal lobes' Overall their analysis of their findings did show a decrease in grey matter volume in the areas studied but a concurrent increase in white-matter volume indicating that while neurons may shrink if not well used or required, connections between neurons continue to expand allowing greater cohesion and comprehension between experience, memory, decision-making and planning

Researcher/source	Findings
Sowell et al. (2002) Study of children aged between 7 and 16 years	Reduction in grey-matter volume and increase in white-matter volume over time. Considered that myelination may be more important than synaptic pruning[22]
Sowell et al. (2002) Study of children aged between 8 and 22 years who had been exposed to heavy prenatal alcohol abuse	The influence of pre-natal alcohol abuse appeared to influence the rate of brain maturation in certain areas as opposed to 'typical' development
Sowell et al. (2003) study of a large group of normal subjects from a community sample representing a wide age range (from 7 to 87 years).	Adolescent maturational changes in grey matter density, for example, occur in spatially and temporally specific patterns, with *parietal* cortices maturing earlier than *frontal* cortices. White matter density also increases with age during adolescence
Paus et al. (1999)) study of structural maturation of fibre tracts in the human brain based on 'an increase in the diameter and myelination of axons'	Found evidence for a gradual maturation during late childhood and adolescence of fibre pathways presumably supporting motor and speech functions. They also note that *post mortem studies suggest that axon diameter and myelin sheath undergo conspicuous growth during the first two years of life*, but may not be fully mature before adolescence or even late adulthood
Giedd et al. (1999) (study is relevant in that this 'surge' mirrors that which occurs in the second year of life)	Found surges in brain activity during adolescence are followed by a post-adolescent decrease and imply that, if this surge is related to a 'second wave' of over-production of synapses, it may herald a critical stage of development when the environment or activities of the teenager may guide selective synapse elimination during adolescence
Harasty et al. (2003) study of 21 post-mortem, adult human cases	Indicated the neocortex on the left secondary auditory cortex was thinner but longer than that on the right side. These studies suggest that the hemispheric differences arise from a so-called 'balloon model' of cortical development. In this the cortex is extended and stretched by white matter growth
Huttenlocher (1994)	Synaptic increase by factor of 10 between birth and 6 months in visual cortex

Researcher/source	Findings
	Dendrite 'spines' density *thought* to be maximum at 5 months and then decline to adult values by 21 months
Thatcher (1994)	Postulated 'growth spurts' nested in 4-year anatomical cycles: Cycle 1.1.5–5 years; Cycle 2.5–10 years; Cycle 3; 10–14 years
Johnson (2001)	Notes that: brain structures 'have the overall appearance of those in the adult by 2 years of age and that all the main fibre tracts can be observed by 3 years of age' (p. 476)
	Maximum density of synapse formation in visual cortex is reached between 4 and 12 months (150% of adult levels)
	Myelination of pons and cerebellar peduncles has begun at birth and by 3 months has extended to 'optic radiation and splenium of the corpus callosum' (p. 476).
	Suggests that children do not seem to 'perceive and process objects in the way we do as adults' (p. 476) until the second year.
Goddard (2005)	Cerebellum grows faster than the cortex – 80% of size by 2 years completing a 'major period of myelination by 4 years'
	Development continues until age 15 and beyond
	'Primitive reflexes' emerge and gradually become inhibited over the first 12 months of life to allow for more 'conscious' movement
Benes et al. (1994)	Myelination of the neurons in the hippocampus demonstrated a twofold increase in the first and second decades followed by a 60% increase between the fourth and sixth decades. They also discovered a gender difference with females showing a significantly greater degree of myelin staining between the ages of 6 and 29 years but there were no further gender differences after that

consider the human face, one side is usually slightly different from the other and yet the positioning of eyes, ears, nose and mouth seems to be both rational and pleasing – although perhaps this is just because it is how we are! Within our bodies however, this pattern continues, two of some organs, one of others.[24] What is interesting is that apart from some relatively rare exceptions, we all carry our organs in the same places, and our hearts in particular point towards the left. We are usually right-handed although a sizeable majority of people are left-handed and most people are right-footed. Speech production is usually lateralized to the left hemisphere while general recognition of faces appears to be a right hemispheric function. The brain itself has its own strange mix of asymmetry and balance – the right frontal pole protrudes over the left and at the back of the brain, the left occipital lobe protrudes over the right (Goldberg, 2001).[25] A majority of women and a smaller proportion of men will automatically hold a baby in their left arm – a position reflected in paintings and sculpture of mothers and children throughout the ages. There is undoubtedly a laterality and coherence in our overall 'design', possibly due to nature's economy and rationalization, just as there appear to be distinct 'laws' of physics and indeed laterality which rule not only our planet but also the universe both macroscopically and micro-scopically. For example, the DNA helix almost always spirals to the right and electrons are 'left-handed'. Social and cultural practices both throughout the ages and across societies all reflect a strange laterality in the way that we organize and think about our world. For example, burial patterns where bodies are carefully placed facing either to the east or to the south, waltzing couples always turn clockwise, blood flows through the heart in a pattern of left- or right-handed spirals so that blood entering and leaving the heart does not collide (McManus, 2002).[26] However, the potential whys and wherefores of bodily symmetries or otherwise is beyond the remit of this subsection. The above examples nevertheless provide a context which reminds us of the wonder, complexity and potential logic of the way we are.

The work of Gazzaniga (1999) describes startling insights into the functions of our right and left hemispheres first noted over 30 years ago, when three patients had their brains literally divided by severing the corpus callosum as a treatment for severe and intractable epilepsy. Each hemisphere appears to mainly deal with the opposite side of the body and appears to have some functions of its own. What Gazzaniga discovered was that patients who were given something to look at in the right visual field (left hemisphere) were able to describe what they saw. However, when another object was shown to the left visual field (right hemisphere) they said they could not see anything. It seemed therefore that vision itself was affected. However, further tests showed that, in spite of saying they could not see anything, 'when asked to point to an object similar to the one being pro-jected', these patients did so perfectly accurately! What was happening was they could 'see' the object in the left visual field, but could not *talk* about it. Gazzaniga and his colleagues found that this also occurred for stimuli such as touch, smell and sound. They also found that the left hemisphere controlled the right hand and fingers, and the right hemisphere the left hand and fingers. However, both hemispheres control the upper arms – providing some interesting speculation as babies look at their hands but would find it more difficult to see their upper arms. Experience, including visual experience may link in with the maturation of laterality of function and strengthen the synaptic connections of the specific motor areas. This could be because hands and fingers also have much finer movements and so may require a much more dedicated 'side'.

Research findings overall seem to point to the left hemisphere being particularly dominant for tasks involving analysis, detail and language, while the right hemisphere appears dominant for visual-spatial tasks. Language in particular has been associated with the left hemisphere, especially Broca's and Wernicke's areas. It must be remembered however that function is never quite so clearly cut as various qualitative aspects of such tasks also can involve 'the other side'as McManus's (2002) book highlights so clearly. For example, a sizeable proportion of the population (about 3–5 per cent) have their main speech centres in the right hemisphere rather than the left, so any information about the hemispheres is a question of generalizations and majorities rather than absolutes.

So, generally speaking, the two hemispheres seem to have different 'information-processing' styles discovered by asking such 'split brain' patients to match patterns with either hand. What transpired was that patterns that were 'easy to describe but difficult to discriminate visually' produced better performance by the right hand (left hemisphere), while patterns that were the reverse were performed more easily by the left hand (right hemisphere). In addition, when given somewhat ambiguous instructions to match various items, the left hemisphere seemed to match by function and the right by appearance. Again, this has a developmental logic in that babies will discover objects by mouthing and touching as well as seeing, so if the right hemisphere is more active and dedicated to visuo-spatial information then this function may remain even when language becomes dominant. For example, babies will recognize a shape first before they associate a colour with an object and, interestingly, studies of patients with Alzheimer's disease at the University of Kent (England) have shown that they more easily recognize an object (for example, a banana) by its shape rather than its colour.

The hemispheres also appear to vary in their ability to find or 'search' for a pattern or object in a particular visual field. The left hemisphere seems to be particularly adept at this and split brain patients actually performed better on such tasks than 'normal' people. The right brain appears to be much 'smarter' at looking at global features than finding specific patterns. Looking at the wider picture, it seems that the left hemisphere is constantly looking for order and reason. The brain – or rather the left brain as well as nature – appears to abhor a vacuum. A good example is how many people are keen to rationalize events that seem out of their control and that finding someone or something to 'blame' will provide a reason for otherwise troubling events. Of course, this propensity has a positive logic of its own. Finding a pattern or logic in events helps to form a stable view of the environment in which we find ourselves. It provides a reason for our need for familiarity and how disconcerting (even if exciting or interesting) novel events can be.

The right hemisphere however appears to be more involved in sensory perception of the world, for example, smells and flavours are rated more highly 'when inhaled into the right nostril and subsequently processed by the right rather than the left hemisphere' (McManus, 2002 page: 192).[27] This hemisphere is particularly important for music and melodies and it is the right hemisphere that provides the 'musicality' of speech, and so damage to this area produces speech which can appear monotonous and atonal. Rhythm and absolute pitch however, seem to be left hemisphere functions with rhythm linking to language. Goddard (2005) describes the right hemisphere as the 'training ground' for the left and is especially good at learning 'with the body', that is, processing information especially through the medium of movement and music.

Emotional words and phrases are also apparently more clearly remembered if spoken into the left ear than the right – again emphasizing the 'emotional' aspect of the right hemisphere. Some aspects of humour and use of metaphor, ambiguity and allegory also seem to depend on normal right hemisphere functioning (Ramachandran and Blakeslee, 1999).

In drawing, too, damage to either hemisphere appears to produce different effects but which nevertheless tie in with the overall picture of global functioning by the right hemisphere and more detail and analysis by the left. For example, in people with left hemisphere damage, patients tend to draw with minimal detail but with an overall idea of the general shape. Conversely, those with right hemisphere damage appear to produce drawings with lots of detail but which lack 'overall coherence' and with poor proportion and spatial relationships between the figures or objects. This provides an interesting comparison to the 'tadpole' drawings produced by very young children where a 'person' is recognizable as a 'person' but there is very little detail. It is only when children are older that they begin to draw fingers, ears, more detailed faces, and so on, and it is around 9/10 years old that most children draw people with necks! The style of drawings may represent a transition from right to left dominance as the left hemisphere's love of detail comes into its own and as language becomes more sophisticated.

What some very early, pioneering work, carried out in the 1980s and quoted by Gazzaniga (1999) demonstrated was, if the two hemispheres were both involved in 'attention' processes and one half was 'working' particularly hard, then it was harder for the other half to carry out a task simultaneously. It may seem somewhat of a leap, but if Schore's (1994) firm belief based on many studies that it is the right hemisphere that is the most dominant in the early years and that spatial tasks are more involved in this hemisphere, it may go some way to explaining why young boys who have a more active behavioural style generally (and this is a huge generalization) are sometimes slower in language development. The male tendency to be more proficient at spatial/three-dimensional tasks could all be part of this picture. The finding of some variation in attentional focus depending on task may also provide a logic for the emotional vigilance of troubled children, which frequently precludes their ability to learn at their optimal level. Their 'searchlight' of attention is focused on their awareness of potential danger and so concentration on a task may be much harder. What emerges powerfully from the research is, first, that we do use all the parts of our brain on both sides in varying degrees dependent on tasks. Second, that the ability to synthesize information depends on the two halves communicating with each other, and this latter function also develops over time as the brain matures.

What is particularly important for those working with infants and very young children is not only that this communication between the two hemispheres has a time element, but also that the ability to 'cross the midline' is crucial for optimal development.[28] The finding that children aged around 4 years find difficulty in imitating contralateral (opposite) as opposed to ipsilateral (same side) actions (for example, touching the right ear with the left hand) may be indicative of the slow maturing of the developmental changes taking place in the corpus callosum[29] (Gattis et al., 2002). However, not only does this potentially illustrate the maturation of connections between the two hemispheres, the capacity to imitate may also illustrate maturing of connections within the hemispheres. Goldberg (2001) describes studies of patients with frontal lobe dysfunction who find it difficult to imitate the opposite of what the examiner is doing (that is, raise a fist when the examiner raises a finger). 'Sorting out' and copying bodily movements, appears therefore to indicate levels of brain 'communication'. Springer and Deutsch (1998) suggest that most of the anatomical differences in brain asymmetry appear to be through differences in right hemisphere development which again has links with the importance of experience in the early years when right sided processing appears to be more dominant. They also suggest that overall the right hemisphere is more involved in the processing of emotional information but with the caveat that the left hemisphere appears to be more involved in processing positive 'approach related' emotions.

Of significance is that the right hemisphere with its more 'global', integrative and holistic style of processing and its apparent dominance in the early years, also seems to have links with the establishment of a sense of self, achieved as it is initially through sensory information and the accompanying emotional context. Damage to the right frontal lobes in adult patients appears to result in subtle changes in behaviour, attitudes, motivation, self-reflection, and abilities to plan and understand the consequences of their actions, in other words, how someone functions as a person.

Does gender have an effect on the brain?

The answer to this question is, as so often, both yes and no. Overall, the consensus seems to be that while some studies demonstrate some differences and others do not, there nevertheless seems to be a recognizable trend towards an acceptance that there are some genuine differences which act more as 'predispositions' towards different activities, styles of behaviour and ways of thinking rather than absolutes. The proviso is, of course, that while there do exist tendencies or predispositions there are also within gender variations which must not be discounted. The area in which there is most agreement about gender difference is in that of verbal and visuospatial skills, with females and males showing different tendencies. For example, women's general use of language, fluency, speed of articulation and grammar, together with perceptual speed, manual precision and arithmetic calculation, appears to be more proficient. Males appear to perform better on tasks that are spatial in nature, in mathematical reasoning and in finding their way through a route, and are more accurate in throwing or catching. Such findings are also echoed and replicated in many studies by Baron-Cohen (2002, 2003, 2005) and colleagues (Baron-Cohen et al., 2002) and form the basis of his theory of the extreme male brain as the aetiology of autism. He builds this on his hypothesis that females, generally are 'empathizers' and males 'systemizers'.[30]

These findings require a reflective approach regarding teaching and overall teaching styles for both males and females rather than a global 'one size fits all' approach. Unfortunately as Springer and Deutsch (1998) point out, discussion about optimal approaches to education is often hijacked by ideology and political and/or social agendas. For example, a generalization can be made that women are not good at mathematics, whereas in fact both males and females can be 'good at' mathematics. What may be variable is the type of mathematics in which each may be predisposed to excel, for example, females may excel at being accountants while males may excel in the world of abstract mathematical theorizing of cosmology or astrophysics. It is not a question of superiority or inferiority but a manifestation of difference, which probably has its roots in our evolutionary roles. The other finding that seems to be generally accepted is that males have a tendency to be more 'lateralized' in brain organization, while females appear to bring a more generalized organization to tasks. The direction of the male lateralization appears to be to the left but the differences are often small.

However, there is one potentially crucial area and that is the rate of male versus female brain maturation, and it does seem that the male brain not only processes information slightly differently from the female brain, but also, as has already been indicated, a small but significant difference in the rate of brain maturation in some areas, with boys being approximately a year behind girls in readiness for more formal skills such as reading and writing (while being potentially ahead of girls in their gross motor and spatial skills). Please note that I am generalizing here across genders because, of course, there are differences within genders as well as between them. While this is a brief overview of general trends, there are implications for both preferred learning styles and type of provision. Sax (2001) puts forward a strong case for many boys not to enter school until the age of 6 years. He states that in a 'modern American kindergarten' the emphasis is on 'paper and pencil exercises, reading and arithmetic' and that the 'first grade curriculum has been gradually but inexorably "pushed down" into kindergarten' (Sax, 2001: 4).[31] Such an emphasis, he argues, plays on girls' strengths and boys' weaknesses because of the well-documented differences in maturation rates, and he suggests that provision should be much more developmentally appropriate.

Summary

The two hemispheres of our brain work together being both complementary and equally necessary for the optimal well-being of an individual. While in most of us, the left hemisphere is the most 'dominant' in the sense that we use language to communicate, the functioning of the right hemisphere provides the emotional colour and depth to our experiences. The ancient structure of our brain, combined with the evolutionary 'new' cortex, provides the framework for our 'mind' and sense of self through the broad organization, distribution of function and integrated relationships between the hemispheres. In addition, the hemispheric 'division of labour' would also seem to be the best use of space of a relatively small organ encased in a rigid skull.

Our particular gender plays a part too, in that it predisposes us to potentially have skills in particular areas of thought or language, which are complementary rather than conflicting. Goldberg (2001) suggests from his research that there are definite differences in the way male and female brains are predisposed to process information. He infers from his findings that there is not only a potential difference in 'degree' but 'in kind' and that 'the two sexes emphasize different aspects of functional cortical differentiation. In the male brain the left-right differences are better articulated than in the female brain. But in the female brain the front-back differences are better articulated than in the male brain' (Goldberg, 2001: 97) He sees these differences as essentially complementary. However, echoing Sax (2001), it raises the very real issue of developmentally appropriate provision for girls and boys which take into account their various strengths and preferred learning styles. The steady trend for girls to outdo boys in General Certificate of Secondary Education (GCSE) results may not reflect any female superiority (sorry!) but instead a much deeper and more worrying 'turn off' from formal education in boys, which begins with broadly inappropriate school-entering ages and a focus on the types of activity mentioned by Sax with emphasis on early reading and writing in more formalized contexts requiring sitting still. Decisions about care, learning and formal educational provision should be based on a rational, ideology-free and compassionate view of the research which indicates that overall there may be different needs at different ages for both genders.

In conclusion, those of you who may wish to read further about the brain itself have a wide choice ranging from the comprehensive, extremely detailed and weighty (in every sense of the word) work of Kandel et al. (2000) and Bear et al. (1996) to perhaps more accessible works such as those by Greenfield (1997, 2000), Carter (2000), Pinel and Edwards (1998) and Smith (2005). I strongly recommend Goldberg (2001) for a detailed look at the frontal cortex.

Finally, to check out the complexity of the human brain, try out a few tasks:[32]

- Imagine a favourite scene where you feel happy and comfortable. See the picture in your mind and hold it for about a minute.
- Tap your fingers one after the other on your desk or chair.
- Remember a time in your childhood such as your first day at school. Can you remember what you were wearing, who might have been with you? Can you remember how it felt?
- Add up a recent shopping receipt.

I have given the information for what is involved in the task of tapping your fingers below. (Don't peep!) The other tasks involve memory, processing of the senses and emotions – in fact, emotions would be involved in the tapping task too as you would be interested, intrigued or simply bemused by the request!

Brain areas involved in tapping your fingers

Tapping your fingers in succession would activate groups of neurons in at least four distinct areas of the brain: the *prefrontal cortex*, where your brain makes the conscious decision to do the task; the *premotor cortex*, where you formulate the instructions for doing the task; the *motor cortex*, a sort of relay station that sends those instructions on to the arm and hand muscles that move the fingers; and the *cerebellum*, which supervises the whole process and adjusts your actions as necessary in response to external cues, such as where your hand is in relation to the desk.

(Balog, 2006: 9)

If there was anything amiss in the workings of our brain in any one of these areas, such a simple task would be difficult, from understanding the instruction, to carrying out the task. Immaturity in any of these areas would also make the task impossible or very difficult. Think about, too, if you were to tap your fingers in time to a favourite tune on the radio or recording...

3 'A world of one's own': the body and the senses

Our senses are indeed our doors and windows on this world, in a very real sense the key to the unlocking of meaning and the wellspring of creativity.

Jean Houston

In the last chapter, the brain's structure, maturation, function, aspects of hemispheric laterality and potential gender differences were discussed. In this chapter, I am going to consider the sources of the information to our brain and will start with movement and touch, then move on to the more traditional 'senses', that is, hearing, taste and smell and, finally, vision leading into an overview of face-processing/eye gaze.

Background

The senses are fascinating because while they are all ultimately processed in our brain as electrical impulses, they remain unique and distinct in their quality. However, as is the case so often with the brain, the picture is not quite so clear cut. There exists a strange phenomenon in some people known as 'synesthesia' where the senses are not so highly differentiated and people experience a combination. For example, the most common is experiencing sounds as tastes, that is, both hearing a sound with an accompanying taste sensation, or visual experiences with accompanying smell. Rarer are people who can 'see' tastes or associate words with postures (Carter, 2000). However, this 'mixing' of the senses does exist in all of us to some extent: for example, when we describe a taste as 'sharp' or words 'jumping out' from a page and taste itself is particularly mingled with smell. Consider when you have a heavy cold how dull food tastes and the way wine or tea tasters smell the liquid first. In addition, what seems to be emerging from studies quoted by Carter – although still not fully explained – is that babies appear to have similar patterns of sensory processing as that seen in people with synesthesia. However, there is logic to such an idea. For example, if we consider there is proximity of the main visual area to the auditory cortex together with the slow process of myelination, 'spillover' as Carter puts it, can occur.

However, our senses do provide babies with a powerful 'kick start' for experiencing our environment via smell, taste,[1,2] hearing, touch and movement. Initially, sensory experiences may be mainly undifferentiated, as above, but as we live our day-to-day infant life the different sensations we experience begin to develop and refine their particular pathways. Again, there is a logic to this, as if we – or rather our brains – did not differentiate between different types of information, we would probably lose some of the richness and complexity that an individual sense can give us thereby allowing us to either enjoy it or change focus. For example, something of visual beauty may make us linger, or the unpleasant smell of tainted food will dominate any visual 'evidence' that the food may be acceptable. Equally, differentiation of our senses into particular pathways ensures that we are not 'overloaded' or confused by a plethora of information warring for our attention.

What is also crucial about a broad understanding of sensory and motor systems is that sensation is suffused with emotional meaning. Touch, for example, can convey information about temperature and pressure, but also can convey a range of emotions from empathy to aggression. Taste can bring with it feelings of happy enjoyment or disgust at something bitter or foul. Smell can invoke memories of tremendous power. Hearing allows us to experience the full range of human and environmental beauty and also dis-cordance, despair, distress, fear or pain. Vision allows us to see our world and through our dreams a self-induced vision of our experiences. We also use our eyes intensively to convey meaning and we assign powerful emotions to the gaze or look of others. Glances can be described as being soft or hard, loving or hateful, flirtatious or pleading. When we attend to our language, we gain insight into the importance of the senses in the way we organize our thoughts and behaviour frequently using vision as a metaphor for understanding (as we do hearing). It is through our senses that we become aware of the 'I' that represents the feeling of having the 'self' that responds to, interacts with, acts upon, thinks about and emotionally reacts to the particular life we live – because the senses are both objective and subjective. The how of what we experience is common to all of us – what we actually perceive as our experiences is individual and unique. Whatever the mechanism may be that transforms the sensory into electrical impulses, which then transform into the meaning interpreted as what 'I' experience, it remains that the senses compose what Carter (2000: 178) calls 'a world of one's own'.

The body, movement and balance

I sometimes think that our bodies (including our heads) get rather short shrift when thinking about development apart from knowledge concerning the development of fine and gross motor skills. However, our bodies provide a rich source of sensation via touch, limb positions, posture and sensations of pain or comfort, both internal and external. As Sheets-   Johnstone (1999: 226) says:

> Fundamental facets of our knowledge of the world derive from our basic kinetic corporeal commonalities. As infants we all explored the world about us. We picked up objects, put them in our mouths, turned them about in our hands, studied them from various perspectives. Through touch and movement we come to constitute the world epistemologically for ourselves; we came to know a spoon, a ball, an apple, a book, a box ... from touching it and moving it directly and/or from moving ourselves in relation to it. Moving toward objects, approaching them from different directions, stopping in front of them, peering down or up at them, grasping them, mouthing them, we engaged the world on the basis of our tactile-kinesthetic bodies.... Coming to know the world in a quite literal sense means coming to grips with it.

What we take for granted is the fact that we walk upright on two legs and this 'bi-pedalism' is unique in the animal kingdom. We are also able to have eye and head/body position independent of one another, for example, we can look to the side, without turning our head or body or turn our heads without moving the body. For us to maintain balance and posture we depend on ongoing information from current body posture and movement including and especially the head and eyes. Before we make a move, there are countless 'pre-movements' made by our bodies to ensure that we do not fall over, for example, when reaching for something or turning to look. We also need to move in order to experience – the baby cannot actively experience a mobile or a rattle without being able to reach and touch. In the womb, the baby is not passive and, especially in the third trimester, demonstrates a range of movements, expressions, thumb-sucking, eye-blinking, breathing, and so on. The baby also is subject to bodily sensations which are tactile (the amniotic fluid and the sides of the womb as well as the baby's own skin-to-skin contact as it lies curled in the womb) and will give information as to body position. In the baby's 'toolbox' the body is the first instrument.

This emphasis on movement may be reflected in the finding that the only sensory system myelinated at the time of birth is the vestibular (balance) system (Goddard, 2005). This system is, perhaps, one of the more neglected sensory systems, whereas its proper development together with body position and movement provide a fundamental aspect of our day-to-day lives. The movement of the head appears, in particular, to be sensed by the structures within the inner ear and this helps track both balance and direction. It is possible that the first step in orienting direction and balance may be a combination of the movements experienced by the baby as it is moved by its carers, the broad movements it makes for itself and for baby to be able to track movement in the carer's head/face. Movement both of the baby and of those around it become a bi-directional synchrony.

Most of us are familiar with the concept of reflexes, especially those of a newborn baby of which the primary ones are rooting/sucking, stepping, startle and grasp. However, there are other less commonly mentioned reflexes, which are, the asymmetrical tonic reflex, the spinal Galant reflex, the tonic labyrinthine reflex and the symmetrical tonic neck reflex. The key point about these reflexes is that they support two key factors for development, that is, interaction with carers and the child's capacity for movement. Table 3.1 shows the usual time frame for the appearance and diminishing of those reflexes primarily concerned with movement.

As the baby rolls, sits and then moves independently prior to standing and walking, the whole system of balance is supported by the appearance and inhibition of the various reflexes. These reflexes appear to me to have a different qualitative function to a reflex such as a tap on the knee, which causes the leg to jerk forwards – although all are indicative of neurological health. They appear to be, rather, 'templates' on which the baby is then able to build from experiences in the womb.

Something that is of particular interest regarding the debate that exists between a 'maturational' or 'interactive' view of brain development, is consideration of the appearance and gradual inhibition of the primitive reflexes. Studies of patients with Alzheimer's disease (dementia) suggest that these reflexes begin to re-emerge in the order in which they were inhibited, that is, the latest in infancy appear first in such patients (Walterfang and Velakoulis, 2005).[3] This also supports a suggestion that these reflexes or templates do not 'disappear' but become incorporated into increasingly conscious action. As patients with Alzheimers gradually lose function in the frontal cortex, it would seem that the mind reverts to an early childhood state – but with the complex influence of many years of experience.

Links between bodily movement and the other senses

As we can see, the movements that infants experience such as rocking, being picked up, bounced and gently 'swung' are exactly those which help the vestibular system to interact with the other senses. For example, Muller et al. (2001) state that the mechanisms for visual development in very early childhood depend on the interplay between the child's experience of looking and movement (or being moved) and the consequent changes in synaptic strength and neural firing patterns – so the instinctive actions of parents when handling their infants provides the stimulation the sensory systems need. In addition, any information on movement processed by the brain is

Table 3.1 Types of reflexes: emergence and inhibition[4]

Reflex	Emergence	Birth	Inhibited/diminished
Moro/startle	9/52 utero	Fully present	2–4 months post-natal
Palmar/grasp	11/52 utero	Fully present	2–3 months post-natal – changes from involuntary grasp to release and fine finger control. Replaced by pincer grip at 36 weeks (approximately)
Asymmetrical tonic reflex (when the baby's head is to one side, the arm and leg on that side are extended and the arm and leg on the other side are flexed	18/52 utero	Fully present	About 6 months post-natal – followed by the symmetrical tonic reflex which emerges around 6–9 months post-natal and which diminishes between 9 and 11 months
Spinal gallant. This can be seen if baby is placed in prone position and the back stroked on one side of the spine. The baby will flex the leg on the side of the stimulus, to about 45 degrees	20/52 utero	Actively present	Between 3 and 9 months post-natal
Tonic labyrinthine reflex (TLR) (forwards)	In utero	Present	About 4 months post-natal
TLR (backwards). This reflex appears to help the baby to 'straighten out' from the 'flexed position of the foetus and newborn'	At birth		Gradually from 6/52 weeks post-natal to 3 years. Subsumed into the later 'postural' reflexes

also intricately involved with sensory feedback as the feel of the body in both personal and further space provides the framework for where hands, arms, legs and head need to move in order to achieve what we want.

The close relationship between the body, sensory systems and movement is exemplified by the existence of adjacent motor and sensory 'maps' in the brain which lie respectively in the motor cortex[5] at the back of the frontal lobe and in the somatosensory cortex at the front of the parietal cortex. These maps replicate the body on a small, variable scale, with parts of the motor map varied according to the precision and/or amount of use of the body parts in question and the somatosensory map on the particular part's sensitivity to sensory information. Each map therefore displays a distorted picture of the body, illustrating clearly the overall importance of each body area and the relationships between them. Incidentally, their positioning reflects the curled foetal position as well as their dimensions relevant to usage.

Three important points to make about these maps are:

- The maps are *fine-tuned*, that is, there is not one single map for either body sense or movement but finely tuned individual maps for the body parts.
- Size and shape can change according to experience, for example the loss of a finger, will lead, over time, to an adaptation of the maps with the other fingers 'taking over' the space.[6]
- As information proceeds from brain stem up into the cortex, sensory information is initially segregated and then, as it moves upwards, this information begins to converge in particular sites within the lobes where complex representations of the information begin to be formed.

To emphasize the last point, even though these maps are arranged on specific regions of the cortex, nevertheless the upward processing of information requires aspects of organization across *all* the cortex and other brain areas. For example, the basal ganglia[7] and the cerebellum are particularly involved in the organization of movement. It does seem that the cerebellum seems to contain timekeeping systems (Levitin, 2006). For example, we can sing songs from memory very close to their original tempo.[8] This mechanism combined with the maturation rate of the cerebellum provides some explanation why it takes practice for a child to learn how to 'brake' when moving quickly and needing to stop or to smoothly and accurately reach for a drink or to learn a dance step. The cerebellum is also involved at working out the speed at which objects are moving – which involves both space and time.

While it can appear to us that when we make a conscious decision to perform an action, the thought appears to be instantaneous with the action associated with it – in reality thought/idea and action chase one another in 'real time'. Some movements, particularly rapid voluntary movements such as throwing a ball cannot be altered by sensory feedback once the throw has started. What seems to happen is that such movements rely on sensory information before the action and it is the basal ganglia which seems to coordinate this part of the process in these types of movements. This unconscious preparatory state deserves some comment as it illustrates the degree of anticipation that occurs before we carry out any willed action, not one that we simply copy.

However, it is only by repeated trial and error, imitation of others and the resultant sensory feedback that our brains 'wire up' patterns of sufficient complexity which, in turn, provide the framework on which our mind/brains can then smoothly anticipate both action and reaction.[9] The ability to repeat an action, practise and imitate brings with it the assumption of the capacity to do so, and this means being able to match our own bodily movements to that of another. This suggests that

- we understand we have a body and where our limbs and parts including facial features are *and*
- we recognize that others have bodies similar to ours.

This is where the 'mirror' neurons mentioned in Chapter 2 come in.

Movement and touch: the somatosensory system

Being touched is an integral part of early experience and is part and parcel of the sensory information received during day-to-day care of the baby and young child. Nothwithstanding the generally universal acceptance that as babies, soothing touching, confident handling and cuddles are a necessary part of care, our perception of touch is complex. This is perhaps because touch is profoundly associated with feelings, and people's experiences can fundamentally alter the way in which they perceive their ability to give and receive affection. People can be very different in their capacity to tolerate touch and even the type of touch or the part of the body where touch is acceptable and/or welcomed. We associate touching with empathy and understanding, yet there are many people who cannot tolerate such touching and see it as unwelcome and intrusive. Some babies too, may be hypersensitive to touch or be aversive to over-delicate handling. In some instances it may not be that the baby is averse to touch per se, but rather to who is doing the touching, as not every adult finds touch in this emotional/caring sense 'easy' or 'natural' and babies sense this. Some children, too, do not necessarily welcome being touched by adults if their experience has been confusing, inappropriate or minimal in this regard.

However, touch is not only associated with emotions, but also with exploration. We discover the world through active touch, that is, we use our hands and fingers to feel our environment (and ourselves). As a newborn baby, someone reaches for our hands or offers a toy or rattle. This may be passive but the grasping reflex means that there is an action of the fingers, which gradually leads to the conscious hand and later finger movements in making discoveries. We use touch and pressure to grasp and hold, we find a key on a key-ring in the dark by feeling for it, we want something out of a bag and we 'rifle' through its contents with our fingers. Active touching includes pulling, lifting, stretching, squeezing, fingering – all of which are in the baby's repertoire for exploration over time. It is interesting that the most sensitive parts of the body for the reception of touch are the fingers, the hands, the tip of the tongue and parts of the mouth – all areas heavily involved in very early exploration/learning.[10] When we touch, we both touch and feel at the same time – a dual process. For example, when the baby 'finds its feet' and enjoys the feeling of the feet in its mouth, the baby is not only receiving information from the mouth but also from the feet, thereby providing a knowledge of what 'my feet' feel like. It is interesting that this ability comes just before many babies are beginning to support their weight, allowing the brain to assimilate the familiar feeling of feet with the new sensation of feet to surface plus weight. Remember when you have had 'pins and needles' in your feet or legs and just how difficult it is to walk when you have lost the feeling in them.

The 'haptic system'

This is a combination of information from the skin and muscle position. It is responsible for the perception of the shape, dimensions and proportions of objects handled (Schiffman, 2001). We can see how the systems link together as we discover the shape, texture, temperature, solidity and weight of an object through vision, smell, touch, hand/finger position and hearing (the sound emitted by tapping on an object often tells us much about the object, for example, if a watermelon sounds hollow, it is ripe). I am sure that the baby's mouthing of objects has links with the baby's handling of objects, which leads to the hand and fingers shaping to adapt to the object as the child reaches.[11] Schiffman describes the haptic system as supporting eating by sensing food texture, but I suggest that mouthing and the ensuing sensory information allied with vision also allows the forming of mouth shape to adapt to food shape. Eating would be difficult if we were not able to do this – imagine eating spaghetti as opposed to eating an apple!

Our bodies, selves and minds

The growing concept of 'my body belonging to me' requires a long period of movement/sensory feedback. If we think back to the discussion on the roles of the different hemispheres, you may recall the involvement of the right parietal lobe in forming body awareness. The 'maps', which are constantly updated dependent on our daily experience, provide us with a body 'schema', which Roberts (2002) describes as a system which represents and coordinates our body posture movement and feeling and this also ties in with the idea of our body 'image', which provides us with the concept of what our body is like and whereabouts everything is. Body image, however, also depends on visual feedback and it is very interesting that young children's ability to recognize themselves in a mirror approximately coincides with the ability to point to their own body parts so they can link both body 'schema' and 'image'. This provides a rationale for a strong link between the development of a physical sense of self and the abstract. In other words, the bodily sense of 'me' is the precursor to the conscious sense of 'I'. There is another link to be made here – as we explore our environment, we receive a simultaneous matching up of sensory experience, associating a touch with a texture and/or a sound and/or a movement and so on, and connections in the physical world may be the early precursors of the child's later ability to make abstract connections between objects, an idea supported by the work of Diamond (2006) which is touched on again in Chapter 6.

We need to recognize that a child's body image and body schema is as much a part of their development and learning as any other area, and needs adult understanding and support. Damasio (1999, 2003) has presented a hypothesis of the 'somatic self' and he argues that what supports our understanding of what 'me' is, where our bodies are and where they start and stop, comes from the general 'sameness' of the bodily signals from day to day, which he calls 'somatic markers', allowing us to have a familiarity with an amalgam of the external and internal self experienced through these sensations. In other words, we know what we feel like.

A paper by Jeannerod (2004) also provides links with brain functioning and understanding of self and other from the discovery of a new visual area,[12] which from fMRI imaging of 'normal' adult subjects selectively responds to visual images of human bodies or body parts – even when partially hidden. In addition, the response was observed even when the subjects were preparing to move or *imagined* the movement. This information makes sound links with understanding how imitation may work as such a powerful learning process via not only mirror neurons, but also the particular responses to self-movement suggested by these studies. A further speculation is whether such neurons also activate when a child is 'daydreaming' and also when dreaming action sequences in actual sleep. Given that very young babies spend a lot of their sleep time in rapid eye movement (REM – 'dreaming'; see also Chapter 4) sleep, this also may provide another 'arena' for practising movement. A further point from the study was that these particular neurons integrate external signals, that is, from what is able to be seen by the individual when moving their own body and the sensations from the actual or imagined movement.

However, this leads to my suggestion that the physical forming of our 'sense of self' in infancy and early 'toddlerhood' is at its most vulnerable and that inappropriate, confusing or dysfunctional experiences and/or processing by the senses may cause a substantial 'fault line' in the initial construction of who 'I' am. Temple Grandin (Grandin and Johnson, 2005) illustrates this in her difficulties in understanding both what her senses are telling her and her sense of space, the relationships between her body, the bodies of others and the objects around her.[13] Another example is given by a respondent in an Internet discussion group on autism who described her 20-year-old son with Asperger's as follows:

> He says he has NO physical sensation that he even has a 'body'. He cannot do anything in which the referent is solely a part of his body. He can do it if one of the two referents is somebody ELSE's body, or an inanimate object, or an animal. He cannot easily locate a pain if he has one, unless he or I can see a wound. He cannot clench his teeth together for the dentist, unless there is a piece of paper, or a device, he can put between his teeth as a referent.

This young man had no sense of his body without a visual or tactile referent – neither body image nor body schema appear to have aligned themselves in his brain.

I suspect it is only as we reach beyond 18 months/2 years with knowledge of body parts and the associated labelling that we can assimilate and 'ground' our sense of who we are, at least until puberty. Puberty with its emergence of new feelings and body changes provokes a confusion in the sense of self which is emotional and cognitive as well as physical/maturational and which needs to 'reassemble' so that the young adult re-emerges with a stronger (hopefully) sense of self which is increasingly less fixed in the physical and more into the abstract.[14]

How it all pulls together

Information from the body is carried in various feedback loops through different brain structures and the cortex. All the different, but nevertheless related types of information – such as when a baby feels, examines, tastes and smells a wooden brick – pass through these neural structures in parallel, only beginning to integrate and merge as they reach the higher brain areas where the apparently seamless and rapid 'knowing' or representation of what we are experiencing eventually occurs. If we remember that sensory information also has a feeling response to what we experience, this will also form part of the holistic integration of sensation to representation.

Another point for consideration is what emphasis or 'weighting' is given to the sensory information arriving in the brain (Sun et al. 2003). This suggests that it is the type, quality, timing, persistence and accompanying sensation of sensory cues that provide the information regarding reliability/stability of sensation and it is this information on which other experiences are then based. Using our hands as 'tools' and using tools as an extension of our hands also requires that we understand the sensory information we are receiving. For example, one of the most common activities in children aged 4–6 years is beginning to cut with scissors, and perhaps one of the reasons that children find this so difficult at first is that we get the sensation of cutting *at the blades of the scissors* (try it). Children need to feel confident about their own hand image/sensations as well as the development of fine muscle movements before they can begin to cut confidently as the sensation of the scissors being part of the hand (almost) may be quite difficult for the brain to 'work out'. However, after a time we expect certain sensory bits of information to be 'in tune' and our use of our hands and the rest of our body becomes more coordinated.

A world of hearing

Being able to hear helps us to detect and locate sound, identify its source, detect its nuances, evoke emotion and, of course, enables us to use verbal communication with its range of psychological properties. We hear via sound waves which are converted by the hair cells in our inner ear into electrical signals which are then carried to the brain. There they are interpreted into the myriad sounds that we identify as a dog barking, someone singing, a child laughing, a bird calling. How the hearing mechanism actually works still remains much of a mystery but what is known is that sounds have features in common, such as intensity, pitch, timbre, rhythm, melody, harmony, tempo, meter and location, and each of these is represented in a different way in the auditory neural pathways – again similar to the stimulus 'breakdown' in vision into colour, form, motion, depth, and so on, and like vision there are overarching organizational principles dependent on the type of stimulus.

A difference, however, is that information from both ears is sent to both hemispheres although most of the left ear's signals do go to the right hemisphere and vice versa. As hearing is particularly important for hearing human speech, it is interesting that human speech is complex for the ear to detect as the level at which speech vibrations occur is less than the low-frequency limit of hearing. However, various receptors in the ear appear to act as 'frequency analysers' so that the different sound peaks produced by different vowel sounds are represented in specific patterns in the auditory system. Sound location is achieved by the brain 'comparing' the differences in timing and intensity between each ear, for example a sound on one side would reach the same-side ear first and then the other ear a fraction later, and location would be based on these differences. A sound presented to the midline however – and most parents talk to their baby looking directly at them – reaches the two ears simultaneously.

Budiansky (2003) points out that before the age of 4 months, human infants are confused by the echoes of sound, for example, an initial sound coming from the right may 'bounce off' a wall or other large object to the left of the listener so that the sound is heard from the original direction plus an 'echo'. After 4 months of age, babies seem to be able to localize much better as the maturing brain circuits appear to 'actively suppress' the echo. I suspect this is a development that has been supported through a myriad of face-to-face interactions which enable babies to sort out sound coming to their ears simultaneously as a 'marker' among all the myriad sounds they hear. In other words, the way that parents talk to their babies[15] with exaggerated mouth movements and vocalizations all support the baby in localizing as well as copying the mouth movements and making the sounds. The exaggerated vowels and highly variable pitch of the carer's language towards their child also helps the baby's brain to organize the sounds of its language as well as the highly charged emotional atmosphere of fun and love such talking often generates. Again, this has similarities in vision – discussed later – whereby babies appear to need to be able to focus to the front first in order to then more accurately locate to looking towards the sides.

By 8–12 months, babies all over the world have learned to discriminate the sounds of their own language, and their acute sensitivity to the nuances of languages they do not experience diminishes (Gopnik et al., 1999). The future ability to produce 'normal' coherent speech is supported by auditory feedback particularly during development producing vocalizations that are matched to the sounds of others, according to Brainard and Doupe (2000), who also contend that this feedback needs to be relatively continuous throughout life. For example, adults who suffer profound hearing loss have a correlated loss of speech intelligibility.

The ability to identify familiar sounds and the common finding that babies 'find their voices' during this same phase, cooing, shrieking and babbling, potentially reinforces Brainard and Doupe's notion of feedback, as the babies may be providing their own feedback experiments, that is, matching their own sounds to the sounds they hear. The emphasis on the role of feedback also provides some speculation about children with autism if they have problems processing facial information as this will affect not only any feedback from seeing facial expressions regarding emotion, eye gaze and so on, but also the lack of auditory feedback to aid speech. The possible lack of meaningful (to them) feedback may then, layer on layer, lead to their own behaviour being seen as less comprehensible by their carers because the main 'template' for their interactions has become primarily *self*-referencing. For example, children with autism have been demonstrated to mimic tapes of their own voices rather than tapes of the voices of other children. Hobson (1997).

Each hemisphere also appears to have a role in sound-processing; the left hemisphere is particularly dedicated to the words, grammar and construct of speech, while the right hemisphere appears to be more involved with the musicality, rhythm and tone of speech as well as in the appreciation of music itself. This right-sided preference again links in with the general assumption of right hemispheric dominance in the first three years of life as it is the musicality of early language directed towards babies which appears to be universal. It is interesting, too, that the most 'primitive' parts of the brain, that is the brain stem and the cochlear nucleus in the inner ear – structures possessed by all vertebrates – are involved in recognizing whether sounds are pleasant or unpleasant – so right from birth the baby is able to potentially discriminate between sounds that appear to be universally pleasing.

A world of smell and taste

Smell and taste are the two senses most involved with our primary needs of hunger, thirst and later sexual activity, and are very difficult to separate and, indeed, smell has been described as 'taste at a distance'. Smell and taste also have strong emotional components as we talk of 'comfort food' and smell has the power to elicit powerful emotions and memories. Research by Phillips and Cupchik (2004) found a strong association between the types of recall of positive reading matter when associated with a pleasant smell and the reading of negative subject matter associated with an unpleasant smell. The interesting finding was that the combination of the two positives resulted in more accurate recall of character details, while the negative/negative resulted in a more accurate recall of settings. This raises some interesting possibilities when considering how infants lay down their sensory memories of their experiences and relationships. Adults often describe how, for example, they remember the smell of their mother's perfume when being kissed goodnight and such associations may all support the infant's positive learning about their carer. However, negative smells such as alcohol on the breath or sweat may instead contribute to an overarching experience of a dangerous/ unpleasant situation in which the personalities involved may then become associated. The dislike/fear by many people of hospitals because of the smell and the associated avoidance of anything to do with hospitals comes to mind. Smell and taste also warn us of danger – we do not eat what disgusts us, either by smell or taste – and such a reaction is often evoked by what would be truly dangerous to us – poisons or rotting substances. Smell and taste, as with the other senses, can become increasingly sensitive – perfumiers, wine and tea tasters being some of the professionals for whom smell and taste are particularly highly developed. While we know that other animals such as dogs have a highly developed sense of smell we often do not realize our own 'normal' sensitivity to distinguish literally thousands of 'odoriferous chemicals'. There also appears to be a gender bias demonstrated in a study by Dalton et al. (2002) where women showed greater sensitivity to particular smells over time than did men. However, these sensitivities to some odours were only distinctive in women between menarche and menopause and the researchers suggested that while such sensitivity had a 'downside', a more positive interpretation was an evolutionary/biological one suggesting that such sensitivity meant a greater ability to recognize infants and other kin through their scent together with a similar heightened ability to find good food sources and avoid toxic substances. Babies are born with a sense of smell and can identify within a few hours their mother's breast milk compared with that of others and the findings in the above study could indicate that not just babies but mothers too can identify the 'smell' of their baby, and there is anecdotal evidence for this. Babies are also born with the four basic taste senses, that is, sour, sweet, bitter and salt.[16] What is interesting, given the controversy over the use of salt, is that hunger for salt and certain other foods appears to be innate but also that aversion to foods can be quickly learned. Smell and taste are biological necessities for our physical well-being but they are also heavily endowed with emotional resonance and, like colour or texture, they can become representations of something welcome or something to be avoided both physically and emotionally. For example, both normally developing children and those with particular needs can develop highly specific (and passionate) preferences or aversion to tastes, sounds or smells.

A world of vision

> The eye is the most refined of our senses, the one which communicates most directly with our mind, our consciousness.
>
> (Robert Delaunay)

The visual system is complex and also highly organized with divergence of different aspects of the visual process, and yet through the reorganization and coherence of its system we have a useful template for considering how all other information is shared throughout the brain. It is a fair assumption that nature is inclined to use what works, for example, the mammalian eye differs little from species to species, with variations being mainly due to differing needs. Furthermore, the fact that vision is not only a 'mechanical' process but also is imbued with psychological, motor and cognitive connections make it an excellent medium for considering the differing relationships between these connections.

We will start by taking Ramachandran and Blakeslee's (1999) perspective by employing that old saying that 'there is more to vision than meets the eye'. To illustrate this, I will take the example they give of a patient who was apparently blind but who could reach for objects accurately and even correctly align a letter to 'post' it in a mail slot. In other words 'vision' involves much more than the, albeit wonderful, 'mechanics' of retinal images and photoreceptors. What we need to understand is that vision and the other senses form part of a symbolic representation of the world and that we 'sense' via a symbolic language created by neurons. What we do is we disassemble the information, which then becomes reassembled into the experience we have of 'seeing', hearing, tasting, and so on – but which is unique to each of us. When we look at something, the different types of information – shape, colour, depth, distance, motion – all activate different patterns of neurons which then pass their information on to the 'higher' areas of the cortex. Ramachandran gives the example of what is termed the Necker cube,[17] which can be perceived either as pointing upward and to the left or downward and to the right – even though the image remains static in reality – as illustrating how what we see is ultimately perceived. When we look at something, we are not even aware of the tiny 'jumps' or saccades that our eyes make as they move across a page or scan a view or gaze into the eyes of someone we love. Ramachandran also points out that his work over many years with people who have sustained damage to different parts of the brain has led him to the conclusion that we create our own reality from mere fragments of information and that what we see is a reliable, but not always accurate, representation of what exists in the world.

The experience of vision, or indeed the experience of any of the senses, exists on two levels – the subjective experience and the objective 'third person account' of what is there. You and I see a table and there will be the objective view of wood (or hardboard and veneer!), four legs (maybe), colour and shape. However, what we experience as we look at the table will depend on our particular context at the time. If I was looking for a new table, this could influence how I 'saw' the table. This applies to whatever we see. When a baby looks at the human face, the baby will actively see the face in the context of visual maturation (that is, the physiological element) and will also experience a sensation dependent on both the expression on the face and how the baby is feeling itself – hot, cold, tired, lonely, playful. The face will become imbued with meaning and associations. In other words, there is a substantial, qualitative difference between how information is transmitted from the eye to the brain and what we eventually experience as 'seeing'. What I suggest is that our emotional 'view' of the world also influences to a greater or lesser degree, dependent on context, the peculiarly personal 'angle of perception' of our visual experience. In addition, there is the very interesting question of 'internal imagery', that is how and what we see when we imagine, and what this may mean for someone whose imagination seems to be impoverished in a particular way. For example, what might be the implications for a child who cannot engage in fantasy role play but can still hold representations of objects 'in mind'? Is this a disability or simply a change in an 'angle of perception' from what is termed the 'normal'? In addition, the actual ability to see requires the combination of a number of segregated bodies of information, the efficiency of which depends on innate processes, which are then promoted and developed by experience.

The visual system itself is highly complex and some of its functions are still poorly understood. However, there are some key points to emphasize to add to the evidence for highly integrated functions both within and between developmental systems. The visual system itself undergoes significant developmental changes over the first few months of life. Newborns can see – albeit in a limited fashion.[18] They can move their eyes and scan objects that appear in their visual field (Hunnius et al., 2006). However, to highlight key maturation areas, I am indebted to Atkinson (2000) for an excellent and comprehensive text based on her own and others' research over many years. This work identifies the following:[19]

- Newborn vision is limited to orientating to single targets especially faces.
- By 3 months, vision appears to be sufficiently integrated for the baby to switch attention from one 'object' to another accompanied by a parallel development of such systems as orientation, motion and colour awareness – incidentally all becoming more sensitive over time. For example, newborns and infants under a month appear to have very poor or absent colour discrimination.
- Around 5 to 6 months, there is visual control of reach and grasp pointing to awareness of 'near visual space'.

Interestingly, a child's ability to reach with one hand appears to coincide with the child's control of the trunk, when it can sit steadily unsupported, usually around 8 months. If you are still 'wobbly' when sitting, reaching is probably more successful two-handed!

- By 1 year, there is visual control of locomotion, which indicates an integration of physical action, attention control and awareness of far and near visual space.
- By 18 months, there is an integration of 'recognition, action and speech'.

What Figure 3.1 cannot illustrate is that the adult visual system takes many months and in some parts, years, before being fully functional. For example, the process of interconnectivity and pruning to 'define the fine structure of receptive fields to achieve the adult values of acuity and contrast sensitivity' appears to continue until the ages of 3–4 years. Atkinson also points out that the retina, the LGN and the visual cortex develop in parallel anatomically. However, a newborn does appear to have a capacity for

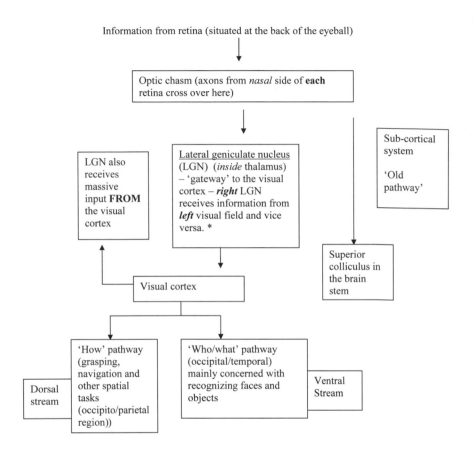

Information from retina (situated at the back of the eyeball)

Optic chasm (axons from *nasal* side of **each** retina cross over here)

LGN also receives massive input **FROM** the visual cortex

Lateral geniculate nucleus (LGN) (*inside* thalamus) – 'gateway' to the visual cortex – *right* LGN receives information from *left* visual field and vice versa. *

Sub-cortical system

'Old pathway'

Visual cortex

Superior colliculus in the brain stem

'How' pathway (grasping, navigation and other spatial tasks (occipito/parietal region))

Dorsal stream

'Who/what' pathway (occipital/temporal) mainly concerned with recognizing faces and objects

Ventral Stream

*Note that left and right visual fields contain information from the left and right eyes, for example the left visual field is composed of information from the nasal left retina and temporal right retina so that information is both ipsilateral and contralateral. The information is arranged in the lateral geniculate nucleus (LGN) in orderly alternate layers providing an exact topographic map of information from the two eyes.

Figure3.1 Broad outline of visual pathways.

reasonably sophisticated eye movements and a good orientating system (Atkinson, 2000) but visual development overall is very rapid, particularly after the first 6 weeks of life (incidentally tying in with when the first smiles reliably appear) and which also suggest a period of adjustment to life outside the muted sound and colour of the womb.

An area of particular interest is the linkage between vision and movement, and even newborns appear to express a preference for moving rather than static objects and also some understanding of direction. Newborns can orient in the right direction towards an attractor and can 'pre-reach', that is, wave an arm in roughly the correct direction for close objects, which means that some manifestation of dorsal stream processing exists. The ability to discriminate movement is important to differentiate one object from another and we also have to learn about the coherence of movement, that is, that objects move as a complete unit and not in disparate sections. We do this via cues which become increasingly more sophisticated as the visual system develops, for example, form, colour, brightness, relative motion and depth. Grossberg et al. (2001) indicate that neonates see partly hidden objects as disjointed but the ability to 'pull together' related objects develops rapidly between 2 and 4 months.[20] In addition, infants and young children need to learn the spatial relationships between objects and it would seem that, while very young babies can roughly work out where an object is in space, it takes many months before they can understand more detailed spatial relationships. For example, children's ability to make a construction of blocks appears to follow a regular pattern with the vast majority of 1-year-olds, who, while being able to spontaneously construct a stack of one or two bricks, are unable to copy anything different. Furthermore children of 18 months who can copy building a stack of bricks have great difficulty copying a design made of a line of bricks. This does not seem to be because of any physiological difficulty in the child discriminating between local features (the bricks) and global features (the design), as some studies quoted by Atkinson illustrated that infants of 3–4 months possess some degree of local and global discrimination. It would seem that the concept of 'next to' requires more sophisticated processing and emphasizes that there is a segregation of visual processing into the ventral and dorsal streams mentioned earlier.

Apart from the powerful links between vision, perception and movement, a further correlation is the link between vision and attention, which pulls together sensory, perceptual, cognitive, motor and emotional information. When we 'attend' to something, it usually means that we have to move our focus from one thing to another – we need to be able both to attend and to change attention otherwise we would become fixated and unable to function. When we 'shift' our attention, it can be either as a response to a novel sight or sound, that is, we turn to look at the source, or it can be 'internally' generated as we actively seek out what we wish to 'attend'. The latter illustrates the links between vision and imitation/curiosity and motivation. What influences early 'attention' is the physiological limitations of vision and context. Babies have a limited visual field and, so, attention is narrow and requires effort to change plus they need adult intervention to help attend to a wider range of objects than would be within the baby's own abilities. Visual acuity and the ability to shift attention become more sensitive with age together with the baby's increasing motor abilities.

However, from my understanding, it seems that we need to learn, as infants, to shift our gaze before we then are able to inhibit our attention when there are competing stimuli – in other words we need to be able to physically change focus before we learn how to choose which of the competing stimuli we wish to attend to. This suggestion arises from the findings that 1-month-olds find it very difficult to switch their gaze from one stimuli to a competing one while the original stayed in view – while 3-month-olds did this much more easily. Where the picture becomes somewhat muddied, however, is that care needs to be taken when thinking about a young child's ability to 'attend' because 'long looking' can simply mean improved information processing. Brown et al. (2003: 1039) point out, for example, that there is intense speculation about the role of neurons in the parietal cortex 'in establishing "body centred" frames of reference for action, i.e. integrating information about head, eye and body position with respect to a target in the environment'. This reminds us that the baby during the first months of life is also learning head control then upper body and by 8 months most are usually able to sit steadily and begin to crawl/shuffle. All of which will stimulate visual/motor/attention/emotional/cognitive feedback loops. Overall, any difficulties or delay in switching focus between stimuli need to be considered within the light of the actual ability to 'shift' gaze and the child's desire to keep looking because what they are looking at is really interesting! A further point to consider when reflecting on the child's abilities to process visual information lies in the type of information that is being processed and whether it is pleasurable or unpleasant. For example a paper by Maljkovic and Martini (2005) suggested that 'human visual short-term memory is affected by a brief "freezing response", followed by a preferential accelerated encoding of negatively tagged information'. It is possible, therefore that negative information may induce an appearance of brief actual stilling in the infant followed by faster processing – which potentially raises the question that 'looking times' may also be influenced by what the target 'means' to the baby as well as the implications and links with the outcomes of the emotional 'tagging' of all experience to the child.

The other facet is that once we have switched attention to a new stimulus we may decide that we wish to turn again to the original stimulus and this again requires a 'shift'. This skill has also been demonstrated as having a maturational, temporal component and, surprisingly, very young infants (under 3 months) have been shown to be able to do this – given very particular conditions and visual parameters (Valenza et al., 1994). This could imply that many of our later developing skills are in place very early on in a 'crude' form – necessitating experience to allow these skills to develop in ordinary, rather than laboratory, conditions. Another point here is that within the required circuitry which appears to be required for these skills to develop, information is never just one-way but information passes between 'streams' and backwards and forwards between the various areas in the cortex and the thalamic 'relay station', which will, I strongly suspect, include emotional feedback loops as well as physiological information from the senses overall. A further dimension is added if we consider the functions of the dorsal and ventral streams. The dorsal stream is involved in visual motor action as it is 'primarily concerned with the spatial location of objects and their relation to each other' (Spencer et al., 2000). This means that the dorsal stream must be involved when paying attention as the child (or adult) has to be able to find what it is looking for. Spencer et al.'s study concerned the difficulties children with autism have in integrating local visual signals to extract a global pattern. Their findings supported previous work illustrating children with autism's superior skills at finding embedded figures in comparison to their difficulties in general motor performance.[21] Incidentally their study also emphasized a maturational component in that, in the 'normal' controls, abilities on the tasks reached adult levels at around 10–11 years, with children with autism also showing increasing skill but still at a much lower level than the control group.

A note about colour

It has been noted earlier that very young babies have poor colour vision, possibly because the womb is limited in colour and potentially this 'saves' overloading of visual information on the very immature brain. They appear to be sensitive to red, yellow and green but not blue until around 2–3 months. However, Schiffman (2001: 298) reports that by 4 months, infants do possess colour vision and that the 'primary colour categories – blue, green, yellow and red – seen by adults are matched by infants'. Atkinson (2000) provides a detailed overview of several studies, which give slightly varying information but essentially the above statement seems as accurate as it is possible to be!

Atkinson (2000: 69) also notes that *consistent* colour naming – 'even of primary colours' appears to be absent in children under 4 years of age. At the same time colour names appear frequently in early vocabulary at around 2 years of age and, as the research shows above, even young infants are aware of colour so there appears to be some delay in the child's ability to link what is seen to what can be named. What colour naming instead appears to provide is what Atkinson (2000: 69) describes as 'a marker of attentional salience with parents commenting that their child goes through periods when all "interesting" objects are labelled with one particular colour name – usually red or yellow'. What makes this doubly interesting is that children with autism sometimes appear to retain a strong preference (or dislike) for specific colours.

Finally

A final point from Atkinson is the anomaly between most of the visual studies which emphasize subcortical mechanisms mainly at work in newborns and the fact that these babies are able to imitate tongue protrusion and mouth-opening when only a few hours old. They also show differential responses to face-like stimuli together with preferential looking towards a familiar face in the first few days of life (Atkinson, 2000; Meltzoff 2002; Pascalis et al., 1995). One partial explanation may be that tongue protrusion and mouth-opening are part of the newborn's repertoire of motor skills and, so, the action presented builds on the mouth movements which are part of the sucking and rooting reflex – which also might explain why imitation of such movements seems to 'fall off' around 3 months. This is coincidentally when many babies are 'weaning' and when the very different mouth movements required for sucking on a spoon are being practised.

To sum up

Information from the body is carried in various feedback loops through different brain structures and the cortex. All the different, but nevertheless related, types of information – such as when a baby feels, examines, tastes and smells a wooden brick – pass through these neural structures in parallel, only beginning to integrate and merge as they reach the higher brain areas where the apparently seamless and rapid 'knowing' of what we are experiencing eventually occurs. The brain appears to group together components which appear to belong to one another – for example, eyes, nose, mouth grouped together form a face. The whereabouts of something is also a 'grouping principle', as Levitin (2006: 73–9) puts it, as we tend to put together sounds which seem to be coming from the same direction.

We must not forget that as sensory information also passes through the limbic system we will also have an emotional response to what we experience and this, too, will form part of the holistic integration of sensation to representation. Another point for consideration is what emphasis or 'weighting' is given to the sensory information arriving in the brain. Greenspan (1997) reminds us that the processing of sensory information is not 'all of a piece' but highly individual and that everyone manifests differences in the way they can appreciate/tolerate or dislike certain types of sensory information, as we saw in the section on touch. He also notes that the normally variable and musical pitch of 'motherese,' which is alerting and joyful to many babies can cause other babies to either react with confusion or find difficulty in simultaneously orienting to the sound while paying attention to the face. Any individual can have variability in their capacity to process any one of the sensory modalities or a combination of them due to either genetic or environmental experiences. If we add the knowledge that the sensory systems individually are also complex in their individual organization, this could suggest that the synthesis of such sensory information within an immature nervous system becomes highly idiosyncratic.

A world of faces

Our faces are the great communicators. Faces are fascinating and yet we never see our own apart from in mirrors/reflective surfaces or reflected in the eyes of others – and, even then, our faces belong in a looking-glass world, for ever reversed. Faces therefore represent both the real and the reflected self. All humans possess the capabilities for the six basic emotions – happiness, sadness, fear, anger, surprise and disgust – and possess in varying degrees the capacity to 'read' such expressions/emotions because of the similar facial configurations used across the world, which correspond to the feeling (Ekman, in Calder et al., 1996).[22]

The skill of recognizing emotional expression supports us in understanding not only the type of feelings but potentially thoughts also – although the latter is a later development. Faces therefore have a strong emotional valence – as we cherish those faces that are dear to us and the sight of a familiar and/or well-loved face can bring profound feelings of emotional safety and security, we feel, in the midst of emotional or physical chaos, that things 'will be alright'. Faces are inextricably bound up with our knowledge of others and ourselves, as it is through the expressions, moods and tone of voice that emanate from the face that we learn about ourselves. Schore (1994: 321) tells us that as long ago as 1971, Izard suggested that 'facial muscle feedback activates central neural activity in the limbic cortex, hypothalamus and brain stem reticular system, which mediate emotion'. Recent research also indicates that while we use the same facial muscles when we smile, we each use them slightly differently, so smiles are as unique as fingerprints and this may be one of the ways in which we learn to identify one person from another (Giles, 2004).[23]

Much of our understanding of how we come to understand and recognize faces comes from work with adults who have sustained brain injury through trauma or disease processes and there is acknowledgement that recognition of faces or the emotion transmitted by faces can be unconscious as well as conscious. This possibility was illustrated in research carried out by de Gelder et al. (2000) who studied a patient who had a 'complete loss of processing facial expressions in recognition as well as in matching tasks'. However, when asked to rate face and voice expressions presented together, it became clear that the facial expressions impacted on her choice of assessment of the heard stimulus. The implication from this both suggests and supports other research quoted by de Gelder of evidence of non-conscious facial processing. What makes such research fascinating are two things. First, it identifies the complex way in which facial stimuli are broken down in that there appear to be separate processes for recognizing facial features individually and for recognizing the face globally. For example, the patient studied in the above example was 'flawless' when questioned about the 'shape of the mouth or length of the nose on a particular face'. In other words, she knew what the features were but could not 'put them together' to form a face.

Second, the finding in de Gelder et al.'s study that facial expression modulated the rating of *vocal* expression potentially illustrates the power with which the expression on a carer's face will impact on the infant. It also adds another interpretation to the finding that babies find non-congruence between lip movements and heard sounds upsetting. Perhaps it is not just the lack of vocal/visual synchrony but also if the expressiveness of the lip movements within the context of the face does not match the sound, a further disturbing dimension is evoked. What is also particularly noteworthy is that de Gelder's patient's matching for objects and faces was 'severely impaired when the stimuli were shown in canonical upright orientation but not when these same stimuli were presented upside down' (de Gelder, 2000: 425). Some insight into this may come from research, which indicates that a component of face-sensitive cells may show differential responses to upright versus inverted faces in 6-month-old infants (Atkinson, 2000; Paterson et al., 2006) indicating a variation in the processing of different views of the face. This is supported by research findings that processing of inverted faces is based on 'part-based' analysis such as the shape of the mouth versus the more configural processing of upright faces (Ganel et al., 2005). This links with de Gelder's patient's intact knowledge of the shape of features – which information again leads to reflection on how children with autism are processing such information.[24] This also links again with the experience of a person with high functioning autism. When I asked about recognizing a face, the remarks included:

> An angle of about 45 degrees from the front gives me the most clues as to depth perception/topography, so it gives me the most input on what the overall shape of the head, chin, cheekbones are. That large amount of information increases the probability that I can connect that face to a memory file. Basically, though, I do not 'recognize' faces.

A further finding from de Gelder's work is that his patient could mimic facial expressions perfectly, which the researchers state supports their previous findings that visual perception and mental imagery are 'functionally independent'. Research by Calder et al. (2000: 139) also supports de Gelder et al.'s work as their research suggested that 'our representation of facial expression is coded independently of our representation of what is face like'.

Their work, interestingly, also indicated that highly exaggerated expressions of emotion – even those that appeared to distort the face – were nevertheless identified and associated with a high degree of intensity. This can suggest that the exaggerated facial expressions that many adults instinctively use when talking to babies is a factor in helping the baby establish both the feel of the emotion expressed and support the neural identification of facial expression. Calder et al. (2000: 118) also suggest that 'facial expressions may be coded at a level that does not incorporate a full representation of the facial image', which may indicate that an infant's processing of expression comes prior to the processing of individual features, the latter I suspect being linked with the ability to recognize the self in a mirror. It also again ties in with Schore's right-hemisphere dominance hypothesis where global processing is foregrounded in the first three years of life and expressions are the global 'feature' of a face. Schore is also supported by the work of Le Grand et al (2003) mentioned earlier whose research found that in adults, face sensitive activation is greater in the right than in the left hemisphere. What may be especially important is that visual deprivation to the right hemisphere in early infancy does seem to adversely influence more sensitive face-processing in later life. Deprivation to the left hemisphere does not seem to have this effect.

Another component is that during these early years, the types of expressions encountered by the baby are more likely to be very clear manifestations of particular emotions. For example, most people smile at a baby and babies are actively encouraged to smile. Laughter through games and tickling are also encouraged. As Calder says, if 'certain facial expression configurations are encountered more than others ... clusters of particular categories would form'. As the infant grows older, other expressions such as brief anger/irritation and sad faces may become more frequent as the child begins to be more mobile and, consequently, begins to explore, demonstrate more independence, and so on, the ratio of positive to negative emotions encountered maybe changing in parallel with a widening of the types of emotions elicited.

Another aspect in Calder's work was that in adults fear and surprise were the two expressions most commonly confused. They felt that this was consistent with previous suggestions that surprise might not constitute an emotional expression in its own right. However, an alternative interpretation may be that in infants surprise may well be associated with some fearfulness as the baby has only the adults on whom to rely to 'check out' the surprising event and therefore such findings in adults may indicate an echo of this fear component in surprise. Consider if someone 'jumps out' at you as a 'surprise' or a baby is presented with a 'pop up' toy. The first reaction may be one of startle/ fear and indeed many babies can become upset at toys that produce sudden movements. The finding that exaggerated surprise faces were rated as more happy does not invalidate this hypothesis as, once the surprise has turned into a happy event (or at least not a scary one), the ensuing emotion will be relief/ happiness. It may also be why many people say that they do not like surprises!

Research by Neuner and Schweinberger (2000) found face and voice recognition were dissociable but not face and voice naming, which may also suggest that the ability to discriminate and differentiate between voices and faces is more important than the ability to label different faces/voices. Perhaps the most compelling finding regarding faces is that human newborns make 'differential responses to a face-like pattern' (Atkinson, 2000), including differential head turning and tracking. Hairline appeared to be a factor, which helped babies to distinguish between faces up until the age of around 3 months, and that by this time infants have built up 'prototypes' of faces (de Haan et al., 2001). It is interesting that the temporal lobe system becomes 'on line' at around 8 weeks and babies appear then to be able to recognize faces in a similar way to an adult. It is damage to the temporal lobe, incidentally, that is implicated in adults who are unable to recognize faces. However, as we have seen in the studies above, even at this early stage, several systems may be at work embedded in the development of the visual system itself and differentiating between feature and expression. These findings have implications for considering the particular problems children with autism have in following gaze and understanding expressions, but also serve to illustrate how experience with a familiar carer supports the interplay between the child and the environment.

In Table 3.2 I have pulled together a range of studies which gives information about the development of face processing during infancy. Faces, emotions and eye gaze/direction form a crucial part of the beginnings of our learning and we will be revisiting aspects of the importance of faces in the following chapters. Particular findings of relevance are highlighted in italics.

Table 3.2 Summary studies of visual processing especially for faces and eye gaze

Source	Firdings
Liu et al. (2002) 'Stages of processing in face perceptions'	Data suggested that face-processing proceeds through, first, *face categorization* and later, *identification*. Emotional expression potentially is processed before either of these
Hood et al. (2003) 'Eye remember you: effects of gaze direction on face recognition in children and adults'	Findings indicate that direct gaze influences both encoding and retrieval for face recognition – gaze direction also influenced the efficiency of face recognition *Note: they also comment that staring is known to activate centres associated with the task of evaluating the social relevance of stimuli. It is interesting that infants under 3 months spend much of their looking time 'staring'*
Johnson et al. (1998) 'Whose gaze will infants follow? The elicitation of gaze-following in 12 month olds'	Study compared gaze following to an adult stranger and a 'soft, brown, dcg-sized … object' which either did or did not have facial features and interactive behaviour. They conclude that by 12 months it is the entity's abstract quality of intentionality that appears to draw the gaze of an infant at this age
* Cashon and Cohen (2003) 'Construction, deconstruction and reconstruction of infant face perception'	6/52 Process two lines of an angle independently 14/52 Process how lines relate to form an angle 4/12 Process features of a line-drawn animal independently 7–10/12 Process correlation between line-drawn features of animal 3–4 months/12 Infants move from processing internal and external features of face independently to processing the relationship between them 4–7 months Similar integration with objects 4–6.25 months Infants 'drop back' to featural processing for both upright and inverted faces

Source	Findings
	6.25 months Infants become sensitive to causal effect between two objects
	7 months Infants regain the ability to integrate feature information – but only for upright faces
* Bednar (2003) 'The role of internally generated neural activity in newborn and infant face preferences'	Newborns and 1/12 olds follow moving schematic faces in the periphery more than other patterns
	Newborns show preference for maternal face to that of stranger
	1–2/12 Respond to facial features in central vision
* Valentin and Abdi (2003) 'Early face recognition: what can we learn from a myopic baby neural network?'	6–7/52 Babies able to process internal facial features and can recognize mother from strangers wearing headscarves
	But – studies on facial attractiveness suggest *babies are able to process internal facial information 2 days after birth*
* Johnson and Farroni (2003) 'Perceiving and acting on the eyes: the development and neural basis of eye gaze perception'	Results from studies indicate overlap between processing of eye gaze, facial processing and motion
	Newborns prefer faces with eyes open
	Tend to imitate facial gestures
	Studies showed preferential orienting to direct gaze from birth
	4/12 Direct eye gaze facilitates perceptual processing of faces
	3–4 months Infants start to discriminate and follow adult's direction of attention
	Studies suggest that babies need contact with direct gaze/upright face before being fully sensitive to lateral motion of the eyes to follow eye gaze
Galaburda et al. (n.d.) 'Developmental disorders in vision'	Face recognition involves the posterior temporal lobes, particularly the fusiform gyrus

Source	Findings
Fox et al. (2002) 'Attentional bias for threat'	Attentional bias in anxiety appeared to reflect difficulty in disengaging from threat-related and emotional stimuli (study of young adults) – *suggests that potentially there is a psychological component to 'sticky fixation'*
Winston et al. (2002) 'Automatic and intentional brain responses during evaluation of trustworthiness of faces'	Assessment of brain activity during this study showed 'task independent' increased activity in bilateral amygdale and *right insula*
Hernandez-Reif et al. (2006) 'Happy faces are habituated more slowly by infants of depressed mothers'	Study examined 3–6 month old infants showed that these infants were less likely to look at the facial expressions displayed by both their mother and a stranger regardless of affective display and *newborns of depressed mothers appeared to take longer to habituate to their mother's face*
Le Grand et al. (2003) 'Expert face processing and visual input'	Their study suggested that the neural circuitry responsible for adults' skills in face-processing requires appropriate early experience and only the right hemisphere appears to be capable of using this experience to develop these levels of expertise. *Links with Schore's (1994) assertion of right-brain dominance in the first three years of life*
Calder et al. (2000) 'Caricaturing facial expressions'	This study appeared to suggest that the more caricatured the facial expression, the more intense the emotion said to be expressed (even when the images were exaggerated so much that they no longer resembled natural-looking faces Caricaturing also appears to facilitate 'facial expression recognition'. *Links with the exaggerated facial expressions used by many carers when speaking 'motherese'* *This study also links with other studies indicating that the processing of facial expression is independent of what is 'face like'*

Source	Findings
De Gelder et al. (2000) 'Covert face processing in Prosopagnosia'	Study of patient with visual face and object agnosia who nevertheless rated emotional expressiveness in the voice according to the type of facial expression presented. *This finding supports the separate processing of sound and vision and that the two are also closely intertwined. This connection could begin (in the typically developing child) with the face-to-face interaction of the carer/child*
Yin (1969) 'Looking at upside-down faces'	In spite of the age of this paper, it presented interesting findings that the difficulty in looking at upside-down faces indicated that there may be a 'special neurological factor which is related only to face-processing.' *This could potentially point to a factor in the findings that children with autism are more likely to identify upside-down faces*
Sinha (2000) 'The perception of gaze'	Suggested that analysis of gaze direction in another used by the visual system is based on 'simple heuristics', that is, the strong correlation of perceived gaze direction with contrast polarity in images. *This has resonance with the following study*
Farroni et al. (2005) 'Newborns preference for face-relevant stimuli – effects of contrast polarity'	This study demonstrated that newborns only showed a preference for an upright face-related image if it was composed of darker areas around the eyes and mouth
Vuilleumier et al. (2001) 'Effects of attention and emotion on face processing in the human brain – an event-related MRI study'	The key finding appeared to be that *amygdala activation for fearful faces was unaffected* (unlike other 'face-related' brain areas) *when conscious attention was diverted elsewhere on various tasks*. Other areas showed some modulation in their activity. This together with other findings did seem to suggest that there is a *sub-cortical process of face-processing which links with other research regarding infant processing of faces*
Adams et al. (2003a) 'Effects of gaze on amygdala sensitivity to anger and fear faces'	This study demonstrated that gaze direction should be included in assessing responses to anger and fear – also see next study

Source	Findings
Adams and Kleck (2003b) 'Perceived gaze direction and the processing of facial displays of emotion'	This study links with that above – and reinforces their finding that both gaze direction and expression are combined in processing 'emotionally relevant information' – direct gaze was said to facilitate processing of 'anger and joy' while averted gaze seemed to facilitate 'avoidance or entated emotions', for example fear and sadness
Haxby et al. (2002) 'Human neural systems for face recognition and social communication'	Provides a model for a 'distributed neural system' for face perception *which also emphasises the role of the amygdala for emotion-processing and the implications for social communication*
Ganel and Goodale (2003) 'Visual control of action but not perception requires analytical processing of object shape'	This study suggests that in order to grasp an object, the person uses information about the relevant dimension without first processing the entire shape of the object – an idea supported by the fact that there are two cortical visual pathways – dorsal (action) and ventral (what) streams. *Again this links in with infant ability to reach and grasp which becomes more refined over time without the infant necessarily knowing what the object is in all its dimensions*

Note: Those studies marked with an asterisk * come from Pascalis and Slater (2003) supplying an overview of the topic.

The 'global' context for development is now set – and now the next phase is to consider how these global aspects come together to provide the beginnings of learning and overall development.

4 Origins

This chapter discusses aspects of development in the first year as subsequent development is initially shaped by these very early experiences. The roots of behaviour in a school-age child, their motivation, view of the world and themselves, their capacity to manage emotions, control their behaviour and ability to play and learn, can all be traced back to the way in which personal and unique life experiences build on the universal aspects of human development. Understanding these forces, I believe, is essential for practitioners working with children of any age – including adolescents.

As we have seen, the very first years of life demonstrate an explosion of development within the brain and as our brain matures so do all our abilities and skills – emotional, social, physical, cognition and in communication. In tandem and closely interlinked, we also develop our own styles of interaction and behaviour, gradually building up a basic sense of who we are. As the process of development is common to all of us this means that, as we learn about the children in our care, we learn about our own story. We learn how we formed our particular behavioural styles, our individual view of the world and our feelings about ourselves. While recognizing that the essentials of brain and body maturation are the same for all of us, we each attain a unique quality that is our particular signature on the world around us. We do not go through life unmarked and unseen – although sadly many people feel that they are 'invisible', unwanted and of no importance. The idea that life has meaning comes not only from religious or moral teachings, but how relevant those teachings appear to us within the context of our feelings about the world and our place within it – we long to belong.

So, how do we, when small, vulnerable and limited in our emotional, social, cognitive, physical and communication repertoire, perceive the behaviours of others directed towards us? What are the mechanisms by which we learn to make our way in the world, to find our place in it, to behave in ways that have a shared meaning and which may promote a sense of belongingness, acceptance and security – or, conversely, to find a world in which we feel alienated and alone, a world where our attempts at communication are met with behaviours which seem consistently discordant with what we are trying to say?

As a child attending a convent school, I had to learn the catechism[1] and the very first question was 'Who made you' (the answer being, 'God made me'). To paraphrase this question, I am going to ask instead '*What* made me –

and you?' The answer is, as we have seen in the preceding chapters, to do with the brain and the workings of the senses. The question and the answer is the same for each of us but it is unsatisfactory because, while we can learn about and understand – at least to some extent – how our brains and senses work, what about our experiences? What do we mean when we talk about 'experience' or 'our environment?' On the whole, I guess we mean everything that happens to us, everything we encounter, react to and relate with, especially our relationships with our carers and any other significant adults, siblings, neighbours, and so on. However, for our 'experiences' to have any meaning, there is an implication of an interaction, so this leads on to other questions such as what prompts us to interact with our carers or want to explore our environment? The answer to this question is probably curiosity and a capacity to attend to something that attracts our attention, but is this capacity innate or acquired or both? We might also ask 'What are the elements that make each of us unique?' The answers begin to emerge, as we can increasingly comprehend from the functioning of the innate capacities with which we are born and the impact of experience.

It all starts here

From the moment of birth, the baby begins its life away from the secure, contained world it has begun to know in the womb and into a world where the boundaries both physical and psychological are different. From the sensations of increasingly close confinement as the baby has moved and shifted in the womb, the baby now moves its arms and legs in space. Nourishment that was 'on tap' is no longer there and the temperature control of the womb environment has also gone. What a strange experience this must be, to emerge into this literally open world via the stressful journey that is birth! From reflecting on these experiences we begin to realize what the 'work' is that all newborn babies have to do and what adults need to provide, and so in the first three months or so of life the stage is set for the baby to begin to establish a rhythm of life in this new environment.

Nature or nurture?

In Chapter 2, I indicated that the nature/nurture debate was somewhat redundant,[2] but there still remains the controversy as to what skills and abilities babies are already equipped with, not just regarding their senses but their ability to make sense in very general ways of their environment and on which the carers/experience then build. Meltzoff (2002) states that in general (in his view) a group of research scientists who believe that babies do have innate ideas about the world, known as 'nativists' have won the battle regarding infant development, but that within this group two 'schools' are emerging – 'starting-state nativism' and 'final-state nativism'. As the terminology implies, the latter group generally (and in varying degrees) feel that infants have the same core knowledge as adults, which gradually emerges via biological maturation and the release of 'performance constraints'.[3] The 'starting-state nativism' group, of which Meltzoff is a proponent, believe that infants have 'powerful discovery procedures for developing adult cognition but the final state is not specified at birth or achieved through constraint removal'. I confess I tend towards 'starting-state nativism' but with a proviso that the 'starting state' is not birth per se, because perhaps some of what are seen as innate abilities in the newborn are based on ongoing learning which has started in the womb – particularly in the third trimester. This also applies to 'reflexes', which would appear to be logically based on early movement patterns created in the womb. However, I also believe that there are 'starting points' for the infant to begin to learn about the world (and itself) and that these are based primarily on the social interactions between carer and child – not only for emotional learning but as the 'starting state' for cognition, physical development and language as well, supported by an innate 'push' for exploring/curiosity and a biologically supported mechanism for imitation. What is certainly true is that babies are far cleverer than anyone thought!

To begin and to provide a starting point for discussion, Table 4.1 outlines the developmental changes that occur broadly in the first three months.

If we look at Table 4.1, it is noted that in the early months, babies also begin to establish basic rhythms in feeding, bodily movements and heart rate and, over time, we develop individual rhythms of breathing,[4] the regularity of our heartbeat, even our rhythm of walking, which is highly individual for each of us. There is also a rhythm to most of our bodily functions including hormone release, urine production, blood flow, hair growth and metabolism. (Consider whether you are able to eat large amounts and 'burn it off', whether your movements, thoughts, style of speaking are quick or more measured). Babies have a high heart rate at birth and it is the mother's voice which seems to support the 'calming' of this heart rate to a rate which is within the 'normal' range. Incidentally, from about 7/8 months, heart rate increases in communication with mother as the excitement level rises. Babies also move in time with the rhythms of the mother's voice, so allowing bodily movements to become more coordinated and smoother over time. The brain's own rhythms rely on its electrical activity which is measurable by EEG[5]s and these rhythms seem to be related to consciousness or awareness itself. For example, coherent, synchronized brainwave activity illustrating the simultaneous firing of neurons across particular areas has been demonstrated in working memory tasks.[6] There is also a link between the electrical rhythmic activity in the brain and sleep because types of sleep echo the brain's 'awake' rhythms

Table 4.1 Development birth to 3 months

Open-mouthed vowel sounds – vocalization in response to speech	Limb position is usually flexed in both arms and legs plus presence of asymmetrical tonic reflex – if one arm outstretched, baby will lie with head turned towards outstretched arm	Will respond to familiar sounds by shifting eye gaze and head movements
Newborns 1 to 5 days old have demonstrated an ability to tell the difference between speech rates		
Levels of alleviation of distress – physical and psychological	First experiences of and reactions to the emotional quality of their experience/ environment	Visual interest for faces moves from periphery to centre and from mouth to eyes, for example, newborns up to 1 month show preference for schematic faces in the periphery – 1–2 months seem to 'pull faces together'
First experiences of sensory integration	Very young infants are noted to have long periods of 'staring' – a period of 'sticky fixation'	Behaviour templates (reflexes) gradually subsumed into more proactive behaviours, for example, startle reflex absent by 3–5 months, replaced by adult-type 'startle'
Rapid brain growth especially in visual and auditory systems 2 months Colour discrimination	Emergence (from 3 months) of open-handed, broadly directed reaching for objects and begins to 'bat' at objects. Note the 'fisted' position of the hands of newborns should diminish by 2 months	Establishment of physiological rhythms (sleeping, feeding, temperature control, heart rate)

and the mystery of sleep is that it is the basic rhythm of life around which all human activity revolves. I now want to provide some information about sleep. Markov and Goldman (2006) state that sleep is not only vital but is also a highly organized process where reduced or disrupted sleep can affect a wide range of bodily and psychological functions when awake. Also, while sleep in infants – or the lack of it – can cause many problems for parents, its potential developmental importance is often not addressed.[7]

Sleep has its own rhythm as it appears to alternate between rapid eye movement (REM) and non-REM sleep in 90-minute cycles.[8] Rapid eye movement or dream sleep is bound up with physiological maintenance, for example, there is increased variability in heart rate, blood pressure, breathing and temperature. It is notable that a baby's sleep is dominated by REM sleep, including at sleep onset (see below), and it is during REM sleep that our own internal temperature regulation is switched off – while functioning during slow wave sleep (Skoyles and Sagan, 2002).

What particularly changes over time is the need for different *amounts* of sleep. Rapid eye movement sleep actually begins in the womb and it comprises 80 per cent of sleep in babies born 10 weeks prematurely and 60–65 per cent in babies born 4–6 weeks prematurely. Greenfield (2000: 146) tells us that recordings of brainwaves of human foetuses at 11 weeks show 'consistent electrical activity that indicates a cohesive, functioning brain. The dominant electrical activity seen is indicative of a special type of sleep ... rapid eye movement which is associated with dreaming'. Babies born at full term are in REM sleep half of their usual 16-hour sleep time – which, if we link with the finding regarding temperature control above, provides a rationale for the need for adults to take care regarding levels of warmth in very young babies. However, this need for 'dream sleep' appears to slowly decline until between 2 to 3 years of age it is about 30–35 per cent. Interestingly, this coincides with the period when children will tell stories which are 'sequentially and causally accurate' and at their most sophisticated when describing emotional content, especially that of fear, distress and anger, (Brown, 2003). This age range is also the time when the fear of monsters often appears.

Rapid eye movement sleep gradually settles down at about 25 per cent by 10 years of age and it stays at this rate until 70–80 years (Kandel et al., 2000), while slow wave sleep – delta sleep – reaches peak levels between 3 and 6 years of age and has a significant 'drop off' during adolescence. I find it intriguing that not only does REM sleep decline between ages 2 and 3 years but that slow wave sleep begins to be more prominent when language development is also at its peak. Sadeh et al (1996) identified that babies, while remaining somewhat erratic in their sleep patterns, nevertheless are inclined to spend more time asleep at night, indicating that the circadian (day/night) as well as the within-sleep rhythms were emerging quite early on. He points out that this could be due to environmental factors, such as greater noise levels during the day, but I would suggest that circadian rhythms are already being established in the womb because mothers are more likely to sleep at night too and so the mother's resting state will impact on the baby.

In addition, Minard et al (1999) highlight correlations between sleep rhythms and cognitive development. For example, babies who on the first post-natal day already showed a significant degree of within sleep cyclicity i.e. the proportion of quiet sleep as opposed to REM sleep was more 'mature' –

had poorer mental scores at six months. Alternatively, those that achieved greater cyclicity at six months had better mental scores at 1 year compared with babies who had not shown this maturing pattern. It would seem that too 'mature' a pattern is as 'unhealthy' for development as too confused or chaotic a pattern. Dahl (1996) also noted that during early development, a child spends more time asleep than waking, and yet the specific role sleep has in development remains a mystery. He argues that sleep may be the primary activity of the brain during the early years of development'.[9] It can be no coincidence that the time of greatest 'dream sleep' is also the period of great synaptic activity, myelination rates and major shifts in key basic developmental skills. Incidentally, the amount of energy consumed by the brain during REM sleep is actually greater than that consumed by the brain during intense physical or mental exercise in the waking state – providing a rationale for why very young babies often need frequent feeding throughout the 24-hour cycle. It could also provide a further rationale for the sleeping 'problems' which seem to occur in some babies. Disturbed sleep, for whatever reason, may interfere with the synaptic activity, consolidation and 'pattern-making' arising from experience necessary for optimal development to take place, creating a cycle of irregularity in both sleep and developmental processes. In addition, boys, who are over-represented in most forms of childhood mental health disorder/distress, do appear, in some studies at least, to be perceived as more problematic in their sleeping generally and sleep disturbance is often a factor in autism, attention deficit disorder (ADD) and attention deficit hyperactivity disorder (ADHD) as well as other mental health conditions.[10]

Finally, if studies show that babies spend so much time in REM sleep and assuming they dream, what is its purpose and is their dreaming of a qualitatively different nature and relevant to understanding development? Dreams are mainly visual in adults so it may be simply what is dreamt about rather than the state of dreaming which is different.[11] Putting together all the above information, it does not seem illogical that REM sleep is the time not only of memory consolidation, as some researchers suggest, but also when the consolidation of the day's synaptic activity takes place. I would suggest that for infants, the necessity for long periods of sleep, and particularly REM sleep, is a crucial part of both physical and psychological development. The dreams of babies may be the way in which the 'memory' of living and non-living 'objects' that the baby has encountered is constructed and consolidated arising from the 'bits and pieces' of form, texture, scent and sound bound by the rich tapestry of emotional and bodily sensations that accompany such experiences. I see such dreams as rather like an 'expressionist' painting of shapes and colour gradually undergoing a metamorphosis into the absolute clarity of a Rembrandt.

What else is happening in these early weeks?

If we look at Table 4.1 again, we can see that the baby is beginning to learn about and explore people and their surroundings. In the previous chapter, we talked about the importance of faces and that faces for the normally developing child provide a gateway to understanding the world of sensory information which is now imbuing the child's day-to-day experience. If we consider the extraordinary richness and complexity of the simple and instinctive face-to-face interaction of parent and baby, we can see how viewing the adult face supports a number of aspects of development including that of communication which also involves imitation – a key item in the 'toolbox' – and it is to communication that we now turn.

Kugiumutzkis (1993) in a longitudinal study of interactions between mothers and babies noted that mothers generally tend to imitate infants more than the other way around until the babies reached the age of approximately 8–9 months when babies begin to imitate more actions. From the extensive studies on which Kugiumutzkis draws, as well as his own, it would seem that mothers tend to imitate vowel sounds more frequently and that mothers naturally build on the infant's vocalizations, imitating, responding and providing the sounds with a meaning – for example, the baby is 'saying' that it is hungry and so on. Consonant sounds, if produced, were less copied by mothers but this did not occur until around the second month. One study where Kugiumutzkis particularly draws comparisons is an old but still relevant study carried out by Papousek and Papousek (1989). The main point here is that Kugiumutzkis agrees with the Papouseks that imitation of vocal sounds by mothers is not used to actually *teach* new or meaningful sounds in the first months. However, Kugiumutzkis disagrees with the Papouseks' hypothesis that this, often playful, imitation of sounds is an essential support for the development of the combination of mouth movements and neural networks that go together to produce further new sounds. He also feels that 'development from pre-speech and coos to canonical[12] babbling is probably more under intrinsic morphogenetic control in the infant's brain and vocal apparatus, not taught by the mother'. What Kugiumutzkis does not fully take into account is that when mothers are imitating the infant's sounds, as well as providing meaning and context, they are also providing a visual and auditory feedback for mouth movements, sound production, localization of sound and the rhythms of speech – hence supporting the Papouseks' hypothesis. Mothers are not consciously teaching their babies about sounds and mouth movements, but the babies are learning it anyway! In addition, imitation of the infant's sounds also draws attention to the production of sound and involves, by implication, the infant and mother in mutual face-to-face interaction. This means that the infant will be attending to the face, mouth, maternal expression and direction of eye gaze. The finding that, in the first 3 months of life, babies have difficulty in turning attention to a stimulus on the periphery of their vision is termed 'sticky fixation', and a particularly interesting aspect of this difficulty is that it may actually support the child's familiarization with a commonly seen face. Parents often talk about the way the baby seems to 'stare' at them and this inadvertently allows more opportunity for the parent to talk to the child during these periods providing those beneficial aspects for vision, hearing and, importantly, emotional feedback. Mothers are not static during these times either, as during interactions they will frequently hold the baby's hands, stroke the cheek or head, cuddle, rock and so on – again providing opportunities for a sensory 'bath' for the baby. Nature really is very clever.

A bit more about Infant Directed Speech (IDS) – 'motherese'

The manner in which mothers (and most adults) speak to children from birth to around 3 years is extremely interesting and has already been highlighted regarding its crucial role in communication. The sound of the mother's voice has a unique tone – as have all our voices, which is why we can recognize someone on the phone – and the baby has already heard this particular voice in the womb.[13] While speaking, IDS has a higher pitch, longer vowels, general short phrases and lots of repetition. Research also shows that babies like it and much prefer it to ordinary adult speech even when they hear it in a language in which they are totally unfamiliar. They are also more responsive to the sound than to facial expression, which is logical as they hear a sound first before they sort out faces. Premature babies appear to be more soothed by IDS than they are by touch (Mithen, 2006). In addition, infants as young as 1 month old will discriminate between displays of a mother versus a stranger's face, but only if the faces were accompanied by the voices – they did not discriminate between silent faces (Burnham, 1993, quoted in Muir et al., 2005).[14]

Mothers also seem to instinctively fine-tune their way of speaking to the child's 'linguistic level'. Mithen also quotes the research by Anne Fernald who has identified four developmental stages of IDS (my comments are in italics to avoid confusion):

a) to engage and maintain infant attention – intense sounds create an orienting response, rising pitch can make the baby open its eyes, while an abrupt pitch may lead to the baby closing its eyes and withdrawing. *Incidentally these responses illustrate an emotional response to the stimulus and so there is the impact of the general style of the carer's speaking to the baby as this will influence what might be the most persistent 'feeling state', for example, if the sounds are usually 'a call to play' or whether the baby is subject to mainly an abrupt pitch or raised voices.*

b) Changes in pitch modulate arousal and emotion, e.g. the sounds used to soothe a distressed child. *Consider the implication if the child does not generally experience these sounds – it may influence the child's own capacity to regulate their emotions and turn to self-soothing in various ways.*

c) The tone is not just pleasurable sounds but now communicate more about what the 'speaker' is feeling, so sounds become much more associated with wanting to stop a behaviour (prohibition), calling attention, comforting and approval.[15]

d) The final stage is subtle whereby the 'specific patterns of intonation and pauses facilitate the acquisition of language itself'.

(Mithen, 2006: 72)

The other factor about IDS is that it appears to be universal as studies have indicated that adults from different countries and cultures adopt a similar style of speaking even in a 'tonal' language, such as Chinese, where shifts in sound can give a word a very different meaning and yet Chinese mothers use the same type of musical speech. Studies quoted by Methvin also indicate that lullabies contain cross-cultural similarities.

A rather charming finding is that studies have also shown that we speak to our pets in the same way as towards infants – except that we do not exaggerate the vowel sounds. This illustrates the 'magic' of the instinctive nature of IDS. Pets do not need to know vowels as they do not need to reproduce them.

The musicality of 'motherese' with its variations in timbre, pitch, pacing, rhythm and duration, which is mainly processed in the right hemisphere, may also serve to 'prime' the speech centres in the left hemisphere as well. It is notable that the 'global' picture of speech develops prior to the production of formed speech sounds – echoing the process of global before specific that seems to emerge throughout development. Such pronounced speech patterns may also help the infant discover endings and beginnings because as we have seen in the chapter on senses, we (or rather our brains) tend to group similar properties of information together. For example, when babies touch and/or mouth, they can combine space, surface and edges in the same way that the baby can also scan the edges of a face and hairlines. It is suggested that this is how babies begin to understand words as part of the sound stream they hear, as they appear to group syllables together by recognizing which ones appear together most often. Studies suggest that they use the same principle on listening to music, being able to identify similar tones – although the debate is whether the 'ear' for musical groupings comes before the language group-ings – I suspect the former. In addition, the existence of this potential innate ability to group information, which, I suggest starts with face-to-face inter-action, extrapolates onto grouping sequences of actions and experiences.

This provides some very sound support for the advice given to parents and practitioners to sing to babies, to use rhythm, nursery rhymes, nonsense rhymes, and so on with lots of rhyming tones which supports not only the relationship, ongoing communication and future language development, but the baby's ability to literally as well as metaphorically 'tune in' to its world. Babies like singing and it does not matter if the adult feels they can not sing – babies are not critics! What they want and need is the reassuring sound of their carers' presence. Thinking about these issues further, it may also be that it is the sound of the caring voice which may be even more soothing to a distressed child than touch or facial expression – remembering that some children neither invite nor offer cuddles.

Communication from baby to mother[16]

Babies, of course, are not static in this scenario and communicate strongly with their carers with both their facial expressions and bodily movements. The wonderful synchrony that Trevarthen (1999) in his lifetime of research on mother/child reactions has discovered, and describes so beautifully in his writings, is composed of the mother talking and singing, with pauses to allow the baby to make its own sounds and movements – it is a 'conversation' imbued with enormous emotional power and developmental beginnings.

The way that babies communicate is via facial expression, bodily move-ments and eye gaze. Babies can close their eyes when it all gets too much for them and they can begin to shift their gaze and turn their head so that they can begin actively to 'manage' the flow of information to them. Nature has done it for them at the beginning by the limitations in vision and that hearing – although developed – is most efficient in face-to-face contact and in the midline. Furthermore, it highlights the importance of an interest in faces as one aspect of language production and development, and the implication for children with autism who may not have this interest in faces means that another facet of their growing difficulties may be coming into play. As vision becomes more acute, head/neck and trunk control also develops, allowing a wider range of response. Of course, carers need to be sensitive to what the baby is doing and it is difficult for babies if their carer seems to misjudge and mistime their interventions on a regular basis.

Some thoughts on imitation

The Kugiumutzkis study we encountered earlier, focused on vocal imitation but imitation itself plays a powerful role in the interactions between parent and child in these early months. During this time, it is the parent/carer who most often imitates what the child is doing, although Gopnik et al.'s (1999) famous study of an infant as young as 42 minutes imitating tongue protrusion has to be born in mind. In Chapter 3, I mentioned the anomaly between this observation and the knowledge that infant visual acuity seems to contradict the ability to perform such an action. While not everyone has managed to replicate Gopnik et al.'s findings with these very young human babies, there is general agreement that imitation is one of the ways in which infants do get to know someone else and is a powerful learning tool both physically and socially throughout the life span – not just in infancy and childhood.

When thinking about the role of imitation, we have to remember that humans are not the only imitators and imitation has been broadly observed in infant apes and monkeys. Myowa-Yamakoshi et al. (2002) in their study of neonatal chimpanzees found that at 7 days they could both discriminate and imitate familiar human facial gestures such as sticking out the tongue and mouth opening. However, by 2 months old, these chimps no longer 'imitated' the gestures but began to 'perform mouth opening frequently in response to any of the three facial gestures presented to them'. They suggest that neonatal facial imitation is most likely an innate ability, 'developed through natural selection in humans and in chimpanzees'. Another study which suggests that imitation might be innate is that of adults who have damage to the frontal cortex which then means they lose the 'inhibiting' role of the cortex and find themselves imitating others in an 'unintended and automatic' way (Kinsbourne, 2002). Gallese (2001) also notes such a finding, including patients who have damage to the orbito-frontal cortex who will imitate an action rather than the actual movements. If we turn this around in infancy, the frontal cortex is not mature and so the tendency to imitate is not constrained and this finding also reflects the way children in the second year begin to be able to imitate goal-directed actions, tying in the maturation of this part of the brain.

Imitation is also used as a powerful form of learning. In Japan, an apprentice sushi master will be observed for up to three years before being invited to make his first sushi (de Waal, 2001) – the point being that watching something over and over again allows action sequences that are remembered to be used very much later, when the opportunity arises to carry out the same task. Just think of how often a child watches their carers doing something – and that it is usually around 12–14 months that the child will want to speak on the toy telephone and later there is a surge in wanting to 'copy' those daily household activities.

What may underpin imitation is both the existence of mirror neurons and canonical neurons (see Chapter 2) which activate when either an action is observed or the movement of body parts with the particular point being an implication of agency.[17] What these neurons fundamentally do is to allow a 'match' between what is seen and the establishing of a pattern of action within the observer's own motor/sensory system. Subsequently, when the observer carries out the action, there is also a secondary match between the actual action and the one observed, so strengthening the neural connections as well as registering the accompanying sensations of whether this feels good, 'OK' or not very nice. I find it interesting too, that some facial and vocal actions have a strong degree of 'contagion' about them, for example, if someone is yawning, it is almost inevitable that we find ourselves yawning too. Consider that opening the mouth is one of the very first mouth movements (and one that the babies copied from Meltzoff, 1999), and it may be that such an action has very deep roots indeed! Laughter, too, is often contagious and it is difficult to remain impervious to it. Carers spend a great deal of time reinforcing a baby's happy feelings and accompanying laughter and, again, this may be a way of establishing positive feelings/facial recognition and positive multimodal sensory experiences for the baby, which in turn reinforce the likelihood that an action may be repeated. As adults, as Rizzolatti et al (2002) points out, we still have a strong tendency to imitate observed actions – as he says, when people watch a boxing match, they often imitate the arm movements of the boxers. What Rizzolatti does not say, however, is that this does not apply to all observed actions as we rarely see people copying the *leg* movements of footballers while watching, so hand/arm and face movements may hold particular significance innately.

Meltzoff (2002a) who has written and researched extensively on the topic of imitation, also suggests that babies use imitation to keep track of people. He and his colleagues carried out an interesting study which fundamentally tried to assess how babies can keep track of people coming and going – and found babies used imitation to do this. This is such a fascinating study that it is worth explaining in detail as follows.

Infants of 6 weeks were presented with mother and a stranger coming and going in front of them. Mother would appear, show a gesture (for example the famous mouth opening) and then go out. The stranger would come in, do another gesture and go out again. The babies tracked the entrances and exits and imitated each person without difficulty. However, if mother and stranger 'surreptitiously' changed places, the infants became confused – new person in old place or same person with a different appearance? Meltzoff (2002a: 26) says that the babies sorted it out as follows: 'Infants stared at the new person, stopped behaving and then intently produced the *previous* person's gesture.'

Meltzoff and his colleagues surmised that it is not just appearance and where someone is that gives clues to who someone is but also the actions they do. The particular implication for carers is that babies with many people around them may find it more difficult to sort out who is who – especially if there are more than two or three people who give primary care. It may well be that the familiar sound, face and actions of someone who is their main carer will also help babies to have a 'baseline' which makes it easier for them to separate out other adults and older children they encounter. Meltzoff's findings also show that at 6 weeks of age, the babies have remembered the previous action – so much for babies not remembering under 2 years! The very famous seminal 'still face experiment' (Murray and Trevarthen, 1985; Tronick et al., 1978) also demonstrated that there is an 'expectation' in even very young infants that there will be some kind of similarity between the way that they are behaving and their carers, and babies are certainly more responsive to people who imitate their expressions, coos, burbles and so on (Nadel, 2002). What we must also bear in mind is that the studies show that babies then respond to their being imitated, so that imitation presents a 'round' of communication involving expression, sound and emotional quality. However, Nadel also quotes a study which demonstrated that infants respond differently to live and delayed video feedback of their own movements. At 3 months, the babies preferred the online feedback while at 5 months, they preferred the deferred feedback (or at least showed more interest). Nadel suggests that at 5 months the babies had already formed a primary representation of the body self and so were more interested in external stimuli. This is particularly interesting because babies become almost compulsive in their efforts to reach and grasp between 6 and 9 months, indicating a surge in interest in the external world. In addition, a study by Gergely and Watson (1999) suggested that mental age matched children with autism seemed to prefer a perfect computer-generated match of their hand movements while 2-year-old 'control' children preferred imitation of their movements which was not quite so 'perfect', echoing to some degree the Nadel study.

To become *aware of* being imitated and to act on it does not seem to occur before around 14 months[18] – so imitation serves as a communication tool supporting turn-taking in these early weeks and months, but not yet a 'knowledge' of what being imitated is.

Imitation remains a powerful part of human behaviour becoming more subtle and abstract in its manifestations. Close friends/partners often mirror one another's gestures, unconsciously shifting position to echo the body attitude of the other, thereby enhancing the sense of mutual understanding. Counsellors and therapists echo back to clients some of their words and phrases in order to establish that the client is both heard and potentially understood often changing tone, pitch and pace of voice to match. Singing in unison is a type of imitation as the sharing of the same words and phrases engenders a feeling of closeness and bonding. We listen to and attempt to reproduce the sounds of those around us. Fans of pop stars or football players echo hairstyles, mannerisms and style of dress in order to feel a part of the person they so admire. Imitation in all its forms engenders a feeling of closeness and belonging no matter how superficial or distant from the source of need. Imagination becomes part of imitation as in psychodynamic therapy for example, people are asked to imagine themselves in the role of another in order to understand the behaviour and motives of the other – so echoing in sophisticated form the imaginative play of children, which is discussed in Chapter 7.

Getting a little older

Between 7/8 and 12 months, imitation shifts in emphasis as the infant is beginning to copy the adult's actions, and, even more cleverly, actions and context are being 'put together' in the child's behaviour, such as, waving 'bye bye' appropriately, trying to hold a spoon, manipulating objects in order to examine them, showing and pointing. However, this putting together can also imply a very early separating out between self and other as the child practises observed human actions upon 'objects' (that is, animate or inanimate). This gives the child repeated opportunities to experience what doing the action of another feels like – built on the experience of previous months when the child was mainly imitated by the carer allowing the visual and sensory integration of action/response. This shift also provides an interesting link between the other changes that are occurring at this age, and this particular period is marked by the emergence of some profound changes which are particularly crucial for ongoing development.

Table 4.2 provides a general overview and I have indicated how the various shifts may be linked together.

I want to particularly discuss the following three items, but dealing with 1 and 2, first:

1. emergence and development of shared interaction/social referencing allied with possible basic understanding/linking of emotions and actions in others;
2. emergence of declarative and imperative pointing – often synchronized with vocalizations which appear important for later development of speech;
3. ongoing brain maturation – evidence of ability to remember location of hidden objects and that out of sight objects still exist

The emergence of shared interactions and social referencing is intimately linked and coincidental with the emergence of declarative and imperative

Table 4.2 Shifts in skills and abilities 7/8–12 months

a) Refinement of facial recognition – links with (b) and (h) and supports (i) and (f)	b) Emergence of stranger anxiety and discrimination of attachments – links with (c), (l) (i)	c) Beginning of concept of object permanence – links strongly with (d) and supports (i)
d) Ongoing brain maturation – evidence of ability to remember location of hidden objects – especially links and supports (b), especially (c), (j), (i), (k), (m), (n) and (o) but is framework for all ongoing changes	e) Earliest emergence of 'mark-making', that is, through hand movements on tables with available resource, for example, food – links with (f) (t) and supports (m)	f) Expansion of sensory world through greater mobility and introduction of new tastes, visual and hearing acuity – supports (k), (i), (l), (q) and (t)
g) Able to localize source of sounds from behind – links with (f) and (m) – supports (h)	h) Refinement of vocal matching to home language – babbling becomes attuned to its rhythms. Some children may understand about 10–25 words and two-word 'couplets', for example, bye bye, pat hands, upsy daisy – links with (f), (g) and (l)	i) Emergence and development of shared interaction/social referencing allied with possible basic understanding/linking of emotions and actions in others – links with (k), (l), (h), (a), (j) and (b)
j) Emergence of declarative and imperative pointing – often synchronized with vocalizations which appear important for later development of speech	k) Imitation becomes more proactive and relates some gestures to appropriate context, for example, raising arms to be picked up, waving when leaving or seeing others leave – links with (i), (l), (j) and (m)	l) Increasing sociability and expression of feeling states through facial expression, bodily movements, vocalizations – links with (j), (i) and (k)
m) Can cross midline of body, that is, able to transfer objects from one hand to the other, and thumb/finger pincer grasp develops between 7 and 9 months – supports the ability to play hand games and imitate carers – links with (k)	n) Increase in mobility – crawling, pulling to stand, first steps (for some) – combines with emergence of simple depth perception in most children by 12 months – this supports all aspects of development	o) 'Parachute reflex' usually appears around 8–9 months and fully present by 12 months – the last 'postural reflex' to occur – links with (n), (s), (t) and (u)

p) Most babies will begin to use both eyes together and judge distances and grasp and throw objects with greater precision – links with (n), (m) and (j)	q) Increasing curiosity allied with growing motor and visual coordination – links with (l), (k), (j) and (d)	r) Ability to 'creep', that is, as crawling but with trunk off the ground – links with (q) and (s)
s) Often able to sit from the standing position – links with (r) and supports (n)	t) Can begin to sit for long periods – links with (q), (s) – supports (e)	u) May stand for a moment without support – links with (o), (s), (q), (r), (n) and (f)

pointing. The reason these skills are so important, is they mark a qualitative change in the way the infant views the world and, secondly, the ability to point has implications for children with developmental delay, specifically autism. In the early weeks and months of life, the baby is in virtually constant contact with its carers and during this time the baby will have not only close interactive and, hopefully, synchronous relationships with its carers, but the carers will also, instinctively and naturally, have been pointing out objects of interest, calling the baby's attention to events, other people, pets, and so on. In the meantime the baby is gradually gaining more control over gross and fine motor movements, visual acuity (including a more refined recognition of upright, human faces), localizing of sounds and general mobility. During this particular phase there is also a surge in brain activity, and all these factors combine to produce a truly wondrous shift in the baby's understanding of self and other. The change is that the baby has its first inklings of 'you, me, we'. I have found that, no matter how often I teach this or read or write about this phase, it never ceases to fill me with wonder as to how this revelation comes about. I do not think anyone really knows how it happens – but it does. The baby realizes that it can draw someone's attention to something that it is interested in – it is the first major step towards a theory of mind (TOM)[19] (Leslie, 1987), which is basically an understanding of other people's mental states, that they have beliefs, desires and intentions that underpin their behaviour. The baby uses a new-found skill of pointing (which obviously has to be allied to physical development with the ability to control the arm movement into the desired direction and related hand/finger ability[20]) and points in one of two ways. The first is 'imperative' pointing, which is really 'I want' – such as pointing to bottle, cup or teddy bear. The second is the more important in a sense, and that is 'declarative pointing' whereby the child points to something of interest in order to draw another's attention to it – such as a pet, bird, balloon, and so on. What is crucial about this ability to point to a shared interest is that this is something that retrospective analysis of the behaviour of children with autism illustrates they cannot do. They can 'imperative point' but seem not to point in order to share interest. In essence, even imperative pointing illustrates some degree of understanding that someone will know what you want but there is a subtle difference in knowing that someone else might share a feeling of interest, even though the child would not be able to describe it in this way.

This ability to point to shared interest is allied to social referencing. This is when the child looks to the carer to assess their response to a new person, toy, event, and so on. In other words, the child literally looks to the face of the carer to assess whether something is to be welcomed or avoided. This provides a link between what the carer feels and what the child then might feel, and so, in my view, also provides the first step towards the later understanding that someone may have likes and dislikes different to one's own. As so often happens in development, we need to experience a 'baseline' on which we can then build more complex and sophisticated concepts. The baseline in this case is that the child is imbued with a shared feeling that has been activated by a specific reference to the carer's reaction to an individual situation. This is more than the general sharing of joyful interaction when playing a game together or having a 'conversation'. This brings in a 'third party' whether it be a person or anything else. It is not just child and carer but child, carer and another/object. The other aspect of this amazing 'triangulation' is that the child is also getting the sense of 'I' as separate from another. The child, as we see in the next chapter, is being imbued with the emotional resonance of being with their particular carer(s) and how that feels, and towards the end of the first year has formed a particular and individually specific type of attachment to them, which in turn also represents the child's burgeoning view of the world. The child has already formed a behavioural strategy to 'cope' with this reality within the context of its available and highly limited repertoire for understanding the meaning of the behaviour of others. The child's sense of self is beginning to emerge and it is a sense of self which is now not only being built on the type and quality of physical and psychological interactions between the child and carer, but also on a sense, which will become increasingly more prominent, of a separate and individual identity. It is no accident that this shift towards social referencing and sharing of information also occurs when facial discrimination is more acute for human faces and thereby the emergence of 'stranger anxiety', which, incidentally, appears to relate more to human strangers than other babies or children (Hobson, 1997), and 'language' is emerging through tuneful babbling which is in the rhythm of the home language. All these combine to make a sense of both identity and separateness – a core facet of the human understanding of self.

Finally, I want to discuss the third highlighted item in the chart: ongoing brain maturation – evidence of ability to remember location of hidden objects and object permanence. Once again, this identifies a crucial shift in the understanding of babies and we need to think a little about what leads up to this momentous discovery which not only brings in the importance of memory, but also coincides with infants beginning to develop the concept of object permanence, that is, something out of sight still exists. This is when babies enjoy the endless game of throwing things out of their pram or high chair and begin to look for it and wait for you to give it back to them, over and over again. Before this particular 7–8 months phase, they tend not to look for the fallen item. Atkinson (2000: 39) states that by 6–9 months infants are 'compulsive reachers' and Schore (1994) also notes studies that demonstrate infants during this period are engrossed with 'tactually capturing' objects. Such studies imply both a curiosity about the world and motivation, being helped along by the infant's propensity for 'canalizing' behaviour, which is when children seem to have a compulsive urge to practise a skill as soon as it emerges. Hadders-Algra and Forssberg (2002) also discuss the ideas of Gottlieb (1991) who stressed two particular points of relevance here. First, Gottlieb considered that, within the brain, all the interactions between neurons, groups of neurons and functional areas will mutually influence one another and, second, he drew attention to the part played by simply being part of a species and having behaviour that is specific to that species and how this could also play a 'canalising role' by exposing the individual to particular experiences. To sum up, once an infant or child acquires a skill they want to repeat it over and over and in turn this 'urge' helps [21] form the particular wiring pattern for that activity.

Researchers have also noticed the particular intensity of the play with objects during this phase which coincides with the finding that children are apparently more preoccupied in their play with objects than in social play (Hobson, 1997). Anyone who has watched a child drop an object repeatedly at around 8 months of age will recognize all the behaviours and intensity described. This example is particularly interesting coinciding as it does with the emergence of object permanence so there is both a physical pattern of being able to 'let go' of an object with purpose and an awareness of the object itself when the child looks for it. In addition, the episode of 'compulsive reaching' may also be a way for the child not only to learn to coordinate hand/eye movements but also to learn how to reach for an object if something else is in the way. Diamond and Lee (2000) noted that children of 7 months could sometimes fail to reach an object because they will withdraw their hand reflexively if something else is in the way and they brush against it – which incidentally links with brain maturation as the development of the frontal cortex allows for inhibition of some of the more reflexive actions thereby allowing purposeful activity. The links with vision are powerful as the infant learns about the size of objects and the need to adjust hand and arm movements plus length of reach or locomotion in order to acquire the desired object. It is also noteworthy that between the ages of 8 and 11 months, 'normally' developing infants appear to show a greater increase in looking longer at objects before they reach for them (Atkinson 2000) than either younger or older children. From careful studies of the way in which children in this age range reach for objects, it appears as if this extended looking time is the beginning of more sophisticated 'planning strategies'. It marks, too, the shift between information gained by the child primarily through taste and smell, to a greater emphasis on visual and then auditory information as language becomes more prominent. Furthermore, the ending of this 'extended looking' period ties in with the beginning of Schore's (1994) concept of a practising period, that is, from 10–12 months and lasting until 16–18 months. As he says, this period also overlaps with Piaget's '5th stage of sensorimotor intelligence' which signals 'the cognitive ability to represent the self and external causation' and also links with when patterns of attachment can also be reliably inferred. Schore points out that as early as 1971, Kagan suggested that the capacity for 'active thought' develops at the end of the first year.

With all this in mind, it would suggest, if we follow my premise that all development is logical, that such 'extended looking' times are the precursors for a shift in more sophisticated information processing, implying a temporal understanding of more causal relationships rather than a straightforward 'do/result'. This also brings in the growth of working memory so that information processing can begin to be built on a greater ability to 'hold in mind' current information. Incidentally, the hippocampus is thought to reach maturity by age 1 year.

A study described by Wellman (2002) carried out by himself and a colleague demonstrated that infants as young as 6 months understood reaches as object-directed, as motions towards a target. There is a shift which begins in this age range and parallels the emergence of more purposeful imitation, towards goal-directed, activity supported by greater mobility, visual acuity and range of hearing, and which seems to transfer over time to expectations of goal-directed actions in others. Gergely (2002) presents a range of studies which indicate that at 9 months of age, a qualitatively new level of understanding of goal-directed action develops in infants, which links with other key shifts in development in this age range, such as social referencing and shared attention outlined above. As we can see, from the foundations of understanding the properties of objects, intentional reaching and 'letting go', seeking and finding (a concept which continues well into the pre-school years) and sharing experiences combine to form the framework for understanding the intentions of others. The game of 'peekaboo', with its links with something being there when out of sight – and being the same object – with fun and shared experience, is one which often attracts babies from their object play and provides, through this simple procedure, a link between emotions and the learning of concepts.

Seeking and finding

A way that demonstrates babies can begin to look for an object which has been hidden in a different place has been through the famous 'A not B' test which I describe below.

The baby is shown an attractive toy which is then hidden under a cloth 'A', in full view of the baby. Babies can usually retrieve the toy in this situation. Next, another cloth, labelled 'B' is placed next to cloth 'A'. The first action is repeated several times and then the toy is placed under cloth 'B'. Between the ages of around 9 and 12 months, babies will search cloth 'A', first, and some will look at 'B' but then go back to searching under cloth 'A'. If babies are allowed to retrieve the toy immediately, more success is achieved. However, by about 1 year, most babies will search under 'B'. This indicates that babies have managed to hold a representation of the toy long enough to remember where it was hidden, when put in a different place. If this might not seem such a 'big deal', think about when you are trying to find your misplaced car keys. You look in the familiar places first. However, you do not think the keys have 'vanished' – or at least you hope not – and you begin to search until you have the 'aha' moment when you find them in your pocket. This ability to find something that has been hidden in a different place also identifies another skill, that of memory which is a fascinating topic all of its own and to which we now turn for a brief discussion.

We appear to have two types of memory – long-term and short-term, or as it is more often called 'working', memory. Long-term memory is itself divided into explicit or declarative memory and implicit or 'unconscious' memory which includes procedural memory. People who because of trauma or illness lose short- or long-term memory can often still learn a skill which is procedural memory or still remember how to do a task such as knitting, riding a bike or tying shoe laces. This helps us realize that memory is not a single item nor is it processed in only one area of the brain but in many areas, and we have many memory systems which serve the basic framework outlined above and in Figure 4.1.

It is important to remember that emotions help us choose what to remember from the amount of sensory information that surrounds us and it is also important to remind ourselves that sensory information is a mix of information from all the senses that are working and to whatever degree. Our initial feeling responses will help attract and maintain or lose our attention and so will influence what we remember. The sorts of information we remember in our 'autobiographical memory', which deals with our own events and experiences, will also be influenced by culture. Smith (2005) points out that Americans remember experiences directly related to themselves while the Chinese appear to remember more social experiences.

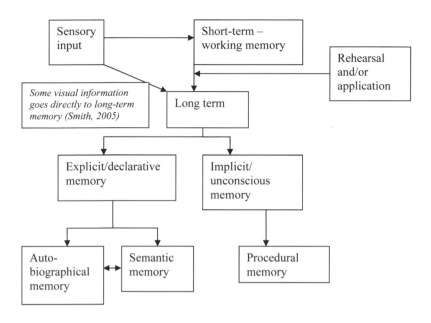

Recall involves information being retrieved from long-term into short-term memory and is essentially a 'reconstruction' of the experience

Figure 4.1 Memory

A mention about 'working memory'[22] which is an essential process allowing us to retain minute-by-minute information so that we can, as Smith (2005) puts it, lend coherence to experience. Without it we would be slaves to the moment as, for example, we would be unable to remember someone we had spoken to a short time before. It reminds me of babies who cannot yet hold the information about the fallen object long enough to realize it is still there and they can look for it. As the infant brain matures, so the capacity to remember the 'out of sight' increases. When babies acquire this as outlined earlier, parents speak of 'velcro' babies who follow them around everywhere. The baby has this new knowledge and so, I believe, rehearses the information by following the parent around almost as if checking this out – as well as expanding their horizons as they move around. Incidentally, this also demonstrates the importance of emotions as it is the baby's need to be with the carer, to be safe and secure, that provides the context which gives the baby the impetus to follow the carer and, in so doing, discovers that their carer exists in the same way in different environments.

I must also point out the importance of autobiographical memory in its role as part of identifying a sense of self. This memory provides the thread that links our existence in the past as well as the present. It is interesting that our capacity to point to our bodies not only links with the recognition of a 'self' in a mirror but also is in close 'timing' with the emergence of language so that the knowledge of a physical body that 'belongs to me' also begins to be linked to a 'me to whom things happen which I can talk about'. In old age or through trauma or disease, when working memory is lost, long-term autobiographical memories can still exist but these can become confused and out of synchrony as there are no longer the links with what is happening in the here and now. Perhaps this is why in dementia, the self – or, rather, knowledge of the self – becomes increasingly blurred and knowledge of people in the present becomes confused with those from the past. Interestingly, too, some studies have found that some people with profound dementia could not recognize themselves in a mirror (Postal, 2005).

Summary

Nobody really knows how babies understand their world, but what is certainly evident is that babies do have ideas about how things should behave very early on, and we revisit this in Chapter 6. There is a lot of data about what infants appear to know at different ages, but *how* they learn these things and what may be innate is still a source of much debate, as is the reason for differences in both the rate of achieving common skills and abilities and the variation in degree. For example, a paper by Sigman and Capps (1997), discussed by Trevarthen et al. (1999), speculated that the differences in joint attention so notable in other research, was felt to be accounted for in some measure by differences in IQ and developmental level. A personal view is that much early learning is centred around the interactions and comings and goings of carers, siblings and, possibly, pets as the sight, sound, smell, feel and taste of these highly consistent and persistent interactive experiences provide the multimodal information on which initial concepts may be based. In the very first weeks, it is almost entirely the experiences the carer provides that shape the first shadowy awakenings of understanding. Gradually, the baby becomes part of the wider family, friends and neighbourhood, and as the baby is participating, observing and absorbing information – the baby is an active agent. The world becomes full of variety but at its heart remains the anchor of the child's existence, the base on which all subsequent information is built, the child's primary carer. We recognize that familiarity and consistency is important and find support for this in research not directly associated with the topic. For example, there has been a finding that babies as young as 2 months of age can remember the arm or leg movement they had made[23] to activate a mobile after an interval of one or two days. However, the crucial thing is that these babies could not recognize the mobile if even one aspect of it had been changed (Bauer, 2002). It seems as if these very young babies are unable to realize it is the same mobile and have to become re-familiarized with the changed mobile in order to recognize it again. This factor perhaps ties in with Grossberg et al.'s finding (2001) (also mentioned later on) that neonates appear to see partly hidden objects as disjointed parts – not pulling the information together until 2–4 months old, when the visual system is also developing rapidly. All these factors strongly suggest that in these early months repetition and familiarity help the baby sort out and retain information and so 'carer consistency' along with familiar objects and routines in tandem with novelty and exploration would seem to me to be a crucial part of a process which envelops social, emotional, physical and cognitive learning.

5 Emotional and social well-being

The hunger for love is much more difficult to remove than the hunger for bread.

(Mother Teresa)

A baby is born with a need to be loved – and never outgrows it.

(Frank A. Clark)

Love is the most important thing in the world, but baseball is pretty good too.

(Greg, age 8)

A child watches another laying out small animals and people on a table, carefully adding fences and buildings. After a few moments the first child comes and knocks over the small world, so painstakingly created. Another child bangs her head hard on a table and retreats into a corner, arms about herself. Yet another approaches two others playing, they make it clear they do not want another playmate and the child skips off to find something else to do, seemingly unconcerned.

All these children are behaving in a way which gives a clue to how they feel inside. In a sense, it does not matter too much what the label is – jealousy, lonely distress or happy confidence – what matters to them is what they feel and what they do to cope with those feelings. In other words, they have a general strategy to cope with the day-to-day ups and downs that they encounter. Such strategies are led by their feelings founded on their experiences and shaped by their ability to make sense of those experiences – in particular a 'push' to make unpleasant feelings go away and feel 'better' inside – strategies which, even as adults, we all adopt in one way or another no matter what the circumstances might be. The strength or otherwise of our emotional health will influence the level of tolerance to minor and major upsets and our ability to overcome them, as well as the type of strategies we will bring into play.

What is emotional well-being/mental health?

In 1995, an NHS Health Advisory Service workshop[1] drew up a definition of mental health in young people, identifying four key capacities as the ability to:

- develop psychologically, emotionally, intellectually and spiritually
- initiate, develop and sustain mutually satisfying personal relationships
- become aware of and to empathize with others
- experience and integrate psychological distress without it hindering development.

Interestingly, this workshop is one of the few that mentions a spiritual dimension to mental well-being and it is also interesting that Maslow's (1943) famous 'hierarchy of needs', which is usually depicted as having five levels (see Figure 5.1), has seven. The final two are the 'need to know and understand' and 'self-transcendence' which is usually interpreted as spiritual needs, reminding us that we are potentially beings who want to know what our place and purpose is in this world. What Maslow's hierarchy clearly illustrates is the importance of emotions and that without feeling physically and psychologically safe and secure we do not progress. It also suggests that the taking away of opportunities at 'higher' levels can also make us regress to an earlier stage and the lack of opportunities may make us 'stick' on a particular level. For example, troubled children may not learn to their full potential because of their constant state of anxiety about their circumstances.

The Primary National Strategy (2006)[2] supplies the following as being important for personal, social and emotional development:

- being social
- being close
- being me
- having feelings
- having friends and relationships.

The original Birth to Three Matters Framework in the aspect: 'A strong child' talks of the child having a 'realisation of own individuality', 'experiencing and seeking closeness', 'developing self-assurance' and a 'sense of belonging'.

All of these emphasize the sense of being an individual secure in their separateness as a self but also confidence in relationships and their place alongside others. This is not intrinsically an easy task and in the previous chapter we saw some of the ways in which all these attributes and beliefs begin to come about.

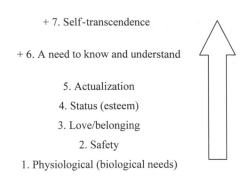

+ 7. Self-transcendence

+ 6. A need to know and understand

5. Actualization

4. Status (esteem)

3. Love/belonging

2. Safety

1. Physiological (biological needs)

Figure 5.1 Theory of needs

Emotions/feelings are not only an aspect of development but are central to every part of it. Nussbaum (2001), for example, begins her book on the intelligence of emotions with the words 'Emotions shape the landscape of our mental and social lives' and if emotions are the shapers of our own personal 'mental and social lives', then it follows that emotions permeate how we behave to one another, how we understand such behaviour and what meaning or significance we ascribe to both our own and others' actions. What is interesting and perhaps surprising is that when we think about emotions and behaviour, the fundamental range is quite limited and can be observed in other mammals. Primates can, for example, deceive each other. An example is of a female chimp being groomed by a 'lower order' male chimp behind a rock so that the lead chimp could not see what was going on (Zimmer, 2003).[3] Although humans appear to have a more complex range of emotions, nevertheless I suggest that even the cruellest behaviour has its roots in one or more fundamental emotions such as fear, rage or sadness. What perhaps does differentiate us from our mammal cousins and other creatures is our ability to reach out beyond the immediate confines of our environment through our speech, writing, art and thought. We do have the capacity to recognize our self as a self, to think beyond our selves, to reflect on who we are and the possible purpose for our existence. It is these questions that can take our minds into abstract places without time or physical constraints. In the early years, in tandem with a growing realization of self as person, there develops the 'theory of mind' which we encountered briefly in the previous chapter and which has been described by Perner and Lang (1999) as a 'conceptual system ... with which we can impute mental states to others and ourselves, that is what we know, think, want, feel, etc.'. As well as reaching into our own minds, we reach into the minds of others and we begin to do this in our pre-school years.

Through this extending use of mind we also can 'move on' our emotions where they can transcend far above immediate need. But – and it is an important but – we do not reach this stage without having literally 'lived through' the acquisition of the skills and aptitudes we require in order to be able to survive within our own human societies and that the emotional tenor of such living will dictate how far we can move from self-absorption to self-reflection. However, the external manifestation of our emotional inner lives will depend also on culture, ability and opportunity.

In essence, feelings are the internal responses aroused by a situation with different parts of the brain organizing the bodily information into the 'emotion'. Cultural norms 'name' the emotions while both social and family norms, as well as maturational level, influence their level of acceptance, variety and type of display (see Figure 5.2). Sadness and happiness appear to have different pathways and different hemispheric activity – the right hemisphere more involved with the processing of negative emotion and the left, that of positive emotions. Behaviour is driven by experiences and shaped by the strategies which are learned from the earliest days in an effort to deal with the internal feelings. These strategies arise from the patterns and networks of connections between the senses and the mediating brain – resulting in the ongoing sense of self as an 'active entity'.

A brief note on gender and emotions

Females frequently express emotion more intensely than males but this does *not* mean that males feel any less intensely, although frequently and erroneously expression is equated with depth of feeling. For example, Marzillier and Davey's (2004) study on disgust, which is one of the basic emotions, noted that while males and females did not differ on the emotional profiles provided by their reactions to both primary disgust items and more complex disgust items,[4] females responded more intensely across all the negative emotions. The widely acknowledged ability of females to talk about their feelings more should also not be confused with a notion that all females are naturally more 'empathic'. They have a greater biological predisposition to understand facial expressions more easily, and young girls often have a strong 'nurturing' tendency, expressed through play, and learn to manage their emotions in social situations earlier than boys. Experiences, however, can support, enhance, diminish or 'skew' this 'natural' tendency. For example, girls (and women) can frequently adopt more 'psychological weaponry' when wanting their own way or in expressing anger, dislike or disapproval, such as targeting someone else's self-esteem.

However, there is a very real reason to consider gender differences in all aspects of development, irrespective of the fact that within gender differences

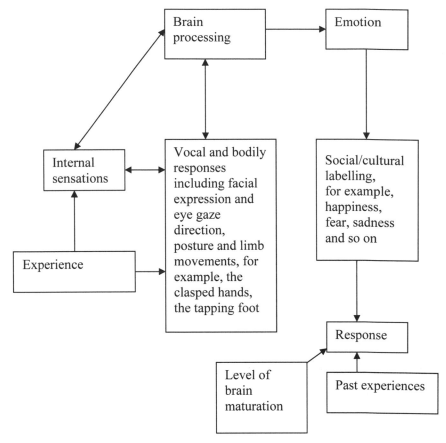

Figure 5.2 A representation of the influences on behaviour

can also be very great. Animal studies have identified that stress can have different effects on males and females, and so there may be biological gender predispositions to react to stress in different ways. The significance is that signs of stress or distress in males and females may manifest itself differently and, indeed, there is increasing information regarding the validity of this idea when considering manifestations of depression, anti-social behaviour, suicide rates and drug and alcohol abuse.

Early emotions

The generally accepted range of 'basic' emotions are sadness, fear, anger, happiness, surprise and disgust, and many of the more complex emotions, for example guilt, jealousy and pride, are thought to be subtle variations, enhancements and mixtures of these – comparable perhaps to the basic palette of colours whereby there are only three primary colours – red, blue and yellow and yet from these an amazing range of shades can be produced.[5]

As we know, babies are not passive beings but express their feelings in a very real way. We have already talked about distress but babies obviously show signs of contentment, pleasure and joy. However, whether emotional expressiveness and basic feelings are broadly the same in babies as adults or whether there is developmental change over time is the subject of much debate and research. Oster (2005) outlines broad areas of agreement among researchers from different theoretical perspectives as follows:

- Affective communication plays 'a crucial role in early social, emotional and cognitive development'
- Infants are 'pre-adapted for social interaction'
- Infant facial expressions and other expressive behaviours have a biological basis
- Cognitive development and experience 'also play a role in the elaboration and refinement of emotions and emotional expressions'

Oster (2005: 262) summarizes the debate thus: 'disagreements have focused primarily on the nature of the information we can infer from infant facial expressions and the nature of developmental changes in facial expressions and emotions'.

The arguments about what can be discerned from an infant's expressions has a very real application in the life of the baby and young child as it is only through our understanding and interpretation of what their facial and bodily signals may be telling us that we are able to discern what a child is feeling and later what they may also be thinking. We then respond according to our interpretation of those signals, and this is the mechanism by which we frame the relationships we have with the child and, crucially, the 'correctness' or otherwise of our interpretation, and thereby our response, will result in the child's reaction – contributing over time to the child's ongoing emotional state and burgeoning sense of self. As adults, we also constantly infer another's state of mind not only from what someone says, but also from a triad of facial expression, body posture and behaviour. These arguments also bring home to us how much we rely on expression/body language in order to communicate throughout our daily lives, which is why a lack of understanding of facial expression and eye gaze can be so devastating.

Back to the brain: making links

As we know, the brain processes all information, with facial processing and emotional expressiveness forming a key part of deciphering both what the world is like and what it feels like to be 'me'. Panksepp (1998); Panksepp and Panksepp (2000) also provides a strong evolutionary perspective indicating that, in his view, emotions are founded on deep, organic, neural activity within the brain. He notes that an area within the mid-brain – associated with consciousness/awareness, the periaqueductal gray (PAG),[6] which has some of the richest and most widespread connections with other parts of the brain – is more active in the early days of life and he sees this as the source from which a variety of core emotional 'states of being' could emerge. He feels these 'core areas' are the fundamental part of experiencing emotions based on the ancient 'gifts' of evolution rather than focusing only on the pathways of bodily information to 'higher' neocortical areas. In other words, he suggests that emotions are part of humanity in a truly fundamental sense and higher cortical structures are not essential for the experiencing of emotion. This brings into focus the potential reality of the internal experiences of babies and the links with what we know about early brain development and key structures within the brain. In Chapter 2, we encountered both the cerebellum and the amygdala, and this latter structure has strong connections with the areas in the brain which subserve memory, the body's 'status quo' and the planning and organizing parts of our brain. Many studies identify the amygdala's crucial role in the processing of emotions but especially fear and anxiety, for example, Le Doux (1998, 2002), Blair et al. (2005), Morris et al. (1996), Wright et al. (2002) and Vuilleumier et al. (2001). The latter study also identified 'enhanced amygdala responses' to emotional as opposed to neutral 'schematic faces'. This is pertinent when we consider the newborn's well-documented preference for looking at faces including schematic ones. This study also suggested to the authors that 'the amygdala utilises relatively simple features to distinguish emotionally salient stimuli from neutral ones' and that in spite of repeated presentations of these simple stimuli, while showing some diminishing of reaction, nevertheless showed 'sustained responses'. The key point about this finding is that usually when we see something frequently, we tend to lose or have diminished interest,[7] so the maintenance of interest in contrast to the usual findings illustrates that there is something about emotional expressions that keeps us alert. While animal studies are more robust in implicating the amygdala in both fear conditioning and recognition, a PET study carried out by Morris et al. (1996) concluded that the human amygdala is engaged in the processing of the emotional salience of faces with a specificity of response to fearful facial expressions. It was also noted that the left cerebellum[8] was activated for fearful faces.

Another study by Ashwin et al. (2006) on processing of anger faces by people with Asperger's syndrome stated that social threat captures attention and is processed rapidly and efficiently and that angry faces 'pop out' in a crowd compared to happy faces. They also found that the study group only differed from controls when the situation was in 'widely varying crowd sizes and when faces were inverted'. This suggests that the noticing and processing of angry and/or fear-inducing faces is very deep-seated in the human psyche and impervious to some degree to dysfunction of generalized face-processing. An interesting study by Cavanagh (2005) found that the amgydala became activated (in adults) to blurry fearful expressions, supporting the notion that even with poor visual acuity it is possible that we are able to react to fearful faces. Cavanagh further points out that earlier studies showed the amygdala responded to such images even in a brief masked presentation that subjects do not report seeing and the right amygdala has even been shown to respond to emotional facial expressions in a patient with no primary visual cortex and no conscious visual experience. In other words, emotional expressiveness may even be 'sensed' in some global way and that we notice an expression even if not consciously aware of doing so.

This idea of awareness of facial expression outside a conscious appraisal further supports the sensitivity we have for emotions and how, even as infants, reactions and responses can be finely tuned. Dr Beatrice Beebe[9] in her work with mothers and babies has demonstrated, through freeze-frame video recording, the speed of infant response to fleeting changes in expression. Research by Muir et al. (2005) which has built on and made modifications to the 'still face experiment' (Tronick et al., 1978) supports Beebe's work by demonstrating how infants as young as 3 months will react and respond to changes in facial expression (for example, from happy to sad) as well as to a still face.[10] This also ties in with the research which has indicated that the actual processing speed of facial processing is emotions first, then recognition of a face and then whose face.

Such studies of the brain provide interesting perspectives on what may be discerned as emerging in this chapter, that is, that there is possibly something special about the awareness of negative emotions. Gerhardt (2005) explains in depth how important love/affection is in order to 'shape a baby's brain' and the toll it places on the child when such affection is not forthcoming, but there is one particular aspect which I want to explore and which, linked with the brain studies, may provide a basic rationale as to why negative experiences produce such a pervasive effect. It may also help to explain why early years professionals have to work so hard with some children to turn negative behaviour around.

To introduce these ideas, I give the following quote:

our brain's specialization for producing social responses seems to have a bias toward negative situations, as though evolution placed a premium on our ability to shrink in submission, bristle in retaliation or retreat from others' indifference. Some of us may register these unpleasant feelings too frequently and in ways that are inappropriate to the circumstances – to our detriment. Thus we perceive others as critical, antagonistic or rejecting. Correspondingly our body states register fear, reactive irritability or dejected withdrawal. Our brains are like hyper vigilant sentries on duty in the dark, perceiving malevolence in every rustle in the bushes.

(Brothers, 1997: 64)

A piece of information which links with the above comes from Damasio (2003). This concerned a woman suffering from Parkinson's disease, who was part of a group being treated by a new method of passing a low-intensity, high-frequency electrical current via the brain stem. On the occasion in question, a current was sent 2 mm astray and produced a rapid response of devastating sadness, sobbing and crying followed by verbal expressions of desperate sadness and worthlessness in the patient – who, incidentally, had no history of depression or any other psychiatric illness. The area activated in the brain stem[11] was one which produced a set of motor responses involved in manifesting the signs of sadness which was followed by feelings of sadness and then sad thoughts – which in turn compounded the feelings of sadness. This rare and intriguing experience strongly illustrated that feelings come before thoughts and that bodily expression of feeling also induces, or at the very least is parallel with, accompanying feelings. Damasio also quotes studies by Paul Ekman who asked volunteers to move their facial muscles in certain ways which – unbeknown to the subjects – displayed anger, fear and so on. Needless to say, the feelings that normally accompanied such expressions were not far behind.

What is interesting is that these suggestions and findings have links with Patricia Crittenden's (1999) contention that the attachment system, which is discussed later, is a system against danger and so looks at the necessity for attachments to primary carers from a slightly different angle. That is, to see the avoidance of harm as the prime mover with children's behavioural strategies developed in order to ensure, in one way or another, dependent on the type of relationship, ongoing contact and thereby some safety with the carer. This is an interesting twist on the idea of attachment formation as providing what Bowlby (1988, 1991a, 1991b, 1991c), the founder and 'father' of attachment theory, terms 'a secure base'.

As we have seen, 'nature' provides the newborn with the basic tools to ensure contact as we literally cling to our carers for support, help and nurture.[12] In addition, a baby's first emotional display is that of crying and it seems to me that the general feelings that accompany such states will also occur. Babies cry when they are startled and/or frightened, and when they are cold, hungry, lonely, and so on. The adult role is both to prevent harm and relieve distress, thereby through their actions encouraging pleasurable feelings. This can be illustrated by our almost instinctive inviting of the child to smile – because that is what we do. We smile at babies, and touch their cheeks and mouths, stroking upwards to induce a 'smile' even in very young babies. We soothe, talk to, rock and cuddle children. In other words, we help the child move from distress for whatever reason, to at the very least a state of reduced crying. From a different perspective, consider Alzheimer's disease. In many ways the manifestation of this disease resembles the slow peeling away of layers of developmental skills, abilities and understanding.[13] All too often, it is also accompanied by distressing states of anxiety such as sufferers wanting to find their way to their childhood home and/or constantly feeling lost and frightened. I wonder if this may reflect the existence of a fundamental, core state of anxiety which exists in infants and that relief of anxiety/distress may be part of the inherent driving force for the formation of attachments. Potential support for this idea and Crittenden's premise, is given by a recent, large study[14] from the National Institute of Child Health and Human Development (NICHD) in the USA which stressed that it was 'attentiveness to her baby's *distress*' (emphasis added) which seemed to be a prime factor in the formation of secure attachments to the mother rather than level of sensitivity of response in other situations such as play, feeding and so on. Incidentally, the researchers also found that 'difficult' temperament in the baby was not a particularly contributing factor.

If we tie together these findings with Crittenden's ideas, plus the fact that babies show distress from birth, there emerges a logic as to why we are so vulnerable to adverse experiences – they 'hook into' a very basic human state. It also provides a rationale for how difficult it is for very young children to learn to deal with difficult emotions such as jealousy and feelings of low self-worth thereby often reacting with anger and distress to situations in which they feel helpless and unwanted.

Links with attachment theory

I am making an assumption here, that readers will be familiar with the basic tenets of attachment theory and its classifications and so will not go into the history of the theory nor how the classifications were established. My previous book (Robinson, 2003) provides a brief overview of these issues and there is a wealth of literature about its history and research as well as Bowlby's own seminal works on attachment, separation and loss (Bowlby, 1988, 1991a, 1991b, 1991c). I am also aware that most training courses for early years practitioners, teachers, social workers and health visitors provide information to varying degrees and depth. However, my reason for including attachment theory is that it is one of the most viable (and well-researched) ways of understanding not only children's reactions to separation/loss but also their 'working capacity' to manage emotions and relationships.

Glaser (2005)[15] provides a very helpful summary, bringing out the key points of Bowlby's work, emphasizing the biological basis of attachment behaviour, that is, the seeking of proximity by a child to their carer in order to provide a 'secure base'. She notes that it is a 'behavioural and affectional system' and is activated by 'internal/external stressors', for example, feeling lost, lonely, afraid or being physically separated from the carer.

A strong motivation to maintain proximity to the attachment figure is probably universal to human infants, as well as to many primate young – and, I would add, most infants of many species. The calls between sheep and their lambs, cows and calves, dogs and puppies, and so on, when separated, literally give voice to the need to be back close to the mother and safe from potential danger. It is interesting that both call to one another – the infant when it is in distress and the mother at the idea of separation and its implications.

This need to build a 'secure base' emotionally is no less strong and just as necessary in those children who may have disabilities. A paper by Capps et al., written in 1994 on attachment security in children with autism, identified that autistic children 'appeared as securely attached as comparison children ... but there was a significant positive relationship between attachment security scores and cognitive, language and gross motor level'.[16] Children with autism – or any other special need – have parents who, like any other parent, will encompass the range of type and quality of care and responsiveness, and so the emotional environment of the child should not be neglected when considering behaviour. This paper also highlights the teasing out of different aspects of attachment development such as how a child with autism forms a representation of their carer(s), and what may be their 'internal working model' of their emotional world. It also emphasizes that all children develop or 'construct' their attachments with the particular psychological capacity they have at their disposal and by that I mean the way in which their sensory information is processed, 'colour-washed' overall by the emotional quality of their relationships and mediated by their general brain function. The level of general 'intelligence' will provide the framework on which all children build their understanding of the behaviour of others and how they develop their strategies in response to their experiences. In principle there is no difference in the process of attachment formation in both typically and non-typically developing children.

The particular behavioural manifestations of an individual's quality of attachment will depend on all the factors outlined above but ultimately the function of the formation of attachments to primary carers is to help the child construct their 'internal working model', to use Bowlby's term (Figure 5.3). It is this internal working model which provides the child with their first understandings of safety and security, inextricably linked to the child's internal feeling state, that is, one of general contentment versus general anxiety or fear or distress – which is the type of feeling we all try to avoid. The quality of the attachment, and consequent world view with its accompanying behaviour strategies, can be reliably measured by the 'Strange Situation'[17] at approximately 1 year of age.

It is important that the internal working model is fully understood to encompass the following:

- the child's general internal feeling state, for example secure/ contentment, anxious, fearful, sad
- their relationship to carer (and consequent tendency to approach and/or withdrawal to other adults dependent on quality of primary attachment and need)
- their behavioural strategy in day-to-day situations.

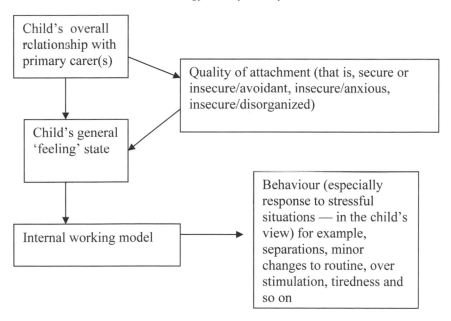

Figure 5.3   Summary assessment

These are formed prior to the child's conscious awareness of a bodily self which has also arisen, as we have seen from previous chapters, via ongoing interactions with carers, especially the use of imitation. The child's sense of self as a 'person' is particularly physical in its manifestation in the pre-school years, only gradually incorporating an assessment of abstract views and own character in the teenage years.

A contentious issue in the past regarding Bowlby's work and attachment theory has been whether babies are able to form attachments to more than one carer. Basically what 50 years of research have probably demonstrated is that the term 'primary attachment figure' refers to the 'person with whom a child develops a lifelong emotional bond and whom they most want to be with when they are frightened or hurt – usually but not necessarily with their birth mother' (Bowlby, 2006). It is to be remembered that children form attachment relationships with fathers too, and in a two-parent situation it may be that it is the father who is the primary attachment figure. However, 'secondary attachment figures' according to Richard Bowlby (2006) are the 'few special people in children's lives with whom they have developed a close subsidiary or secondary attachment bond, such as siblings, grandparents, nannies or childminders'. Having these additional close relationships provides additional support to the child and increases their resilience to stress. Stress itself has become something of an issue as raised stress levels have been found in children in day care. What is clear, however, is that most children form specific attachments to a limited number of people, and this is logical when we think of the developing brain and the immature skills and abilities of young children. Children cannot cope with everything that happens to them or adults inflict on them – although they try and it is often how they form their coping strategies in confusing situations that manifests in behaviour 'problems'. Practitioners dealing with children who are deemed 'out of control' at ages 5 or 6 are potentially dealing with a child who is hanging on to behaviour which serves an emotional purpose for that child given their circumstances.

It is important for practitioners working with children across the age spectrum to realize that attachment behaviour is a universal phenomenon and its manifestations can be recognized in many different cultures. The differences are in the way these behaviours are expressed and dealt with by the mothers and how they respond within the confines of their particular culture. The needs of the children remain the same.

What might be the behavioural outcomes for insecure attachments?

The following is a list of symptoms which can indicate insecure attachments. They will obviously vary in their manifestations in individuals in type, degree and developmental stage. They do not all necessarily coexist as a child may only demonstrate one or two of the symptoms:

- affectionate with strangers or wants to leave with them
- learning problems
- hyperactive, overactive, attention deficit
- destructive to self, others and/or property
- cruel to animals
- daily lying or lying in the face of the obvious (crazy lying)
- provokes hostile/dislike reactions in others.

All these factors emphasize how important it is for adults to support infants from the beginning – to promote a robust sense of confidence, a sense of self – which provides the wherewithal to become 'strong'. Perhaps in a strange way, our vulnerability to fear or anger may be the optimal way in which we do gain strength as our carers help us to deal with such feelings. Even in adult life, it is perhaps no accident that it is often through adversity that we feel we 'learn' something and find coping mechanisms. However, when we are small and vulnerable in every sense, the way in which our carers react and respond to us becomes increasingly crucial, for it is they who help us to build the strength which we can then use in the future. Without these early building blocks, the normal phases of emotional development become fraught with difficulty. Glaser (2005) notes that the probable sensitive period for developing stranger wariness is in the first three years of life – remember that in typically developing children this occurs around about 8 months – and that if children do not form selective attachments by around 3 years 'children may become disinhibited in their approach to strangers' – incidentally, a strong finding in older children adopted from Romania. Again, this is understandable because if we have not formed an early secure base then I strongly believe we continue to look for it and children will seek what they desperately (and unconsciously) need and, as they get older, this can be in increasingly damaging ways – anything to fill that psychological 'gap'. In tandem, there is a growing recognition that there are strong associations between adverse childhood experiences and later physical as well as mental health. Large-scale studies, for example the Adverse Child Experiences Study in the USA (ACE)[18] find that rates of teenage pregnancy, suicide, alcohol and drug abuse rates were all high in these groups. Furthermore, maltreatment victims were also more vulnerable to cancers, heart, lung and liver disease and diabetes – possibly because of risky lifestyles but chronic stress alone in childhood may also contribute to these findings.

On a more positive note, older children can and do make attachments and, indeed, we all make attachments when adults to our partners but our relationships with them can echo those early foundations. It is also possible for an older child or adult to become 'learned secure' but it often takes a long time and much mistrust and 'testing out' of the particular person involved.

Attachment and place

A further dimension to attachment is that we not only form attachments to persons but also, in strong but different ways, to places (Spencer, 2004). Spencer says that individual identity arises from being shaped by others' responses to oneself as an individual and from a biological self-awareness from infancy. He also adds that people (and certainly children) have an emotional relationship to place. A very simple example which may illustrate the power of this idea is when, as adults, we attend a training session. How often do we choose a seat which feels 'comfortable' in a psychological sense and is the seat we will continue to use throughout the day, and can sometimes feel resistant if a group activity requires us to change places. This emotional attachment to place is the sense of 'home' and although the saying 'home is where the heart is' can mean that we can feel safe with loved ones in different places or where we feel at peace, there is nevertheless something about the place where we are 'brought up'. I also think – although I have nothing to prove it – that our place attachments reflect our emotional attachments. I, for example, have never been back to my childhood home and had a very strong resistance to even visiting my home town, although I did with a great deal of trepidation about four years ago. Incidentally, I know now that I was an 'avoidant' child. What our childhood home can provide is a sense of stability within change, as can going to the same school throughout school life. Those of us who perhaps did not equate our childhood home – which encompasses both the bricks and mortar, decoration, outside areas and community as well as the people within it – with security, may find, as adults that we are more protective of our 'home' and often less able to cope with intrusions, people who 'drop in' or long-term visitors. For adults, our childhood memories can revolve around home, school or favourite places where we could be away from adult eyes such as dens which can be even under a stairwell. It is a complex subject because, as children, we often need to make such a space and practitioners and carers need to provide the opportunities for children to create a space for themselves within a space. Perhaps as Spencer says, the easiest way to grasp this concept is to think about when it is disrupted, for example burglary, when people often feel as they themselves have been violated – not just their home. Moving house can create a very strong sense of emotional as well as physical disruption, as can moving to a new school from nursery or going to college. Both children and adults often need help on such occasions and frequently it is the continuing existence and availability of familiar items such as 'comfort objects', which may be a soft toy, a blanket or even a small ornament in the case of a child, whereas for adults, we can hang on to a favourite tea set, an old diary or wallet, photographs – all to provide a sense of continuity with what we have left behind – no matter how positive the change or move may be. It is notable how, as adults in a totally new environment, we can try to re-create what made us feel secure, hence the group identity and the tendency for the English abroad to want pubs and chips!

This has implications for us when supporting children through change – some children have a very strong sense of place and become very attached to what they see as a familiar and well-loved place, be it their space in their bedroom, a favourite chair or, moving into their wider environment, their nursery school and so on. Some children find such transitions from place to place difficult and all of us feel some 'tugs' when leaving the familiar. We need to understand why even older children may still carry some comfort object in their pocket or become distressed at someone borrowing a favourite pencil. It is all part and parcel of our need to feel safe, and as adults we need to remember our own needs, rituals and comfort zones and respect those of the children in our care. This sense of place must not be confused with spatial awareness – something discussed in the next chapter – which is our location in respect of our selves in relation to others and objects in our environments.

Emotions changing – thoughts emerging

Understanding emotions and understanding minds follows a developmental thread, beginning with the development of both emotional display and feelings followed by a gradual growth of understanding intentions and the feelings of others during the second year of life which, in turn, influences how a child begins to change its strategies of behaviour adapting to new-found knowledge and skills. However, I believe that early experiences do not go away but simply change their form, becoming subsumed into the growing sophistication of language, wider interactions, more complex thought processes and adaptive behaviours. This idea is based partly on personal history as I can vouch for how very early, pre-verbal experiences set the scene for my personal view of the world. Of course, I did not know why I had screaming tantrums on being told that it was 'time to go home' or told 'crazy' lies or gave away items so that others might be my friend. I only knew what I felt – lonely and continually anxious and/or fearful. This led to the adoption of various strategies to deal with this situation, gradually replacing the physical giving of items to people by more abstract forms of giving, that is, choosing nursing as one of my careers and, as told about in my first book (Robinson, 2003), running soup kitchens, working in India[19] and so on. Understanding did not come until much later and again it can illustrate how thoughts and emotions intertwine because it was only when opportunities arose to think about my feelings and actions and reflect on their beginnings that I was able to 'move on'. To paraphrase T.S. Eliot, pre-verbal experience is like music heard so deeply that it is seemingly not heard at all. In other words, our inability to recall very early experiences does not mean that they have not left their mark on us, but simply that it is lost to conscious recall. The emergence of language allows another dimension to experience. It frames concepts, ideas and feelings into sounds and symbols that we can share with others. Prior to this, our experiences leave their mark in ways identified in the preceding chapters – a sensory memory built up of sounds, tastes, smells, bodily and limb sensations. Knowledge of 'me' is buried in this sensory landscape, a landscape in which we stumble on its furrows and ridges at those times when we feel and react beyond our understanding – like sending oneself a valentine card, destroying the painstaking work of someone else or only turning to the self for comfort.

As already indicated, during the early years, children's strategies for dealing with their day-to-day lives are built up by what they have experienced and Gerhardt (2005) comprehensively describes how positive or negative emotional experiences profoundly influence the way the brain 'wires' itself and sets the pathway for the tempo and outcome of future development. As we can surmise from the chapters on sensory information and the brain, competing signals help make the patterns for neural connections based on sensory experiences and, as Gerhardt indicates, emotional experiences will undergo the same competition and result in a patterning of emotional responses unique to that child embedded in the context of growing skills and abilities. Panksepp and Smith-Pasqualini (2005) says what emerges during development 'is the higher capacity to regulate emotional states and to construct more complex behavioural strategies to cope with emotionally challenging events'. In general, feelings and greater awareness of another's feelings and ability to empathize with them appear to arise in conjunction with the recognition of the self in a mirror and the capacity to correctly identify body parts and point to them appropriately.[20] Gradually, over time and into the third year, there is the beginning of an adaptation of behaviour in response to experience with a secondary goal in mind. An example would be a child, A, who wishes to play with an attractive toy, held by another child, B. Child A offers B another attractive toy and when B takes it, A grabs the first toy. This potentially illustrates that child A has worked out a strategy of how to obtain the desired toy, through an understanding of what another child might find attractive and how they might respond. In addition, such a strategy also indicates a basic understanding of a sequence of events in time – that is, if *this* happens now, *that* might happen next.[21] While this example illustrates a growing complexity of understanding, it must also be noted that other aspects of development are available to the child in order to carry out this strategy. For example, the child had to be able to physically move and accurately reach and grasp in order to fully achieve the desired goal. In addition, the example offers up further questions as to the foundations of the child's own desires, understanding and behaviour, for example the potential for a sequence of development that culminates in the initial understanding of another's mind as well as self-awareness. For example, Barna and Legerestee (2005) point out that at around 4 years, children produce a variety of internal-state terms when describing what people are doing and use words such as 'believing', 'thinking' and 'feeling', while at age 3, children are more likely to be confident about 'wants'. Barna and Legerestee are also likely to see the transition in modes and styles of thinking as emanating from 'primitive mental states' to more complex understanding indicating that the origins for the growing understanding of wants and later beliefs can be traced to early infancy. Nielson (2003) describes in detail the child's development of spatial relationships and the perceptual field, and notes how the child's ability to move independently supports the burgeoning understanding of self, object, space and position. Such a process of acquiring a perspective of the physical self in relation to objects is suggested to be the starting point of the eventual complex and sophisticated ability of mental perspective-taking, that is, of understanding other minds. Gallese (2001) provides a link with brain activity as he associates the existence of mirror neurons to the ultimate development of empathy, which brings the role of observation and imitation back into the equation. Babies and young children watch what others are doing and will imitate and be further imitated in their turn. Gallese's paper points out that while we do not necessarily produce an observed action, our motor system acts as if we were executing that very same action that we are observing. If we think back to the previous chapters, we can see how not only are activity, vision and the capacity to imitate the building blocks for the child building a sense of self, but also noting how others react and what they actually do. We do not live in a static world, but as infants we are surrounded by people who reach for things, who speak in various ways to each other, who move about, who have a variety of facial expressions and body language. Gradually through learning about what people are doing and then slowly beginning to understanding intentions – something that seems to emerge towards the end of the first year and into the second year – the child gradually learns to apply this knowledge into interactions and communication with others. The child also learns to manage their own emotions – over time! – by the constant support and help of the adults around them. Their emotions are very strong (and sometimes frightening) and it is the adult's ability to tolerate and understand the behaviour which helps the child understand that feelings are tolerable and that they can modify how they behave. What is crucial is that adults acknowledge the reality of the child's feelings first before helping the child find ways to deal with them. An angry child needs to feel that their anger is understood even if the accompanying behaviour is unwanted. Adults help the child understand that feelings are neither good nor bad but what is important is how we deal with them. A child whose anger or distress (as well as their happiness and joy) is not acknowledged may think that they are 'bad' for feeling in a particular way rather than understanding that it really is the behaviour that the adult may be concerned about.

Self-regulation

As we can see from the preceding information, emotional well-being includes the capacity to regulate our own behaviour, that is, to adapt our behaviour to the circumstances rather than simply reacting – such as having a tantrum when a desired toy is not forthcoming or when having to wait for a turn on a slide. The adult's ability to manage the child's emotions gradually helps the child manage their own emotions and establish ultimately a degree of self-regulation which in its true sense, is the ability to modify behaviour according to an internalized 'set of rules' which govern whether, for example, you will notify the shopkeeper that you have been given too much change, or whether you keep it! It is important to recognize that this ability to self-regulate also follows a developmental timescale which is closely linked to how the brain is maturing. It is also interesting how self-regulation links with both stress and attachment, as securely attached children are found to be more resilient to stressful situations but children who are rated as having low self-regulation also displayed higher levels of stress in challenging situations (Bruce, 2003). A picture emerges of the insecurely attached child when faced with criticism or a want unfulfilled being more stressed and less able to cope, and so is more 'reactive'. Link this with the fact that experience physically shapes the brain and influences the types of connections made, and Maslow's hierarchy, and we can see that the child's fundamental emotional state impacts on not only how the child behaves but also provides insight into why. This may be especially helpful to bear in mind when working with older children as, between the ages of 5 and 8, children are naturally more sensitive to criticism and this will be compounded by the state of their 'internal working model'.

The following gives an overview of the developmental progression of self-regulation:

1. neurophysiological modulation 0–2–3 months
2. sensorimotor modulation 3–9 months
3. control 12–18 months
4. self-control 24 months +
5. self-regulation 36 months +.

What this means is:

1. modulation of arousal, activation of organized patterns of behaviour – for example, mother's voice will help calm and soothe baby, rhythmic kicking in tandem with rhythm of voice
2. change ongoing behaviour in response to events and stimuli – reaching for a toy, responding to a stranger
3. compliance and self-initiated monitoring – beginnings of responding to simple requests, for example 'no', 'stop', 'come here' – child may also begin to inhibit an action themselves such as stopping half way to reaching for something
4. behave according to social expectations in absence of external monitors – for example, child may not touch a desired or attractive treat, even if no one is watching
5 flexibility of control processes that meet changing situational demands – child can begin to adapt their behaviour according to different situations and contexts.

What is notable is that by the age of 5 years for example, the child has only had a limited amount of 'practice' at controlling their own behaviour and, as we have seen, many other factors can influence this ideal progression. Practitioners, teachers and so on need to be very aware of the 'newness' of these skills and that even in well-balanced and secure children, some upset in their lives such as a house move, a new baby or rows in the family can disrupt their ability to cope.

To conclude, I briefly return to separations. When children are separated from their carers, even for the most positive of reasons such as going to nursery, the reality of the separation will cause a grief response in the child. The level, duration and intensity of this response will depend on the child's experiences and what the child has already learned 'works' for them. Some children may be relatively briefly distressed but are mainly confident and ready to explore, others may be distressed for weeks and yet others may not outwardly show any distress at all. Each child needs support from adults dependent on their particular need but the reality of the feeling must not be discounted. Separation is a mini-bereavement and with it comes the same stages of any bereavement, that is, denial ('my mummy doesn't want me to stay here'), anger, sadness and, finally, acceptance. It is our responsibility to acknowledge the child's potential grief and to acknowledge how this hurts *us* as we deal with it. I will talk about this more in the chapter on the adult role, but a distressed child is painful to see and we adults also have our strategies to deal with our discomfort – and these too depend on our experience, insight and awareness.

Finally, human happiness/contentment seems to depend not only on close social relationships and a sense of place, but also arises out of a sense of achievement, of obtaining a goal. Our brains seem to be 'hard-wired' for motivation, goal-seeking and successful outcomes (Swanson, 2000). A child who is demotivated, whose actions and attempts are not appreciated, encouraged and supported, will be losing one part of the jigsaw which makes up emotional well-being.

To summarize, Figure 5.4 provides an overview of how all the different aspects link together no matter what age of the child. Then, Figure 5.5 is an example of a potential 'time line' for emotional development and leading into how thoughts become conjoined with feelings.

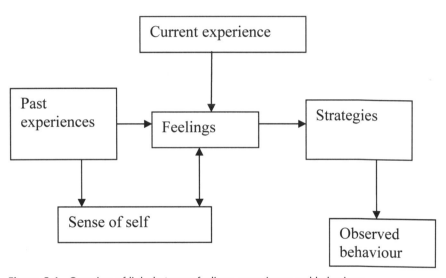

Figure 5.4 Overview of links between feelings, experience and behaviour

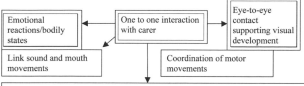

Growing sense of self physically and psychologically, formation of attachments, object permanence, imitation shifts from primarily carer of child to child imitating carer, discrimination of language and greater discrimination of human faces, shared interaction – supports the growing awareness of a 'self'.

During second year – recognition of self in mirror, recognition of basic feelings in others, recognition of different likes and dislikes, development of pretence and language, imitation of adults and peers very powerful, strong episode of nurturing type play (17– 19 months approximately), emerging feelings of embarrassment and guilt as adults increasingly provide social and emotional boundaries to the child's behaviour through their disapproval of unwanted behaviours and support of those they encourage. The need for strong boundaries and for adults to 'manage' the child's behaviour is very important as the child gradually learns to tolerate their own strong feelings.

Third year: Emergence of fantasy/role play – allows child to take on the role of someone else, practising what someone might do and how they would react in different situations. Encourages 'what if' thinking and supports the growing (but still vulnerable) understanding of another's likes and dislikes. 'Self-talk' as child carries out activities also gradually supports the framing of 'internal' thoughts. Through play, children learn about accommodating someone else's feelings and behaviour, but require continuous adult guidance.

Fourth year onwards: emergence of 'theory of mind' with growing understanding of 'false beliefs.' The complexity of fantasy play which continues into the fourth and fifth years (then games with rules become popular too) – allows the further understanding of another's 'mental states'. Children of this age and into the fifth year begin to understand that someone can be thinking *about* something. This links with a growing ability to manage own behaviour through understanding another's feelings and ultimately thoughts recognising that others can have another point of view (by around 6 years) but still seeing the world in very 'black and white' terms. The child will gradually begin to enforce rules themselves and in the early school years can become quite serious. Stress of any kind can make the child 'regress' into earlier behaviour – everything is all still very new!

Figure 5.5 Time line

6 Learning and development

Some of the skills which we value most highly in our education system are thoroughly alien to the spontaneous modes of functioning of the human mind.

(Donaldson, 1978)

In order to understand we need to know. In order to know, we need to experience and, in order to experience, we need to have opportunity. In this chapter, using the language of the current Birth to Three Matters Framework, I reflect on some aspects of how we become 'competent learners'. This includes thinking about the tools available to help us – such as curiosity, the ability to attend, the continuing role of imitation and the influence of the child's physical environment on their learning. This chapter also reflects briefly on language development and thinking, number and acquiring knowledge of the world around us. There are strong links in this chapter with Chapters 5 and 7.

Some background on approaches to understanding cognitive development

Prime, and in many ways continuing, influences on understanding cognitive development has been the work of Piaget (2002), who together with Vygotsky (1962) still comprise the essential reading for those undertaking training courses especially in education. Piaget emphasized three processes crucial for an infant/child moving from one developmental stage to another – assimilation, accommodation and equilibration. Assimilation refers to the way in which new information is fitted in with existing ways of seeing the world, while accommodation refers to how these perceptions are adapted to make room for the new information, and equilibration encompasses both of the other processes. This is the cornerstone of Piaget's conception of how the child's internal world increasingly becomes allied with reality. The essential difference between Piaget and Vygotsky's views of development was that Piaget concentrated on the within-child processes, while Vygotsky emphasized the role of the social and cultural context. Vygotsky's approach is encapsulated in a quote as follows:

Any function in the child's cultural development appears twice, or on two planes. First it appears on the social plane and then on the psychological plane. First it appears between people as an inter-psychological category and then within the child as an intrapsychological category ... Social relations or relations among people genetically underlie all higher functions and their relationships.

(Locke, 1995: 103)

Much of the more recent research on infant, toddler and pre-school capabilities can sometimes demonstrate greater levels of understanding earlier than might be anticipated by 'classical' theory. Meltzoff (1999), in particular, states that new findings have led to the gradual weakening and finally the collapse of classical Piagetian theory – a rather strong view I admit and one which would be contested by 'neo-Piagetian' theorists such as Demetriou et al (1994). Meltzoff proposes that there are three alternative models to explain cognitive development in what he terms a 'post-Piagetian era':

- modularity-nativism, as exemplified by Chomsky (1980) and Fodor (1983) which emphasizes 'innate ability' with 'behavioural and communicative change attributed to maturation or automatic triggering by environmental effects'
- connectionism (Elman et al, 1996) which, according to Meltzoff, is 'good at explaining behavioural change' but weaker on explaining the recently discovered innate competencies, which we will be looking at later in this section and some of which have already been touched on
- Theory-theory (Gopnik and Meltzoff, 1997; Gopnik et al., 1999) which Meltzoff describes as a 'thoroughly developmental view founded on a rich initial state' while at the same time 'embracing qualitative developmental change'

All these approaches have the same basic aim, which is to tease apart how our minds develop and, as we have seen from Chapters 2 and 3, any ideas we have or preference for theoretical ideas about learning must be viewed in the context of how the brain and the senses mature. A further point, to be emphasized again in Chapter 8, is that thinking about these approaches is important for practitioners. In one way or another, whether expressed explicitly or implicitly, how we think children's minds develop will influence not only our attitudes towards them but also the particular focus of the style of resources and opportunities we provide.

What does being a 'competent learner' involve?

The Birth to Three Matters Framework sets out the following components as being part of a 'competent learner':

- representing
- making connections
- being creative
- being imaginative

In the framework, they are not given in any particular order as each component has its own developmental trajectory but I have ordered the components with 'being imaginative' as the 'latest' in the spectrum because in order to be imaginative, the child needs to be able to represent, to make connections and be creative. Incidentally, this emphasizes one of the main tenets of this book, that is, that aspects of development build on and complement each other. As we saw from the previous chapters, any aspect of development involves a functioning brain, information from sensory systems *and* emotional responses. Both Piaget and Vygotsky emphasize the role of 'affect'[1] in cognitive development and yet, as Locke (1995) points out, this role has been systematically excluded from developmental psycholinguistic theory and often from literature focusing on broader cognitive concepts as well.[2]. Hobson (2002) states that many psychologists find it inconceivable that the development of thinking might be so dependent on feelings, but Hobson is supported by others such as Damasio (1999, 2000, 2003), LeDoux (1998, 2002), Schore (1994), Panksepp (1998), Fonagy et al (1994) and Sroufe (1995) in the view that emotions are the engine that drives both thoughts and behaviour. Paradoxically, play or playful experiences and hence, hopefully, pleasure and enjoyment are used by cognitive researchers in their findings. For example, in investigating an infant's understanding of object motion, attractive toys are used as there is a tacit recognition that such objects are interesting and fun, and provide the type of appropriate context in which the study can take place, that is familiar and safe. At the same time, this aspect is frequently left out of the discussion of the results. Only if an infant has become distressed, and therefore the findings are not included, does the mood of the baby or child come into overt awareness. It is interesting to speculate how far 'performance' is influenced by the amount of fun (or otherwise) the child has had during the study. One exception is research on mastery and motivation, which does include the influence of affect when assessing exploration and persistence in infants and toddlers (for example MacTurk and Morgan, 1995). Yet as we already know, Maslow (1943) emphasizes that emotional needs come before learning and indicates that they are also a requirement for learning and imbue every aspect of it – something that many early years practitioners have known for some time!

So, when we talk about learning or cognition, what is generally meant? For much of society, 'learning' is intimately linked with 'education' but as we know, learning is an extremely broad concept, beginning in the womb as the growing foetus experiences its surroundings such as the walls of the womb when it stretches and kicks and the initial pathways of the senses are laid down. Essentially, what is usually thought of as 'cognitive development' develops in tandem with learning about ourselves and other people, and has to do with understanding wants, wishes, desires and how people may be thinking and feeling, which we have encountered in the previous chapter. It is this latter aspect which encompasses a 'theory of mind'.

A narrower version of cognitive development involves:

- those skills and abilities which are to do with planning, problem-solving, and self-monitoring[3] and are termed 'executive functions'
- other 'high level' functions including comprehension and use of speech, visual perception and construction, calculation ability, attention (information processing)

As we have seen from previous chapters, all these more formal aspects of cognition are laid on the foundations of understanding self and other, aided by the capacity for imitation and also play which will be the focus of the next chapter.

Not only does every child need the opportunity to learn but they must also have the *capacity* to learn, something which is not a 'given' but depends on a whole raft of factors which include our innate abilities both human specific and our individual inherited genetic make-up. These are then combined with the quality, duration, intensity and persistence of the experiences that we encounter. Social and cultural influences in a particular society will serve to distinguish which aspects of cognition will be enhanced, prized, neglected, devalued or discouraged, as will the attitudes and values of communities within that society, such as neighbourhoods and family groups. For example, reading, writing and numeracy are powerful requirements in our society, but in aboriginal society the ability to remember a verbal history of immense length and complexity, to find water and to have a profound sense of 'space' and direction would be paramount. Attitudes to learning itself within a particular family or neighbourhood may also influence the level to which skills and abilities are encouraged. For example, a child may have the skills and interest to be a great musician but if their skill is seen as unimportant and devalued within their family, opportunities to fulfil that potential may be limited or non-existent. It is interesting that people who are deeply involved in a particular topic or are studious are currently labelled 'geeks' and/or 'nerds' in our society or 'anoraks' if they have a particular passion. These are all rather derogatory terms and imply a somewhat mixed attitude to learning and achievement.

In spite of cultural and social mores and inhibitions, there are fundamental aspects of learning, such as knowing that one is an individual with feelings and thoughts, having a means of communication, a knowledge of the properties of people and things, and that there are emotional, social, cultural practices and behavioural rules. These are essentials in any society at any level.

Dispositions for learning: getting to know the world, being curious and paying attention

Nielsen (2003) describes in great detail how a child learns about the existence of objects and, as she says, in order to learn this, the child must be able to move and objects must be within the child's reach. From early exploratory movements, the child receives sensory feedback and this together with repetition allows for not only a pattern of movements for the particular action, but also a general pattern in the feedback which allows a sense of consistency to arise. The first steps in processing the existence of objects and the formation of object concepts, is to do with shape, weight, size, surface, auditory, tactile, movable and visual properties. Over time, the infant learns that different feedback can come from different directions, introducing a sense of things in different places in relation to the self – the first inklings of spatial awareness. Knowing where something is also becomes associated with what you need to do to get it – so linking movement with learning and knowledge. The child exploring the properties of different objects gradually learns the differences between them and then the child learns that objects can have a purpose (for example, a cup for drinking), that they may be combined to make another object and that objects have names. This very broadly sets out Nielsen's stages for learning about objects. Other researchers such as Renee Baillargeon have spent many years researching child and infant understanding of objects, which includes findings such as 2.5 month-old infants do expect an object that is hidden to reappear but that they expect it to reappear no matter what size object and what size 'occluder', that is the thing that hides the object. Again, in very young children, around 3 months, there seems to be an expectation that if any size object is balanced on a surface, then it should remain stable – even if balanced just on one corner. However, by 12 months, they seem to have grasped the idea that the object needs something reasonably in proportion to itself to be balanced (Baillargeon, 2002) and, incidentally, show a preference at this age for grasping smaller objects (Newman et al, 2001). Children demonstrate and practice this new found knowledge by beginning to build with bricks – which can also have a link with Newman's findings – and learning what balances and what does not. Such activities will also help children understand about shape and size – what fits. They may extend this into a balancing-type 'schema' (see later sections) which involves them discovering balance through their own actions, for example, children consistently try to clamber over furniture once mobile.

In essence Baillargeon believes that infants have innate 'rules' about the basic properties of objects and, later, more sophisticated knowledge builds on these rules. That all such learning begins in infancy is also supported by Quinn (2002) who studied whether infants can identify different categories of animal, for example, whether an animal is a cat or a dog. We do need to categorize objects and much time is spent in pre-school with activities that help children categorize into many different concepts such as colour, shape, weight, texture. For example, it is estimated that there are 7 million colours that can be discriminated, yet most languages reduce the wavelength continuum into a dozen or fewer basic categories. This skill is a tremendous saving of 'thinking resources'. If we know what a dog or cat is, or what fruit is like, then we can begin to identify, discriminate and compare without constantly working out what something is and how we should respond. Quinn's studies seemed to indicate that infants as young as 2–3 months could form 'separate categorical representations for cats and dogs' (Quinn, 2002: 85). It seems that we do learn about the world from the global aspects of the properties of objects first and that object concepts of older children and adults begin with the perceptual (that is, through the senses) tracking of object categories by infants. It is obvious just how important the opportunities for exploration are for all children, including those with sensory impairment and/or learning needs. These studies also consistently emphasize that learning begins in the earliest months of life and, correspondingly, if opportunities for such learning are not available, how the stage is set for difficulties that may not manifest themselves until much later in the child's life.

Starting the process: curiosity

I would add to Nielsen's earlier ideas above that objects (and people) must also be interesting in one way or another. We learn to pay attention in the first place by being attracted to something that interests us – by being curious about it – and it is certainly likely that we are born with a capacity to be curious. While emotional needs and interactions have been discussed in the preceding chapter, there are strong links to be made with curiosity – proposed here as being one of the driving forces for learning – as it is encouraged and supported by the responses in the wider environment. Curiosity is crucial because being curious about something usually means we want to find out more – we will pay attention to it – it motivates us into focusing on something in particular and thereby moving our attention away from the self or other aspects in the environment towards something else. In other words, being curious invokes paying attention to something/someone. It may be that this form of attraction, this 'pull' to explore, is one of the first ways in which sensory information is brought into some kind of coherence and encourages exploration of the environment – whether it is scanning a face or reaching for a toy.

Some studies which link emotions and curiosity/motivation are those by Alessandri, Sullivan and Lewis, quoted by Barrett and Morgan (1995). These studies were of babies aged between 2 and 8 months who were either unable or able to control a slide music display by moving one arm. If the findings are considered in a maturational context it is not surprising that, for those babies who were able to move the display, the organization of their behaviour to repeat the action improved with age. However, the interest is in the responses of the babies whose arms were not connected to the stimulus or were in the stage of the experiment where the arm pulls no longer worked (extinction). Most of the babies showed an angry facial pattern, fussing, crying and increased movement of the conditioned arm, but there was a percentage of babies who instead of showing angry facial patterns showed sad facial patterns and decreased their arm pulls – almost as the researchers put it, as if they were 'giving up'. The angry babies were still trying to either gain or regain control over the stimulus while the others perhaps were illustrating an early propensity for a different strategy in face of challenge, such as 'learned helplessness'. A useful comparison is that in the first year of life, emotionally laden cognitive as well as affective strategies are being formed in response to environmental circumstance, for example, the child is forming attachments and in parallel will also be experiencing a range of opportunities for play and exploration which will echo the type of emotional relationship with the primary carer.

Panksepp (1998: 145) refers to a 'Seeking System' and in this system he includes 'interest, curiosity, sensation seeking' and later 'in the presence of a sufficiently complex cortex, the search for higher meaning'. The particular area of the brain involved in the 'seeking system' is particularly served by the neurotransmitter, dopamine, and it is dopamine which seems to be especially associated with feelings of engagement and liveliness. If I understand his work correctly, this system is associated in the animal kingdom with sensations prior to 'consummatory' acts such as search, foraging and investigation. If similar circuits are at work in the human brain, as they seem to be, it is interesting that one of the human infant's first acts is the rooting reflex and feeding. Once this innate system has got to work with the ensuing 'consummation' of milk, there also comes with it, as we know, the overflow of sensory experience. In turn, this ordinary care-giving act allows the whole plethora of between-person or 'intersubjective' communication to occur between infant and carer, allowing for the infant's curiosity and interest to be aroused through its senses via the human face, voice and touch.[4] This also provides the initial emotional and physiological feedback to further encourage the infant's interest in and curiosity about its surroundings. In studies of adults when this particular brain pathway has been stimulated, the reports back indicate 'a feeling that something very interesting and exciting is going on' (Parksepp, 1998: 149) – and if this is the case for babies, then it seems logical that this combination of neural, physiological and psychological circuitry is set in motion by the early reflexive activities of the infant. What may also help is that these sensations are apparently 'lingering', indicating more successful neural transmission. Furthermore, as Panksepp says, such a system also helps with the development of understanding of the world and this system may be a crucial part of how we learn.

To illustrate this, in Ramachandran and Blakeslee's (1999) end notes, they describe a patient, 'John' who had suffered damage to the visual system and became completely blind by the age of 40. After two or three years, however, he began to 'notice that whenever he touched objects or simply read Braille, his mind would conjure up vivid visual images, including flashes of light, pulsating hallucinations or sometimes the actual shape of the object he was touching' (Ramachandran and Blakeslee, 1999: 298). Ramachandran and Blakeslee go on to suggest that the 'tactile signals evoked in John's somatosensory area ... are being sent all the way back to his deprived visual areas, which are hungry for input'. This last phrase intrigued me as it suggests the radical idea (as the authors admit but do not elucidate) that we, or, more specifically, our brains, require experience in a way that is truly fundamental to our being. We happily acknowledge that brain maturation requires experience and that experience influences the outcomes for thinking, feeling and imagining, but how deep is this necessity for experience and how far does it contribute to the infant's need to know about the world? In essence, is 'curiosity' an innate attribute driven by a brain which, if it does not receive information, attempts to 'fill in' the gaps? Indeed, this does happen in the physical domain. If there is dysfunction or disability in a limb, imaging of the brain's 'body maps' shows that neural growth from a functioning limb will 'take over' the space for the non-functioning limb. Locke (1995) describes research with kittens indicating an age-dependent seeking for a particular visual stimulation. Such research he feels poses the questions: 'do infants work for stimulation in order to "feed" developing areas of the brain? 'do babies "know" what sensory nourishment their brain requires to develop fully the capacity for behaviour that evolutionary changes have provided for?' (Locke, 1995: 279).

Schore (1994) talks of a 'practising period' for the child's emotional and social development between the ages of 10 and 12 months (think back to the changes outlined in Chapter 4) and extending to 18 months, which leads to the 'self regulation of affect'.[5] Putting Locke's and Schore's ideas together, leads to the potential extension and broadening of the concept of a 'practising period' for a particular aspect of social and emotional development and to suggest that there are 'practising periods' between each developmental shift and for each aspect of development. The infant and young child's motivation for repetition of specific activities and the, often unconscious, potentially lifelong searching for emotional security – if not attained in the early years – lends some support for the idea that humans *are* equipped with predispositions to seek out and engage in those experiences which will support their overall development or meet a basic need. The reflexes of the newborn child, which invite both interaction and proximity, also support the idea that a seeking for stimulation/experience is essential for optimal developmental maturation. However, the quality of the outcome for the child ultimately depends on the qualitative nature of these 'interdevelopmental shift' phases, together with the opportunity to practice and rehearse skills that such periods offer as well as the efficacy of integration between the different parts of development at any one time. In addition, some deviation or dysfunction of any one aspect of development during these transitional phases will influence the way in which other aspects of development emerge.

Putting all this together, it does not seem to stretch too far a point to consider that, similar to a biological impetus for attachment in the domain of emotional development, there is a parallel behavioural mechanism to ensure environmental input to assist the developing cognitive system. Curiosity and exploration allied with imitation would be sound candidates for the components of this system with a co-occuring need for positive emotional feedback – pleasure and interest make what is learned much more memorable.

If there is such a parallel cognitive mechanism, it is possible to speculate that in infants and very young children, the drive for experience – to 'fill in' the environmental 'gaps' may not continue indefinitely in a deprived environment where experience may be sparse, brief and lacking in warmth, and with minimal feedback to any overtures made by the child. The implication is that a child's initial curiosity and interest which could be described as an innate 'thirst for learning' can be hijacked by a lack of appropriate opportunities, lack of encouragement or by chaotic sensory input, for whatever reason. Development in such circumstances will be shaped by the boundaries of the individual's specific emotional, social, cognitive and physical environment, with the child's neural pathways becoming increasingly more disturbed, dysfunctional or desperate for experience dependent on which pathways are at their most vulnerable during the time of deprivation and/or chaos.

The opposite of curiosity is an external manifestation of apathy which can lead to a dampening down of the wish to explore, to discover, to reach out. However, the brain's potential push for input of any kind might mean that the child forms their own strategy to find out about the world or meet their particular interest. Being a child, they will have neither the means nor the maturity to either fulfil or express this need in positive ways. An unfulfilled child on many levels is often an angry child. This again reminds me of the pattern of responses to bereavement and, indeed, a lack of opportunity to be curious and explore is a 'loss', and it could be argued that when deprived of care, concern, support and encouragement long term, or faced with seemingly incoherent and chaotic information, infants and young children may progress from angry 'searching' to becoming developmentally 'passive' or disinterested or obsessive in one particular area. Ultimately, for some, this may mean withdrawal into some internal world where the child uses itself as the reference point. An alternative scenario is that the child becomes attracted to everything and nothing, leading us to the topic of paying attention.

From being curious to paying attention

In the first instance, in a 'typical' child, it is the face of the carer which is the lodestar for many aspects of development, as we saw in Chapter 4. Being attracted to or curious about something, and then paying attention to it, provides a way in which we can begin to both gather and sort out information. To be able to pay attention is crucial because without this skill we would be constantly distracted and distractable, which is why it is so important that carers interact with a child as they provide an interesting 'first point' of focus. Factors that can influence a capacity to pay attention may be that the child has particular sensory, emotional and/or cognitive difficulties, such as a child with autism. An early paper by Shah and Frith (1993) notes how children and adults with autism appear to continue to process information globally with potentially a disturbance in the ability to filter and select salient information, and parallels can be found in children. Other children who are unable to 'pay attention' may also have sensory and/or motor and/or emotional and/or cognitive delay or dysfunction. Environmental factors play a part, too, as some children may not have had the particular opportunities to enable them to initially focus and separate out information coming at them. Another influence on how well the child can pay attention is the amount of 'clutter' in the environment. It is often easier to pay attention to something if:

- it either stands out from the other items
- is not surrounded by too many other items
- or is within the range of vision when looking ahead (rather than the periphery)

This sets up some interesting comparisons when thinking about infants paying attention to something that excites their curiosity, which is usually something novel or unexpected. For example, infant toys are usually brightly coloured and/or differently textured and may emit sounds as well. All these factors excite curiosity and encourage exploration and, incidentally, encourage exploration of a single object at a time. Carers support this by identifying the particular factors or pointing out a particularly attractive toy. Mobiles, cot rattles and 'treasure baskets' for older infants all serve to attract and sustain curiosity, and thereby attention and the growing ability to focus. These factors are also embedded in the infant's and very young child's growing visual acuity and ability to focus and attend within the context of what they are able to see. This also begs the question as to how an infant or child might allocate their curiosity/attention if surrounded by overwhelming or chaotic stimuli. Such factors if part of daily experience may be the precursors to difficulties in focusing attention as the child gets older. This is logical if we think about what we know regarding the ongoing myelination of axons and early information processing being generally more diffuse and 'fuzzy'. In addition, if adults are unavailable to help a child to 'choose' between a plethora of sensory information, they may ultimately develop different strategies to deal with the situation. All this equally applies to infants, toddlers and older children in a nursery or school who may be confused and disorientated by too many transitions, changes in environment and/or ill-defined resources and/or resource areas. The responses can include:

- 'switching off' and become almost totally passive
- becoming agitated and/or distractable, that is trying to respond to everything and nothing
- focusing totally on one or two objects in order to provide a sense of stability amongst the chaos of competing stimuli

Townsend and Courchesne (1994) found that patients with damage to the parietal lobe show particular difficulties in focusing attention, which is pertinent given the parietal lobe's role in spatial information processing. We need to know where something is in order to pay attention to it, which links with Nielson's (2003) stages of how children learn to understand objects. Great similarities were found in the Townsend and Courchesne study between these patients and people with autism, who had similar difficulties focusing attention and were therefore inclined to focus instead on one particular object with an accompanying further difficulty to shift this attention. We must also remember from the section on vision in Chapter 3 that children can typically go through periods when they normally 'fixate' on a colour (but also, incidentally, on a story book or character) and that this 'fixation' was linked to finding objects in the environment that were particularly interesting. It is possible that if such fixation becomes soothing in the face of overwhelming stimuli, this naturally tendency may lead the child to become 'stuck' in the visual/tactile/emotional feedback loop that such a fixation may generate. Attention becomes an obsession.

Being curious and thereby moving one's attention to what has 'caught your eye' (or ear) is also a first step on the spectrum of decision-making. Once we are able to move our attention to one thing, we can then decide to turn our attention back to what we were doing before. There are a number of issues here, as we need to have the visual acuity to be able to physically 'shift our gaze'. We would also need to be able to 'hold in mind' the first item of interest, indicating an active memory system. It also potentially supports a growing sense of self-agency embedded in such physical/sensory maturation as the child is increasingly able to explore items of interest to them, and as the child matures finding out about the world becomes increasingly important. Practitioners must bear in mind that for some children, what the practitioners may see as interesting may not be what the child notices. For example, on a 'bug hunt' there may well be the child who may prefer to look at the leaf on which a ladybug rests rather than the bug itself! Such individual perceptions may especially be the case in children with special needs such as autism (Klin et al, 2004).

To sum up, Figure 6.1 suggests possible pathways concerning the development or inhibition of curiosity and attention.

Getting to know the world: from imitation to intention – making connections – schemas

We saw in Chapter 4 that infants can direct their actions towards objects and the very momentous shifts which happen in the second half of the first year. The infant acts with intention – he or she has a goal in mind. The next step is understanding not only what I might want to do, that is, *my* goal-directed action, but also what *you* are intending to do and this has been described as being found in older children – for example, in the second year. A study by Meltzoff (1995) showed that children of around 18 months were able to re-enact a witnessed scene where the adult acted as though trying to pull a toy dumbbell apart but failed to do so. The children when asked to repeat the action carried out the apparent intended action, which suggests not only that the children were able to imitate the action but also that they understood what the adult wanted to achieve. The second interpretation was strengthened regarding adult intention because the children did not complete the action when a mechanical device made the same 'mistake'.[6] If we reflect on the finding that the child in the second half of the first year begins to imitate more proactively the actions of the adults around them and then 16 to 18-month-olds frequently actively imitate or copy their carers' actions as they go

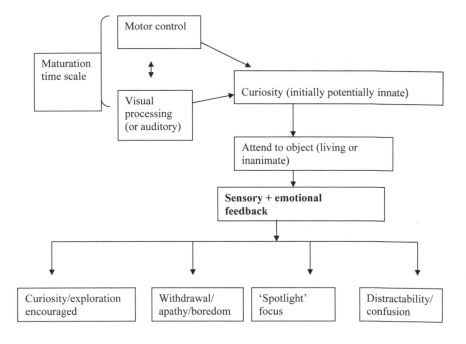

Figure 6.1 Potential pathways of curiosity development or inhibition

around the house, it suggests that the capacity by children to imitate adult actions is potentially embedded in an innate capacity to imitate. This develops into a medium through which another's actions can be both learned and understood – that is, understanding the goal of what someone else is trying to do. Furthermore, such imitation gradually becomes integrated into play situations where the child increasingly uses these well-known actions but in a way where the child has the control and can expand on the original actions in the context of a continually developing brain.[7] However, the ability to comprehend has taken months of witnessing, performing and imitating actions in order to pull together the vast diversity of day-to-day experience.

The implication from research is that intentions are first understood to relate to the physical world and, secondly, to the 'mental' world. It is this 'transfer' from the physical to the abstract which seems to be the fundamental way in which we learn over time. We extrapolate what we have experienced into what we then 'know'. What children are also building on is their capacity for making connections. This has been happening from birth as babies 'connect' their sensory/bodily feelings with the experiences with which they are increasingly associated. As they mouth, taste, feel, shake, bang and generally explore objects, listen to sounds and observe people, pets and objects in the environment, they begin to connect and make associations between the different qualities and characteristics of the world they are encountering. Diamond (2006) in a somewhat complex paper emphasizes that even very young children (9 months) can recognize a conceptual relationship between two objects if there is a physical connection between them. The example she gives is of older children (18–22 months) who were aided by a landmark in finding a hidden reward if the reward was placed *in* the landmark (in this case, an armchair) – and even younger children could do this – but **not** if it was placed *near* the armchair. What the task required was that the children were able to link two pieces of knowledge: first, that there was a reward and, secondly, that in order to find the reward, they are told that an armchair is the landmark. How do we learn to connect two pieces of information? The implication is that very young children may need to have a 'halfway house' of a real physical connection before they can fully link an abstract connection between two pieces of knowledge. There may be parallels in the child's use of a 'comfort object' when away from home. The physical presence of the object links the security of home with being safe when away from it.

Gradually, over time, these connections become less tied to the physical but become slowly more abstract, for example through pretend play and imitation. Making connections also supports the growing ability to think about things, which is intimately connected with the capacity to make a symbolic representation of an idea. This does not mean only thinking about people and objects within the environment but understanding the idea of the environment itself, that is, spatial awareness and relationships or connection between symbolic representations such as models and maps with their real counterparts. Research appears to indicate that young infants tend to orientate to look at or find where something interesting is, in relation to themselves – but as they get older, that is, from the latter part of the first year, they begin to identify the location of people or objects from an external frame of reference – termed allocentric, but these very young children often need quite powerful cues such as colour to help them work things out (Liben, 2002). However, as children get older, they can rely more on finding their way about by using external clues as reference points, such as the home corner is always near to the door to the classroom. Understanding that something 'stands for' something else appears to arise in children around 2.5 to 3 years of age (DeLoache, 2002), which, incidentally, is also when pretend and fantasy play are in full swing. Playing with a doll's house shows understanding that the miniature furniture is representing real furniture and a child's skill in 'furnishing' the house will give some clues as to how they understand relationships between objects and contexts. However, the child's skill in making connections to a real situation might be shaky. A group of 4 to 6-year-olds, were shown where some toys were to be placed in a room by showing them a map of the room first. Then they were asked to put the real toys in the real room in the places indicated. The children had great difficulty doing this and tended to just heap the toys in the room (Uttal, 1996). As Bell (2006) says, children use different strategies to explore, interact with and solve problems in spaces of different size, and they adapt these strategies to different settings. This may explain why some children are more comfortable and confident when playing and learning in large and/or outdoor spaces, while some children prefer to feel more enclosed. It may not just be personality/temperament but also how they cope with the idea of space and scale and understanding of their 'place' within it.

Thinking about these issues may also help when children seem confused or reluctant to go to other places in a building, as their understanding of location is still tentative and they also have to deal with spaces of different sizes. We only need to remind ourselves how confused we may feel if finding our way around a hotel or building we have never been to before and how we work out where we need to go. When taking children out for a walk, it is useful for practitioners to take the time to allow children to stop and look back and to notice landmarks, particularly useful for older, rather than younger, children. However, there is another developmental issue here, as working out locations and scale relations involves a degree of understanding lines and angles and shapes, which is the beginning of understanding geometry.

Schemas: a brief overview

A schema is the general psychological term, coined by Piaget, to describe cognitive structures which children (or adults) have internalized from the environment. Athey (1990) quoted by Meade and Cubey (1996) defines a schema as 'a pattern of repeatable behaviour into which experiences are assimilated and that are gradually coordinated' and so the use of the term 'schemas' often relates to how a child behaves in order to consolidate their 'mental structure' about a particular concept. For example, Manning Morton and Thorpe (2001), also building on the work of Athey, describe examples of learning schemas such as 'transporting', 'enveloping', 'trajectory (diagonal/ vertical/horizontal)' and 'rotation'. A child who has a strong 'rotation' schema may 'be fascinated by the spinning washing machine,[8] love anything with wheels, roll down a hill, enjoy spinning round or being swung around' and may also draw, paint or create circles, as we see in the drawing examples in later parts of this chapter. Schemas also cover such concepts such as graphics and space such as lines, curves and space orders such as on top of, behind and so on. Again we can link this with the way children use different media, actions and play in order to understand all the different aspects of the world they are trying to learn. Schemas can also be linked to emotions in the sense that an 'internal working model' is a schema of the child's emotional responses to the world.

A summary of schema development is as follows:[9]

- Each concept is an abstraction of all the individual instances we've encountered.
- Even the most abstract conceptual schemas have their origins in sensory experience of, and motor activity towards, the outside world.
- Abstract schemas are the most 'detached' from their origins, that is, communism, a soul, relativity.

In essence, schemas are internalized thought processes which have arisen out of action on the world and closely allied with language.

Making connections: thinking about thinking

As children are practising these ideas, transferring physical activity and experience into internal thought, it becomes obvious that the way children think is different to that of adults. We have already seen some examples when considering the notion of 'theory of mind'.

Some key notions about children's thinking:

- Thinking processes/structures change with age – *think about the rate of maturation of the different brain areas themselves.*
- They have more limited capacity and speed, and attention skills – *think back to the process of myelination which takes time and occurs at different rates within the different brain areas.*
- They are more limited in how many pieces of information they can process simultaneously (in parallel). Young children can only cope with simple instructions and it is not until nearly school age that they can cope with understanding more complex instructions from adults.
- They reason from their own perspective, their own interpretation of language and the salient features of a situation for them.

Early 'thinking' may be in images but later becomes 'words in the mind', although some of the most creative and innovative thinkers found images before words to encapsulate their ideas. For example, Einstein's theory of relativity was based on imagining riding on a beam of light. Greenspan (2004), in his discussion on the development of speech, explores how speech allows children to separate perception from action. According to Greenspan, by doing this the child can develop a freestanding perception that can become associated with experiences and thus form the basis for later use of symbols. His use of the term 'freestanding' is useful because if the child can separate out the attributes of a person or object and apply them to something else or think about them in their absence, then the perception is indeed 'freestanding' and can be manipulated according to the child's or adult's capacity to do so, that is, through 'pretend'. This capacity to separate perception from action can be illustrated by a deaf child's ability to form signs, the hearing child's ability to use gesture associated with different contexts such as waving 'bye bye' or to indicate a want or need by turning the head when no more food is wanted or using the hands to push away a spoon. This action is the use of a 'familiar gesture to represent a meaning' and if we consider the word 'represent' it is possible to extend this into much more sophisticated ideas. For example, consider a newspaper, which has print, pictures, cartoons and, perhaps, a map to show the whereabouts of a sale. We use calendars to represent the days, weeks and months and clocks for time. Children have much to learn and understand about representation.

The notion that early thinking is symbolic is supported when considering the mark-making/pictures of young children who begin to draw arcs and lines before shapes and then from around 2 years 'start to make separate yet linked shapes' (Matthews, 1999), which in themselves are reflections of the earlier actions that babies do as they reach and grasp – after all to reach and grasp is making a profound connection between what is seen, desired and obtained.

Children of this age and older will begin to layer colours adding to the understanding of one object behind another. The care that children take by either using carefully segmented colours for different shapes and/or placing their marks carefully on the page suggests the importance of this procedure, and children often are quite ritualistic in the way that they will place their brushes or felt tips as they draw. The marks have intense meaning and the older child will often talk about their drawing during the process which often symbolizes a dynamic action of some kind, for example, water down a plughole, someone swimming, as well as pictures of family or pets. Mathews tells of a child just over 3 years whose 'travelling zig zags' are 'clouds moving along slowly'. If we reflect on this, we note that this is also the age when children are becoming very involved in fantasy and role play, so such play plus their opportunity to express ideas and thoughts on paper or in playdough, plus verbal expression, allows children to think, know, understand and begin to reason. These drawings also allow children to further understand the properties of the world around them as children may draw a representation of previous play, such as drawing interconnecting circles to revisit a spinning game or when they have been spinning objects or watching clothes go round and round in a washing machine – and see 'schemas' above. Children are also interested in 'going through' and will look through tubes, crawl through tunnels in the playground, pass sand and water through grids, colanders, mesh. Looking through and going through a structure also allows different perspective-taking, as does climbing on a frame and sliding down a slide or slope. Children are now combining, in a much more active sense, their physical experiences with their capacity to make meaning out of them and increase their knowledge and understanding. Children also use drawing combined with play to understand concepts such as higher and lower as they place the objects in their drawings higher or lower, to the side, at the edge, at the top and the bottom, which is also, incidentally, helping them understand location and spatial relationships. Their language becomes richer at the same time as they explore these ideas and begin to work out why there maybe differences in textures. The paint drying over time also supports their understanding of time passing, as does the greater emphasis on helping children notice the passage of time through routines, changes in activity such as 'now it is snack/tidy up/story/going home time'. Of course, their other play activities will also support this intense learning as they notice if objects sink or float, how to build more complex shapes, how something small might also be heavy and or that something large can be light in weight. Hanging dolls' clothes on a washing line can help to sequence items, and stories and songs help to establish a time line for events and support different perspective taking – a concept discussed further in Chapter 7. This active learning eventually leads into the child of 6 or 7 years who is then able to learn through more formal media as basic concepts have been established in these early years. The importance of 'active learning' through play, being creative through paints, sand and water, and clay/play-dough is demonstrated by the links between activation in the area of the brain associated with 'higher-functioning cognitive tasks' – the prefrontal cortex and corresponding activity in the cerebellum which has long been associated with movement (Diamond, 2000). She notes that there is a correspondence between the long and slow development of the pre-frontal cortex and the equally protracted development of the cerebellum. It seems logical that play/learning will support the growth of these important brain areas. It is also noteworthy that children with learning difficulties frequently have motor difficulties as well.

Different types of thinking: the emergence of executive functions

Zelazo et al. (2003) describe executive functions as generally referring to processes that are involved in the conscious control of thought and action with related skills and abilities which are to do with planning, problem-solving, and self-monitoring.[10] Ozonoff et al's (1991: 1083) definition is 'The ability to maintain an appropriate problem solving set of attainment of a future goal ... [which] includes behaviours such as planning, impulse control, inhibition of prepotent but irrelevant responses, set maintenance, organized search and flexibility of thought and action'. It is fairly easy to see from this definition the links between emotional development and learning, and we have already seen from Chapter 5 how emotions and the emergence of the ability to think – allied with language – are so bound up together. Children learning to wait, to take turns and to share in the latter part of the pre-school years are all working their way towards these 'executive functions', and are supporting the development of moral thinking – that is, what is acceptable and unacceptable, what is hurtful and what pleases others. Between 5 and 7 years children have built on their early experiences, both emotional and cognitive, and links can be made between a greater acceptance of play with rules to the more abstract concept of 'fair play', although a sense of fairness to oneself is still stronger!

Children are increasingly able to work out what 'tools' they may need to carry out a task, such as organizing their paper and paints ready to draw a picture, or use scissors for cutting out shapes for a classroom display – thereby displaying a greater understanding of planning which also indicates a stronger sense of future. This also links with an increasing sense of understanding time by around 5 years and a knowledge of days of the week. By learning to use tools, children also learn more by using them – it extends their context for learning.

Some 'high level' functions: the use of speech and calculation ability

As vision and attention have already been discussed in this and other chapters, this section briefly considers aspects of language development and number.

Language development

I have discussed early communication in Chapter 4, but this section deals with an overview of the development of verbal language.

The interesting thing about language is that speech and other forms of communication are initially signals and then become 'signifiers' of thought because words, both spoken and written, are symbols of what is going on inside us and another medium from simply sounds and body language to enable us to communicate with others. Children will use signs or gestures far earlier than speech and deaf children using sign language produce their first signs from 6 months but on average at about 8 months. As we know, this is when hearing babies are beginning to babble in the rhythms of their own language and deaf babies 'babble' with their hands too. It is suggested that babies get control over their fingers earlier than their language 'apparatus' and this may be the case because later stages of language development appear to 'follow a common timetable' – see below.

Milestones in language acquisition[11]

- 8–10 months: word comprehension
- 10–12 months: word production
- 16–20 months: vocabulary burst
- 18–20 months: word combinations – most children have established a basic vocabulary of about 20–50 single words
- 2–3 years: grammar – children are supported in using grammar by hearing the language spoken correctly by the adults around them. The left hemisphere is most active in grammatical processing
- 5+ years: discourse organization – and a vocabulary of about 2000 words or more for most children and the ability to acquire new vocabulary continues throughout the school years and across a lifetime.

Words are important – and children need to be supported in finding words to express their thoughts and feelings – a child (or adult) who cannot express themself is frequently frustrated and can become angry or withdrawn.

Understanding meaning – semantics – appears to be robust and generally insensitive to experience but grammar (syntax) and pronounciation (phonology) appears to be more vulnerable and affected by late exposure and so there is an overall 'sensitive' period for language development, that is, earlier rather than later. Blakemore and Frith (2005) suggest that learning grammar after the age of 13 years is much more difficult.

Trevarthen et al. (1999) describe a brain surge in the left hemisphere between 2 and 5 years when language normally has its most rapid phase of development, but it is also when the child has growing understanding about different likes and dislikes, feelings, control of bodily functions, introduction into pretend and fantasy play and when the child is experiencing more inhibition of its own actions as well as a parallel increase in actual and desired independence and self-awareness. Hobson (1997) notes research which points to a child's earliest use of personal pronouns such as 'I', 'you', 'me', 'mine' (very popular!) as beginning around 2 years. Interestingly, children of this age can understand 'your' as referring to themselves but do not appear to use this in relation to someone else. The earliest uses of 'my' and 'mine' have been found to be mainly produced when children were acting on something, that is, reaching, grabbing or claiming – something that many parents and practitioners are fully aware – but not to body parts which seem to come later, for example 'my tummy'. It may well be that the growing use of language also helps the child to integrate more facets of the developing sense of self and that children who want something and grab it, saying 'mine', may be working out what is 'mine' in relation to 'yours'. This is one of the reasons, potentially, why it is so difficult for a child to share in these early years. Sharing is seen as a desired behaviour (rightly) by carers and practitioners but expectations of the child's capacity to do so are sometimes out of line with the child's development and level of understanding.

Children with more than one language

There are many children in the UK who either speak more than one language or where English is not their 'home' language. Practitioners sometimes have to deal with this situation compounded by the fact that children within the particular group may well be at different stages in the learning of their *own* language as well as trying to learn English. As we know, children broadly follow a timescale for language development but still have individual rates of both acquisition and ability. Roberts-Holmes (2001) describes a family where 5-year-old Shah is of British Bengali heritage and he understands Hindi and Arabic, speaks Sylheti (a language from northern Bangladesh) and speaks, reads and writes English and Bengali. His family speak both English and Sylheti at home and he moves backwards and forwards between the two languages, with sometimes the context dictating which language is used. For Shah's family, speaking his 'home' language is not only something that is useful and comforting but also part of his identity. It is important for practitioners to realize that a language is often not only a means of communication but is tied up with a sense of who someone feels they are and a sense of belonging. Siraj-Blatchford and Clarke (2000) provide an overview of some of the stages of bilingual learning. As such learning is complex, they stress that this is guidance only and such stages can be very flexible.

- New to English: staff and English-speaking children model English but support the children's use of their home language.
- A period of silence: what may be surprising to many of us, is that silence can be part of normal behaviour as children start to learn a second language – they are listening and watching, linking words and contexts, just as babies do.
- Repetition and language play: 'developing bilinguals' often imitate and use phrases/chunks of language that they hear most frequently, such as 'happy birthday', 'hello, how are you', 'OK', 'good morning'. Many settings have small rituals of greeting or phrases used at particular times such as 'snack time', 'tidy up time', and these are more easily recognized as the context is also very clear. Repetitive rhymes

are also very helpful, with lots of interaction, so again, words, context, actions all help to link meaning.

- More complex English: children, whether native speakers or bilinguals, will make mistakes and for both it is much better to model the correct or common usage rather than point out a mistake. For example 'she wented out' could be responded to by saying, 'yes, she went out'.

The key issue for practitioners is that children will learn their new language in the context of acceptance and affirmation of their home language and with opportunities provided to speak both. Children seem to learn English better if they are confident in their own language, and it may be useful for practitioners to be able to get some understanding of how the child is developing in their own language in order to support them best in learning a new language. Young children are very flexible learners and the nub of the matter is that their learning will be optimal if they feel respected, reassured and allowed to learn at their own pace. This applies to all children who are learning not just language, but moving on to the more formal communication methods such as reading and writing. Children need to feel confident in the skills they have so that these can then be built on in a secure environment at a pace which is not out of kilter with overall developmental expectations and individual skills and needs.

Numeracy: the shape, pattern and rhythm of life [12]

It can be assumed that a knowledge of number is something only grasped in the later pre-school years – an assumption built on much of Piaget's work, especially his experiments of conservation, which seemed to show that 3-year-old children, for example, judged 'how many' by appearance. However, Blakemore and Frith (2005) describe an ingenious experiment where children were first asked which of two rows of marbles contained the most (one had more marbles but placed closer together, while the other row had fewer marbles but placed wider apart). This emulates Piaget's classic experiment. Children of 4 years frequently answered that the longer row contained more marbles confirming Piaget's findings. However, the researchers repeated the experiment but this time using chocolates and did not ask for a verbal response. They simply asked which row the children would prefer to eat and they found that children as young as two chose the row with the most chocolates no matter how they were spaced! So even very young children can have an idea about 'more' and 'fewer' but need a link to help them – in this case they could eat the experiment! This ties in with Diamond's (2006) studies where a physical link between objects helps children with the abstract connection between them. There are also interesting comparisons between the chocolate conservation study and studies of number knowledge in primates where the primates' matching and sorting tasks were often linked with food rewards (Boysen, 1998).

So when do children acquire a sense of number? Blakemore and Frith (2005) state that there are studies which indicate that even young babies have a concept of number, that is, that $1 + 1 = 2$, and Butterworth (1999) also sets out research indicating an innate sense of number. However, counting and understanding what a sequence of numbers relates to in quantity comes much later and children can use the words 'one, two, three' and so on around 2–3 years of age but often do not relate this as corresponding to one, two or three items. However, Butterworth points out that children can learn about one-to-one correspondence at around 2 years when a child will quite happily give one sweet to one person,[13] but equating a number word with the object or whatever takes longer and some children take longer than others to do this. It is not until around 4 years that a true understanding of counting equating with 'how many' appears. A further dimension is that both human children and primates can approximate quantities but exact calculation depends on language, which may explain why it takes a while for children to link their newly found vocabulary with the ability to correspond their counting words with quantity – both are relatively new concepts.

Children retain links between movement and learning in number when counting because children all over the world will count with their fingers (as do many adults) and will often use finger counting rather than words (Butterworth, 1999) even at 4+ years. Children appear to use finger counting independently and will have their own system as to which hand they use and which finger they start with. There are also links between number and spatial awareness – as we think about numbers in what is termed a 'number line'. Without this idea, it is difficult to add or subtract, and this is where the knowledge about geometry comes in. People with good spatial ability are often good at mathematics as well. The parietal lobe in the brain (see Chapter 2) is involved in both spatial awareness and number.

Summary

What may be discerned from all the previous discussion is that from very simple, yet profound, beginnings the capacity to learn and to think becomes increasingly more sophisticated. Earlier forms of learning do not get replaced but become extended in tandem with increasing brain maturation, physical maturity (allowing for greater exploration of a wider environment), expansion in forms and types of play (discussed in the next chapter) and the emergence of language. Children's experiences are framed initially by the opportunities that their primary carers provide. They will be exposed in varying degrees, to shopping, holidays, family trips, festivals, visitors, activities such as swimming, going to 'burger bars' and other restaurants, and so on, as well as access to a range of media such as television and computers in addition to opportunities for play both indoors and outdoors. In other words all those everyday factors which make up the lives of many UK children and which, without conscious effort, expose them constantly to countless experiences of the written word and recognisable symbols associated with 'environmental print' – such as the 'M' for McDonald's or the names of the well-known supermarkets, signs at bus stops, toilets, exit, no smoking, and so on. Those children who go to playgroups and nursery will also be introduced to children from a potentially wider range of backgrounds, together with unrelated or unknown adults, with all their different approaches and styles of interaction as well as expectations of behaviour. Throughout all this 'growing up' and widening of horizons, the child still has to 'manage' their ongoing experiences dependent on their level of brain maturation and consequent levels of understanding based on the 'internal organization' of earlier experiences. The mind is growing built on previous bodily experiences borne out of 'adaptive actions upon salient aspects of the surrounding environment' (Klin et al., 2004). This approach, called the 'enactive mind', also implies that any 'derailment' or dysfunction in the way experiences are managed in the past – which will also include what the child has paid attention to – will have an impact on the 'shape' of the individual's developing mind and ability to learn. This mingling of developmental achievement emphasizes the 'holistic' nature of learning in these early years and implicitly suggests that 'formal' learning practices, which tend to focus on 'reading, writing and arithmetic' to use the old phrase, are not appropriate – worksheets for 2-year-olds are not helpful! There is also the emergence of a possible discrepancy between the child's ability to act in social situations, that is, their understanding of other people's thoughts and feelings and their actual learning ability. There is a suggestion that while emotions themselves can promote or inhibit a child's desire to learn, the skill of a 'theory of mind' can develop independently to a person's level of intelligence, curiosity and ability to pay attention. We have all met people who seem highly intelligent in a particular field of study or technical ability, but are far less able to converse, see another's point of view or understand how someone else might be feeling. This falls into Gardner's ideas of 'multiple intelligences'. What must not be confused is that a limited ability to empathize means that an individual does not 'feel' and can be just as crushed by inappropriate comments on them as a person whether aged 5 or 35, no matter how impervious they might seem to the feelings of someone else.

Ultimately, we have seen that the foundations of learning are embedded in the capacity to imitate, emotional context, opportunity for experience and the encouraging of the child's curiosity and desire to explore. Hurst and Joseph (1998: 29) provide a summary of how emotional well-being in particular influences the capacity to learn thus:

> Self doubt makes it harder for children to learn as the battle is lost in advance, while optimism that one has the capacity to do things is encouraging to a learner. Valuing and respecting others' ways of doing things makes it easier to learn from and with others. Having the self discipline to put aside some aims in order to achieve others ... enables learners to persist even when there are difficulties.

They add that optimism, self-confidence and the courage to use one's imagination, plus perseverance 'when grouped together form powerful predispositions to achievement'. Of course, as we know, all these arise from the respect, care and loving interactions in the early months and years.

Finally, to summarize the task of an adult – whether carer and/or practitioner – is to be aware of the following:

- the need for communication – infants and children need to be talked to
- to have an ethos of sensitivity towards individual children and their needs – recognizing children as individuals in their own right with all the range of likes, dislikes, anxieties and joys
- that a learning environment must include warmth, security and care
- that play is the key medium for learning – including Key Stage 1
- the need to build on what children already know and can do – including recognizing the skills and abilities babies may have

Therefore, effective learning for the child involves:

- feeling safe and secure
- mutual respect between child and adult – boys especially need to like their teacher
- having a positive self-image
- being able to make positive relationships
- having a friend
- developing a disposition to learn by being encouraged and supported
- having the opportunity to learn and different children may require different means of engaging their desire to learn

This can all be summed up by the four Ss:

- stimulating experiences which are developmentally appropriate
- supportive interventions

- seeing the individual child
- sensitive interactions

We all learn through the following means:

- experience
- observation
- imitation
- rehearsal
- practice

Throughout we can see that visual, motor and other sensory systems, together with opportunity, support and encouragement, combine to help children develop their capacity to know about the world and to actively participate in it. Nothing happens in isolation – it is the whole child at work – and in the next chapter we discuss one of the greatest supporters of learning – the capacity for play.

7 Playing and imagining

It is paradoxical that many educators and parents still differentiate between a time for learning and a time for play without seeing the vital connection between them.

(Leo F. Buscaglia, American guru (1924–98))

It is interesting that Hindus, when they speak of the creation of the universe, do not call it the work of God, they call it the play of God,

(Alan Watts, 1997)

To play is to explore, to discover, to experiment ... play gives children the opportunity to develop and use the many talents they were born with.

(Instruction sheet in Lego© toys (1985) in Panksepp, 1998)

Play, pretend and imagination are a natural and integral part of growing up, developing and learning. The importance that is given to play is represented by the wide range of texts and articles on the topic and the advice, guidance and training often given about the provision of opportunities for play. This chapter reinforces the need for play in all its forms.

Play provides the bridge between all the different aspects of development. It is the medium by which the links between different aspects of learning embedded in a maturing brain become established. A capacity for play or playfulness and its precursor and 'associate' – imitation – together with the child's curiosity, are central to the way development is 'organized' in the early years. Carers intuitively use play, in tandem with nurturing activities, to establish contact with their babies – through imitation, singing, tickling, blowing raspberries, making faces – all those lovely, silly things adults do which are all part of the daily experiences of many babies. From the beginning, playful interaction and games are used to stimulate and amuse children. Such interactions, together with the accompanying mutual smiling and laughter provide an emotional context heavily weighted towards the positive. As we saw in Chapters 4 and 5, much of an infant's experiences involve the reduction of distress and a corresponding search for the baby to be in a state of contentment and pleasure. Play provides another dimension in which such a state can be achieved in tandem with care and nurture. In addition, the provision of a variety of resources from conventional toys, treasure baskets, stack rings, puzzles, bricks, toy animals as well as boxes, pots and pans and everyday objects, with opportunities to feel, taste and smell, provide the arena for exploratory-type play. This establishes the framework for getting to know the properties of things, for example, roundness, hardness, softness, cold, hot, and so on. Such play provides not only an opportunity for mutual play between adults and children, but also for children being able to play on their own, inducing their own feelings of pleasure and mastery, which will, in turn, further their motivation for exploration and learning. In this way it is possible to see how play does bridge emotions, learning and development.

The child, through play, is learning more about their relationship with their carer. However, play also provides another piece of the jigsaw that supports the child's sense of self through the ongoing, parallel development in their understanding of both an emotional and physical self as the play is accompanied by pleasure or frustration as skills and abilities are tried, tested and, hopefully, mastered. It is as if the properties of 'me' are being established as well as what constitutes the world outside.

Bruce (2005) sets out 12 features of play:

- using first-hand experiences
- making up rules
- making props
- choosing to play
- rehearsing the future
- pretending
- playing alone
- playing together
- having a personal agenda
- being deeply involved
- trying out recent learning
- coordinating ideas, feelings and relationships for free-flow play

Obviously, not all of these features will be involved in each child's play but will depend on the level of maturation, age and context. However, these 'features' emphasize the active nature of play – play is not passive – and are an excellent framework for observing and evaluating play for practitioners across the age range and in many contexts. In Newberger's (1999) discussion on play characteristics, he suggests that play not only requires such active engagement and has a 'symbolic aspect' but also is:

- intrinsically motivated
- freely chosen
- pleasurable

Play engages the child's self and, for both parents and practitioners, the child's capacity to play with its invitation to enjoyment provides one of the best means of not only supporting the child's development but also getting a picture of the child's actual level of maturation. Perhaps more than anything else, the shifts and style of play in which a child is engaged reflects more accurately how the child is developing than any other type of assessment. This is because play has its own developmental journey which potentially begins with the child being able to imitate. As we already know, babies appear to have the capacity for imitation soon after birth. Imitation has its neurological basis in mirror neurons, discussed previously, and it remains a powerful part of human behaviour. This strongly suggests that the capacity to imitate is essential for human development and, as imitation in the early months is often in the context of play, playfulness itself is probably also an innate and essential component of development.

The different forms of play

One of the most notable things about play is that we humans are not unique in our desire and capacity to play. All animals play, although Iwaniuk et al (2001) suggest that play is more likely in larger-brained species such as primates, monkeys and so on, and chimps can incorporate stones and twigs in social play. I watched a young chimpanzee at the Primate Sanctuary in Dorset spending several minutes watching water trickle into a hole and scraping around it, appeared to be fascinated by the different patterns. However, (Dugatkin, 2002) indicates that not only primates, monkeys, dolphins, cats and dogs play with objects such as balls and hoops, but also turtles have been known to do so, as have ravens. Young ravens, in fact, appear to spend nearly all their time playing with almost anything they can find! This type of play is 'object play' and it seems to answer the question 'what can I do with this?' rather than simple exploration, which is more about 'what is it?' A baby exploring a treasure basket and then shaking and banging as well as tasting and feeling, could be incorporating both types of 'question', while the older child rolling a car along the floor, loading toy bricks into a truck or making a complex structure with different sized blocks is perhaps incorporating more of the 'what can I do with this?' type of play. It is certainly the type of play involved when children have resources which they can dissemble and reassemble. The quest to find out what something can *do* as well as simply finding out what it *is* implies an innate wish to explore, supported by the existence of this type of play across species. This may be one reason why young children quickly lose interest in toys/resources which appear to have only one apparent and/or repetitive function, rather than 'open-ended' resources such as cardboard boxes, bags and scarves, and why the opportunities for exploratory, investigative and curious play are essential for learning, and build on the essence of curiosity which we encountered in Chapter 6. However, it has to be noted that while play and exploration are closely associated, they are not the same. Children can play without exploring and can certainly explore without playing. In fact exploration – the 'what is it?' and maybe 'is it safe?' may need to come before 'what can I do with it?'

Another type of play common to humans and animals is 'locomotor play', that is all the leaps, jumps, twists, somersaults, chasing and rolling that can be achieved. Anyone who has watched lambs leaping off all fours will attest to the general 'springiness' of this type of play – it is also difficult not to detect an element of joy in all the shenanigans! Dugatkin raises a serious point when he suggests the various hypotheses as to the reason for this type of play. He implies that it supports the animals getting to know their terrain – all the lumps and bumps in the ground, as well as developing motor skills and balance. This would seem to make good sense for humans too. If we cannot negotiate uneven terrain, we become strictly limited in not only where we can walk or run but also how we walk or run. Research linking brain development and play in mice shows a clear correlation between play and the growth of synapses in the cerebellum – providing a link in how play supports quality of movement. Children climbing, balancing, swinging, spinning and doing handstands all help establish balance and awareness of where they are in space in order to orient themselves. Orr (2003) notes the importance of such locomotor play for children with disabilities. He observes, too, that the more disabled children were, the less likely they are to be 'thrown about'. A desire for movement was touchingly illustrated by a young woman with severe cerebral palsy whose dream was to be a ballet dancer. Her school invited a professional male ballet dancer to work with her and with an ingenious suspended harness, she was able to be lifted and moved. He danced with and alongside her as she moved gently in her harness. Her delight in the fulfilment of a dream was a joy.[1] It can be easy to forget that people with limited movement, of whatever degree, may long for an opportunity to experience the different sensations that simply spinning or feeling the bumps and twists on different terrains can give.

Children who are able will clamber up walls and trees, spin on a roundabout or spin themselves until they are dizzy or try to swing higher and higher – and virtually every mobile child I have ever encountered wants to walk along a wall (even me– as long as the wall was low – I was very timid). At 18 months most children are trying to climb and clamber, and it seems almost instinctive how children want to learn how it feels to be in different body positions and move in a variety of ways. The constant, dynamic feedback that the brain is receiving from the body reminds and reinforces that the body exists – and that it exists in the same way when hanging upside down from a climbing frame as it does when standing up. Nishida (2004) includes a category of 'social locomotor play' which seems to be similar to 'rough and tumble' as he describes a young chimpanzee climbing a tree, followed by one or more youngsters, hanging and falling or jumping down to the ground and that they repeat the entire sequence over and over again. The element of imitation is strong and reminds us of children who will play 'follow my leader' as well as just imitating another's actions in order to 'join in'. Nishida goes on to describe how these young chimpanzees will mix 'circling' (and somersaulting on the same spot each time!) with 'wrestling or play-fighting'.

A further dimension to active, physical play is given by Panksepp who stresses the importance of 'rough and tumble play' and describes it as the 'brain's sources of joy'. Panksepp's lifelong focus of his work is linking the workings of the brain and emotions and he states that: 'increasing numbers of investigators are beginning to realise that an understanding of play may reveal some major secrets of the brain and yield important insights into certain childhood psychiatric problems such as autism and attention deficit disorders' (1998: 280). Rough and tumble play is often called 'play-fighting' and in both humans and animals there is a qualitative difference between true 'fighting' and play-fighting. I turn to Panksepp again because of his extensive research on this topic and this appears to indicate that there is no clear evidence of a continuity between rough-housing play and 'adult forms of aggression' – an important point for many practitioners who often seem to equate the two. There appear to be distinct 'motivational substrates' for these two factors and rough-housing perhaps is more likely to be transformed into sports with lots of competition and athleticism such as rugby, football, basketball, hockey or boxing, which are rough-housing with rituals and rules! Incidentally, watching such sports involves a great deal of emotional arousal in spectators.

This confusion between 'rough-housing'/'horseplay'/play-fighting with aggression also led in some day-care settings to the 'zero tolerance' attitude towards 'war, weapon and superhero play' as described by Holland (2003). Holland's excellent book about her research, does appear to indicate that some practitioners' negative attitudes to boys' play especially, seemed to arise in the 1980s. These attitudes appeared to parallel a growth in awareness of gender differences in play which were almost totally – and mistakenly – attributed to social and cultural reasons rather than anything to do with brains, biology and differing developmental needs. Holland (2003) says that perceived sexist patterns in children's play clearly presented themselves as an area in which women could take some control. Such 'control' was unfortunately rarely based on any actual research of connections between what was perceived as 'aggressive play' and male violence. As Holland points out, perhaps it is more useful to think about what are the play 'themes' that underlie the styles of play rather than their overt expression. Fortunately, such extreme views are being modified as more research and understanding of broad gender differences in both styles of play and learning are coming to the fore. The truth is that boys can be just as upset as girls if any type of play degenerates into genuine bullying and aggression. There has also been a fairly recent but less strident trend considering competition between children as potentially negative, which again has rather worked against boys, who often learn better in a competitive environment as it matches their somewhat natural tendency in that direction. It is certainly true that competitiveness can be subsumed – often by pushy parents! – into wanting to win at any cost. However, competition can also support someone wanting to do or be their 'best'. It is possible to want to win and to be fair. The winner who is gracious to opponents and realistically accepts both strengths and weaknesses has learned just as fine a lesson as the child who has learned to accept failure without emotionally crumbling or wanting to retaliate.

Newberger (1999) also suggests that play helps children develop self-control, especially during 'rough-housing', as the excitement is intense during the play but then the child has to learn to 'settle down' and adapt their behaviour once the play is over – whether it is with other children or with adults. As children also 'pretend' to be angry, fearsome, distressed, happy or sad in play, this also supports understanding the facial expressions and gestures that will accompany such pretence as the child can more easily relate the frequently exaggerated expressions and gestures with the stated feeling as well as 'trying out' such emotions in the play. This can be compared with old silent films when every emotion was 'overplayed' to increase understanding of the story.

I have spent some time discussing this aspect of play, because Panksepp, whose research is exhaustive, stresses the importance of active, physical play. It is a way in which children can ascertain strength, agility, balance and coordination. It can be used in imaginative contexts, and can encourage self control and ultimately self-discipline. For example, in animals, rough and tumble helps establish boundaries as the stronger make allowances for the weaker and learn not to use their full strength. Such play can support a child in reading facial expressions and body language more easily as signals that one wants to withdraw or continue are learned. It can also help to encourage empathy as the winded child is helped to his/her feet, dusted down and comforted. Adults need to be sensitive to when intervention is necessary but allowing children some freedom in their ability to rush around, wrestle, push, shove and chase is also part of the practitioner's role as is, perhaps, allowing children to learn to deal with the mixed emotions engendered by competition rather than avoiding them.

Dugatkin's (2002) paper also discusses social play in animals, which he says is the most studied of all types of play including carnivores as well as chimpanzees and other mammals. A delightful example from other research is that of bottle nosed dolphins in Western Australia who permit visitors to stroke them and throw them fish – the dolphins then reciprocate and will 'toss their visitors a fresh herring or piece of seaweed' (Singer and Singer, 1992). Of particular interest, however, in Dugatkin's (2002) paper is the social play he cites of antelopes who prefer same-aged play partners and the evidence apparently suggests that this provides them with a reasonable comparison from which to gauge their own development. This finding seems very interesting when we consider young children playing together and it is not an aspect I have seen particularly emphasized in the many excellent texts on play. It seems logical that such play allows children to react and interact with people their own size and approximate level of maturity, strength and physical ability, and so provide them with a different perspective on their own capabilities. It is interesting that as children grow older, for example, by ages 7 and 8 years, same-sex friendships become predominant. This may provide a further important dimension to building up their view of themselves *within* their own gender as well as making absolutely sure that they have all the same bits and pieces!

Pretend and fantasy play

Where humans depart from other animals – as far as can be surmised – is in the ability to pretend and imagine, which also supports the later development of reading and writing because of the ability to understand symbolic representation. You may say 'hang on – what about the deceiving chimp described in an earlier chapter?' The capacity to deceive would suggest that the chimp had a basic 'theory of mind' through being able to understand how another chimp might react – and might this imply a degree of 'imagination'? It is also certainly true that my two dogs can also deceive each other by 'pretending' to chase one thing, so that another toy can be retrieved! However, a parsimonious explanation may be that there is an understanding of wants rather than minds or thoughts as this type of deception is found in children around 16 to 18 months. Nevertheless it is interesting that the development of the following precedes the emergence of more complex fantasy/imaginative/role play and runs parallel to the emergence of pretend:

- understanding likes and dislikes
- the beginnings of understanding another's feelings
- a surge in the levels of imitation by children of adult actions as well as a means of communication between each other
- the emergence of understanding goal directed actions
- the emergence of verbal communication
- a greater awareness of the self as a self, for example, recognition of the self in a mirror

So, what might come before the emergence of pretend itself in the early part of the second year of life? As we know, a great deal has happened in the first 14 months or so, including vast amounts of imitation both by carers of children and then, from approximately 8 months, of carers by children. In Chapter 4, I outlined the enormous shift in skills and abilities that takes place between 8 to 12 months, including the development of 'object permanence' and 'shared attention'. For a child to be able to pretend, there must be an understanding of the properties of 'objects' in the real world, their reliability and consistency across contexts. The child has first learned about the consistency and presence of carers in tandem with the exploratory-type play mentioned above. Then, with the understanding of objects still existing when out of sight, comes the development of remembering that an object can be moved – and found – in a different place (the 'A not B' task in Chapter 4 illustrates this development).

These particular shifts in knowledge and understanding appear to set the scene for the emergence of the ability to pretend. A child would probably not be able to substitute a small wooden brick to represent a cake or an animal or anything else if the child was not confident in the real properties of the brick. However, there is much 'pretending' that is an intermediary between imitation and more complex representation, that is, substituting one thing for another and that is when the child uses a real phone to 'pretend' to talk to a parent or friend or pretends to go to sleep during a play situation by lying down and closing her eyes. The classic form of pretend uses objects to extend play and which also allows for the representation of one thing for another – literally *re*-presenting. A much used example is a plastic banana being used as a telephone and the key point is that the child needs to hold in mind two items of knowledge: first, that the object is a plastic banana and, second, that it is, for the duration of the play, also a telephone. Alan Leslie's seminal paper in 1987 on 'Pretence and representation' dwelt on his puzzlement as to how very young children can make one object stand for another without getting confused, and it is his theory of 'decoupling' which helps to make sense of the fact that children are not confused and can switch easily from 'pretending' back to the 'real world'. Leslie suggests three aspects which can identify whether a child is actually pretending or simply imitating adult's actions with props and any one of which can indicate 'pretend':

- Has one object been made to stand for another?
- Has a pretend property been attributed to an object or situation? (His example is if a child says that their dolly's clean face is dirty.)
- Has a child said that an object is there when it is not? For example, there is milk in an empty jug which the child then 'pours'.

If the child 'pretends' to eat a plastic banana, this dual representation still takes place but at a simpler level, when the child knows that this is a toy that represents something that the child can eat. The plastic banana replicates the real banana but the child knows (hopefully) that they cannot actually eat it. It is this simple representation that can be termed 'concrete' play, whereby the child uses replicas of real objects to support pretence, for example a toy tea set, a doll, small world toys. Such items can, of course, become part of fantasy play too, as when a child uses them as props in an elaborate story where the animals, for example, have characters, different voices, adventures, and so on.

The crucial thing is that in order for the child to pretend, certain developmental skills and abilities need to be in place and the additional information that Leslie did not have when he put together his original paper, was the existence of mirror neurons which could suggest that there is a way in which the brain itself 'pretends' when the neurons within it fire 'as if' an action was occurring when it is only being observed. This provides a neurological basis for thinking about how pretend may come about in the sense that there is already an 'as if' mechanism at work, albeit beyond the control of the individual. These neurons provide a bedrock on which to understand how very early imitation can occur but also, if Leslie's premise is correct, that pretending has more to do with being a precursor to understanding other minds (see also Figure 5.5 at the end of Chapter 5) than understanding objects. Such neurological activity may provide a basic framework on which all the other skills and abilities around this age can converge to provide the impetus for pretence. It is possible, that just as they have grasped by the early months of the second year that people's actions have goals, so it is highly likely that they will have built on their early knowledge of objects as outlined in Chapter 6. For example, they will have learned that if something is not supported it will fall down, or if a cup is full and falls over the contents will spill out. Children through their extensive imitation and observation of daily activities can then move on to their own conscious form of 'as if'. For example, I am pretending to pour milk out of this empty jug as if there was milk in the jug. The fascinating part of pretend play is that children seem able to understand when another child is pretending and will join in the game, such as a teddy bears' tea party with even the most minimal of props, perhaps a row of soft toys. The cakes, drinks and any other items are simply in the minds of the children with perfect understanding between them – invisible and yet seen clearly in the 'mind's eye'.

Leslie and other researchers have wondered why, with this capability, it takes so long for children to understand the possible 'false beliefs' of others, that is, not until around the age of 4 years, but it is possible that it simply takes that long for the child to practice and begin to comprehend this concept. I imagine that in play situations some discrepancies in the focus of the play do arise and that children put each other right, and in my own observations of pretend play this has indeed been the case. For example, one child decides that teddy has a 'tummy ache' and is not going to eat his tea. The other child says crossly that teddy is going to eat his cake because it is his birthday. This simple exchange nevertheless indicates that one child's thoughts are heading in a different direction from the scenario in the mind of the other child. This example also provides an illustration of the children having to negotiate a solution to their problem, such negotiation often being part of the children 'stepping out' of the play situation and returning to their scenario once the problem is resolved. Such negotiations provide another example of the links between play and cognitive development and communication. Perhaps it is through many repetitions in this kind of play as well as in real-life situations, coupled with the growing language skills and widening experience plus 'rehearsal' through greater imaginative play that this wonderful ability to recognize that someone 'might not know something I know' becomes possible. Perhaps it is no accident that children with siblings are sometimes found to recognize 'false belief', that is, have acquired a theory of mind, a little earlier than others because of the greater opportunities to link different experiences together on a daily basis as they play, argue and negotiate together (Lillard, 2002).

In between the emerging capacity for pretend and the emergence of an understanding of 'false belief'/theory of mind, there emerges what has already been touched on, the capacity to imagine, that is, when the child no longer needs props to enter a world of their own – or if props are used, they can be anything the child wants even if they have no resemblance to the 'real thing', for example, a stick can be a horse. An intriguing parallel is that if we remember from the discussion on sleep in Chapter 4, dream sleep begins to reduce at around 3 years of age from the very high levels in early infancy. Pretend emerges as dream sleep diminishes and perhaps it is not too fanciful to consider that pretend is a waking version. We do in fact refer to 'daydreaming' when the child is absorbed, 'far away' and not 'paying attention'.

To return to imagination, another facet of this play which most likely feeds into this growing understanding is the child's enthusiasm for taking on the role of someone else, whether it be mummy or daddy (frequently the first forms of role play), others in their social world and then figures from television or film. In imaginative play, children imitate the common phrases, behaviours and attitudes of the adults in their family and it is from this that they can then move on to add their own 'twist' to the situations as their play becomes more self-determined and wider in context, embracing more characters and situations. It is often the feelings engendered through imagining the self as another that allows the more insightful thoughts about motivations and intentions to potentially emerge for both adults and children. Simone Weil (quoted in Smith, 2005) felt that we humans needed to reorientate ourselves, to decentre or 'unself'. She said that 'Each man imagines that he is the centre of the world' and this is certainly the view taken by the average 3-year-old whose thinking is strongly – and rightly – focused on 'working out' the self. However, such fantasy/role play allows the child to 'decentre', to move from this natural occupation with the self to trying out another perspective. It is an extension of the 'decoupling' of real and imaginary objects to an abstract version of this process. I strongly feel that imaginative play of this type is a necessary prerequisite to the capacity to understand the minds and thoughts as well as the feelings of others and so, delay, dysfunction or lack of opportunity in this area can potentially disrupt the quality of this ability. Lillard (2002) provides a comprehensive overview of the links between pretend play and cognitive development but also notes that research indicates that securely attached children are more likely to engage early in pretend play and that secure attachment is associated with better 'theory of mind performance'. It is interesting that these findings are linked to the idea that parents of children with secure attachments are more likely to use language associated with feelings and reason, and children are able to build on these communication skills during their play and all that goes with it.

Panksepp (1998) emphasizes that play is a primary emotional function of mammals' brains and this is logical when we again consider its presence and persistence across species. Positive emotions must be involved or no species would play, plus the fact that negative emotions such as fear, as well as hunger in animals can eliminate play temporarily. For example, after several days of isolation, young chimpanzees become despondent and exhibit relatively little play when reunited with each other. Comparisons can be found with the diminished capacity for play in human children when upset and/or fearful. These findings, and a wealth of other animal research quoted by Panksepp, stress that the capacity to play appears to rest on the basis of a warm and secure environment with abundant parental involvement. This certainly reflects my own experience of direct observation of the quality of play in a group of children from troubled backgrounds aged between 4 and 5. Instead of the rich fantasy/role play which children of this age frequently demonstrate, their play was 'fixed', i.e. either very 'concrete', that is, pushing a doll around in a pram and occasionally brushing its hair (and smacking it), or brief episodes of 'locomotor' type play. The most imaginative play seen over several weeks was in making some 'cakes' with play-dough but this, was very brief.

Harris (2000) discusses language and imagination extensively, and describes how the emergence of language in tandem with the emergence of pretend play builds on the child's cognitive ability to create a model of a situation, something which I believe they have practised through imitation of adult actions. Children can then produce language which includes what they have done and what they are about to do – allowing the mind to move between past, present and future. The situations that children will often re-enact are situations that they themselves have experienced and so experience a narrative that flows in time. They are helped, of course, by storytelling, especially fairy stories, which traditionally begin 'once upon a time' and end with 'they lived happily ever after' bringing in something that does not exist in the present time but once (past) and which will be (future). Children need to understand the flow within a story and within play so that they can understand their own 'autobiography'. It is interesting that the ability to recall more about past events occurs around this time, perhaps not only because of language development but also because of the 'practice' they are getting in play. Stories also support the child in taking the point of view of someone else as they listen to the tale which is written from the point of view of someone else – whether a child or a chicken! The frequent acting out of well-loved and familiar stories also helps in this growing ability to take a different perspective and leads to understanding another's thoughts.

Playing imaginatively is possibly the apex of the capacity to play, to shake off the here and now and enter a world of 'what if' incorporating past experience and future plans. Imagination helps us to conjure up pictures in our minds of what we hear or read, which is often why, when a film comes out of a well-loved book, we may be fearful of how someone else has 'pictured' our hero or heroine and their surroundings. As a child, listening to *Treasure Island* on the radio, I had a picture in my mind of exactly what Blind Pugh looked like as he tapped menacingly along the path to the Admiral Benbow Inn. Ultimately, imagination allows us to roam around the universe if we so wish. It sets us free as some of those held in solitary confinement can attest, such as the man who played a complicated game of cricket in his mind, giving characters to all the different players while he was alone and uncertain of rescue, and this activity kept him from despair and mental collapse. Imagination also supports us in empathizing with others as imaginative play not only involves the child's emotional world, but also enables the child to rehearse the emotional world of other people. Panksepp (1998) also says that play allows children to 'project their behavioural potentials joyously to the very perimeter of their knowledge and social realities' but that this 'pushing' may also lead children to begin to be genuinely angry or distressed. This is where appropriate adult intervention is so important. When children have reached this limit they turn to the adult, often tearful and/or angry, perhaps with complaints about the other children. They have encountered emotions in a play situation that are just beyond them and they need the adult to help them cope. This aspect of helping children deal with potentially more complex emotions is another important facet of play. It is also possible that the opportunities for children to sort out and manage their emotions through the 'testing out' of roles and relationships are much reduced if they are unable to participate fully in all types of play and, furthermore, may diminish in some way the capacity for the quality and depth of the ability to think about the self, others and the world in general in later life.

The notion that play and pretend are essential for sound human development is reinforced in the finding that it does exist across cultures, although culture will influence the type of play themes that may be most prominent. For example, Lillard (2002) quotes studies illustrating that American and Turkish children engage in more pretend play than Guatemalan and Indian children do, Korean American pre-schooler's play emphasized family roles whereas European Americans' play emphasized danger and fantasy. The important point is that in all the communities studied, pretending did occur and the levels did seem to relate to parental attitudes towards play – useful, important, a waste of time, and so on.

Reality and pretend

As we have seen, pretend play needs:

- an understanding of the real world
- an ability to switch from reality to pretend and back again
- an ability to sustain reality and pretend at the same time

As practitioners, we have to remember that the child's understanding of the world is growing in parallel with the development of pretend and fantasy play. This ability to 'decouple', as Leslie would have it, is very important, and is perhaps an indication of how important pretend play is, that it does occur at such an early stage when so much 'practising' of other skills and abilities (that is, language) and so on is going on. It perhaps reinforces the supposition of its essential nature as the medium in which all aspects of learning are able to be both rehearsed and reinforced.

However, Lillard (2002) points out that children can become confused between some fantasy situations and reality. This can happen when there is a cultural endorsement, for example, Santa Claus or if there are people who purport to be witches when witches are supposed to be in stories, or if a situation has little or no real-world reference for them, such as an unfamiliar animal portrayed doing domestic tasks. Another situation where children can become confused is in 'scary' situations and Lillard describes a study where children avoided a box which had contained an imagined monster. It may seem a truism but being scared is scary and this heightened emotion may confuse children. The original source of their fear is from their imagination, such as when children are fearful of something under the bed or the dark at the top of the stairs. We need to remember that as older children and adults it can sometimes take us a little while to 'come down to earth' if we have seen a particularly frightening film. We can experience being disorientated for some moments if we have been closely involved and identified with the hero or heroine, and often need to talk about the film itself when we emerge from the cinema to 'settle' our own emotions. It is not surprising then that children can be equally disorientated when presented with situations that are frightening, even if the child has instigated scary play with roles as monsters and witches. This is where adult involvement is crucial as the child needs the adult to help them sort out their feelings and put the monsters back where they belong.

Play in older children

Play enters another phase when older children starting school tend to become more involved in group play, which is usually play in teams with accompanying rules. Of all the animals studied, Nishida (2004) suggests that it is only humans, and possibly dolphins, who actively play in team/group play. Dolphins have been noted to act in groups against one another in competition for a female. This is not to suggest that animals such as chimpanzees do not come together in a group or 'team', but it is usually in situations of conflict, for example, that a group of males will attack a lone ex-alpha male. In other words, it is only humans who seem to play in groups for the play's sake. Children can and do initiate a game of football, for example, without any facilities, using a can for the football and anything as a marker for the 'goal' and will simply play the game together. It is interesting that the move to this type of team game coincides with the gradual and increasing shift from the focus on the needs and wants of the self to reaching out to others in increasingly more complex ways. Children's happiness as they reach the ages of 7 or 8 becomes more bound up with having friends, and team games or activities can often help to foster such friendships. If we link this with the tendency to prefer same-sex playmates at around this time too, we can begin to see how group play becomes a medium for expanding social understanding. Fears are also more reality based around this age as opposed to the fears of monsters, for example, in younger children. It is perhaps at this age that the influence of parents is beginning to be modified as the only important figures in the child's life, as the importance of friends and other adults assumes more significance. Borland et al. (1998) describe from their research with this age range and older that having no one to play with was seen as something to be 'avoided at all costs'. Children's understanding of emotions also becomes more sophisticated and it may be that in group play they encounter and experience a much more complex array of feelings. They are more able to understand that an angry face, for example, may not be matched with an angry 'internal' feeling but that someone could be feeling sad or lonely instead. Team games do seem generally to fit boys' tendency to have 'larger and looser' friendship groups than girls, although there are always individual differences.

Key points and implications for practice

To sum up, playful activity will incorporate some, if not all, of the following:

- emotion
- movement
- communication
- a seeking for understanding/curiosity
- interest
- involvement

Recurring play themes have been found to be:

- treating and healing
- averting threat
- re-enactment of domestic events

Young children explore issues of:

- being left behind, hiding and being discovered
- going away and coming back again

Older children explored the same issues through themes of:

- escaping, killing, dying and coming to life again – often the type of play that boys will engage in

We must not forget that laughter and fun are frequently part of pretend, fantasy and all other forms of play, and adults can spoil play – especially pretend – by 'taking over' the world that the child is creating. Play and pretend are ways in which children manage many of their experiences including situations where they may be distressed and anxious as well as supporting cognitive development through role taking, negotiation and language. In their pretend play, they make their characters speak, they decide who is good or bad, who wins and who loses. For brief moments they are in charge, powerful in a world that they have created. Adults who enter too far into this world bring it into their control, and so the child becomes powerless again and often will stop their play and not return to it. An example is of a child who had an imaginary 'friend' (often a normal part of development). A grandparent became too enthusiastically involved 'directly' with the imaginary friend – and the child ceased to have this friend. Remember, one of Tina Bruce's (2005) features of play is that children make up rules as they go along, thereby keeping control of their play. This idea of the children being able to control this part of their day is vital for them on many levels.

Older children do not, as is often supposed, give up on pretend play but will continue, although team games become more prominent and imagining possibly becomes subsumed in other activities or diverted into games and books dealing with fantasy. Consider the popularity of Harry Potter and the Terry Pratchett books and the enduring popularity of classics in children's literature such as the Beatrix Potter stories, *Wind in the Willows*, *Alice in Wonderland*, and so on. As adults we imagine through daydreaming as well as being able to imagine consequences of real actions.

Play is how we, as children, learn to plan, implying a knowledge of past experience, present happenings and future time. It helps to create a coherent and consistent image of what is happening to us on a day-to-day basis – the growth of our own autobiography – and it helps create a consistent and coherent expression of who we are both as individuals and in reference to others; think about same-age playmates for example.

Supporting play is vital for practitioners and carers in providing opportunities for play indoors and outdoors, open-ended resources and supporting children in telling their stories by writing them down, taping them, and so on. Allowing children to engage in *all* types of play is important too, not just pretend. Children need to play to learn about themselves, their bodies, their abilities and skills in moving as well as the expansion of their minds.

Some final points about play:

- Play is active and exploratory.
- 'Aggressive play' is not necessarily aggression.
- Play appears to support brain maturation (especially the cerebellum which deals with balance/coordination and procedural learning).
- Play helps children to learn about winning and losing.

Practitioners need to:

- understand the role of play
- be sensitive to potential gender differences
- ensure equal access to all types of play
- be aware of their reactions and responses to play they do not like
- provide resources which reflect the interests of the children including comics, car manuals, brochures and factual as well as story books
- have fun too!

8 The role of the adult: to understand the 'heart of the intended communication'

Effective practice in the early years requires committed, enthusiastic and reflective practitioners with a breadth and depth of knowledge, skills and understanding. Effective practitioners use their own learning to improve their work with young children and their families in ways which are sensitive, positive and non-judgemental.

(Primary National Strategy, England)

What's done to children, they will do to society.

(Karl Menninger)

What a child doesn't receive he can seldom later give.

(P.D. James, *Time to Be in Earnest*)

Caring adults count more than resources and equipment.

(Birth to Three Matters Framework principle)

Where did we ever get the crazy idea that in order to make children do better, first we have to make them feel worse? Think of the last time you felt humiliated or treated unfairly. Did you feel like cooperating or doing better?

(Jane Nelson)

The purpose of this chapter is to reflect on the role of the adult who works with children and the vast responsibility to do the job well. The particular issues discussed are, consideration of interactions, interpretations of children's behaviour, the need for observation of children and of our professional practice, and a brief review of the role of the key worker in day-care settings, and the teacher and the commonalities in aspects of early years work. Although the emphasis is on care and/or learning settings, aspects of this chapter are relevant for social workers, health visitors and allied professionals.

Working in care and learning environments is different from other work because it involves working with people who are vulnerable. Professionals such as nurses, social workers, health visitors and teachers, as well as early years professionals have a duty of care embedded in their professional role and 'care' brings with it an emotional reaction and personal involvement. This means that there is an interface between the personal and the professional, and that practitioners own beliefs, attitudes and values will permeate all that they do and influence their motivation in carrying out their responsibilities. Numerous writers and researchers such as Benoit (1997), Crittenden and Claussen (2000), Crittenden (1995), De Wolff and Van Ijzendoorn (1997), Karen (1998), Kogan and Carter (1999), Robinson (2003) Schore (2001), Goldschmied and Jackson (1999), Elfer et al, (2003), Manning-Morton et al (2001) and Gerhardt (2005) emphasize the importance of interactions between children and their carers for the child's emotional, social and learning well-being. The Scottish Birth to Three Framework (Scottish Executive, 2005) sets out three key features for effective practice and these are Relationships, Responsive care and Respect – applicable to children of all ages in reality! All these researchers and/or studies stress in different ways that carers must not only understand the impact they have on the child but also how and why. Stern (1985) suggests that parents compose an 'ongoing biography' for their baby that influences how they see their baby and, ultimately, how the baby sees itself. In my experience, child-care professionals also compose biographies for the children they encounter and, as with parents, such biographies also influence the meaning given to the child's behaviour. Parental perceptions, and by default professionals' perceptions, can result in a particular style of adult interaction. Such perceptions, if negative or distorted, can impede an understanding of the child's emotional and developmental needs. Common themes identified by Lieberman et al, such as destructive, wicked, independent or never satisfied have their echoes in the language occasionally used by teachers, health visitors, social workers and day-care practitioners, that is, 'the bad child', 'the aggressive child', the 'good (independent) child', the 'attention-seeking child' and 'the invisible child'. To highlight the latter example, during local training sessions on understanding children's behaviour, attendees – who are usually teachers in both pre-school settings and schools plus day-care practitioners – are asked to think about the children in their class or main group. Almost invariably, there is one child who is 'forgotten' and this child often turns out to be either the very quiet, compliant child or the 'independent' child who appears not to need much adult interaction. The fact that a child can be 'invisible' allows an opportunity for practitioners to consider whether or not their 'view' of that child affects the way the child's needs may be met and so leads to reflection on their general attitudes, beliefs and values. They often come to realize that potential variations in approach to children can be based on their own internal world rather than that of the child – and, of course, their internal world carries with it echoes of their own parental history, the influence of their environment and the key people they may have met along their own life trajectory – but especially, as we know, in their early years. This 'personal baggage', because of the emotionally laden nature of the work, mitigates the quality and style of interactions, interpretations and rationale for not only the way a child might be behaving, but also their own particular emotional (as opposed to professional) responses to different children in different contexts and situations.

There are two other strong recurring themes which arise during these training sessions. First, behaviour may not only be an adaptive response to circumstances but also a direct communication from the child to the adult about the child's current understanding of the world. Second, there is the recognition of the frequent mismatch between expectations of behaviour and a child's capacity to understand and comply with such expectations. I return to this aspect later on but first, I want to discuss interpretation of behaviour as communication and tell you about a particular situation which will illustrate and explain the subtitle of this chapter.

Three years ago, while observing a group of children with autism in a special school setting, a child whose behaviour was classed as particularly 'disturbed' repeatedly caught my attention. He had no speech, only sounds, and was very active. However, he became still when looking through the pages of a large book which he would repeatedly feel and fondle, running his fingers along the edges and especially the corners, all the while staring upwards. When moving around, he would repeatedly jump up, raising his arms. The focus of the staff appeared to be to try to help him manage his behaviour and be more 'controlled'. They were consistently kind, patient, attentive and caring but with hindsight I wonder whether any of us ever really considered whether his overall behaviour was trying to tell us something about himself and how he was actually experiencing and seeing his world rather than his behaviour being a 'symptom' or manifestation of his 'autism'. Over time, thinking about this and his fascination with the edges of the book pages, I came across a study by Penn and Shatz (2002), who describe how the edge of a page of paper 'can correlate the firing' of many nuclei in the retina on which this 'linear image falls simultaneously'. Was it possible that the child's behaviour, looked at in the context of his sensory, visual, emotional, and cognitive processes, was a direct communication of his potential lack of understanding about his body and spatial awareness? I was too lacking in understanding to think about it then, but reflection since suggests that behaviour can be interpreted as:

- a direct communication of personal meaning, which can be as complex as in the example above or as straightforward as a hug, punch, laughter or tears
- a 'by-product' of other processes, such as a reduction in eye contact in a child with autism

- a mixture of both the above in varying degrees at different times, dependent on context, mood and ability

What was also apparent was that this behaviour had a strange, emotional 'flavour'. It engendered in adults various levels of anxiety, dismay, helplessness, warmth or aversion. Anger, too, may have been present but never expressed. What emanated from the child, in my perception at least, was anxiety and a shadowy sense of despair. These feelings together with my own well-remembered feelings of helplessness as an observer reinforce my current assessment that what we were witnessing was a desperate attempt to communicate, but perhaps in a 'language' that we were not able, ready or prepared to understand. The interpretation of his behaviour by the adults around him may have had only a partial resemblance to what he actually wanted to 'tell' us. In addition, his absolute reliance on our abilities to understand him reflects how we all start off in life – as beings only able to communicate in ways available to us, reliant on the adults around us to understand what we mean. Kinsbourne (2002) notes that rhythmic activity that is confined to oneself, for example rocking, spinning, finger tapping and leg shaking, may replace arousal with a sense of calm. The child in this example did 'calm' briefly when repetitiously and compulsively feeling the edges of pages and it may be that children who are not understood and who feel little or no connection with others – for whatever reason – may turn to a rhythm they self-generate in order to feel soothed in a way that is more fundamental than simply an act of releasing tension. Kinsbourne (2002) also notes that over-arousal may constrain attention to the most important available cues and encourage high-frequency, repetitive responses 'adaptive to the internal state rather than the environment'. In other words, did this child's internal state – physical, biological and psychological – preclude him from being able to react and interact with his environment, leading to a focus on repetitive behaviour which gave him some respite from chaotic sensory information? At the core of all this is the meaning adults give to a child's behaviour and how far such interpretation coincides with the reality of the child's existence for them. In other words we need to pay attention to what Mary Sue Moore (1990) has termed 'the heart of the intended communication'.

I now turn to the second recurring theme for practitioners, which is the expectations of children's abilities and behaviour, and emphasize how important it is that such expectations are realistic and link with the maturational level of the child. However, in the hurly-burly of day-to-day life, practitioners in a range of settings and roles have to balance the demands and needs of parents, curricula, inspections, assessments, local authority requirements and the 'instant' needs of the children involved. This potentially means that the complexities of being a child who has to adapt to the competing expectations, attitudes and behaviour of a range of adults can sometimes be overlooked. In particular, it is adults who mainly dictate the pace, quality, content and range of experiences for the child. For example, think about a practitioner who was seen in a setting feeding three babies at the same time. The primary consideration in this case was 'getting through' feeding the babies rather than using such a care routine as an opportunity for close and positive interaction. Without reflection on the power of the quality of experience, the potential emotional detriment for the individual baby can be neither understood nor acknowledged. This example also brings into relief not only the reality of poor practice but also the practitioner's own reactions within that scenario. How did she think about what she was doing? Did she even consider how the babies might feel, or was the 'task' the primary concern? If she was concerned, she may have felt powerless to do or say anything within the setting which provides a link between the internal worlds of practitioners with the ethos of the setting and the attitudes, beliefs and expectations of parents and/or colleagues, whether the context is the parental home, day care or school with their attendant league tables.

To enable practitioners to think about these issues further an exercise, which has proved to be particularly illuminating for practitioners, is simply to think about a typical day, for example in a nursery or classroom but from five perspectives:

- transitions
- instructions
- the environment
- their own behaviour
- the overarching ethos of the setting

Transitions

Reflection on transitions allows practitioners to link emotional well-being and behaviour, because how a child deals with 'change' will arise from how they have responded to and made sense of their overall experience of life – their ongoing 'internal working model'. What happens at home influences what happens within the setting, and what happens within the setting can influence what happens at home. It is the totality of all these experiences, which supports and strengthens their 'internal working model' positively or negatively. Transitions bring with them different expectations of behaviour. For example, carers may have a different set of rules and boundaries from the setting, different instructions, demands on a child's growing skills and, for both very young children and babies, different sensations, including tactile, vestibular and proprioceptive. For example, the child who has been happily choosing their own activities, when the parent arrives at home time, may be

strapped into a buggy and literally 'carted off' either to home or the super-
market or to another house. This leads into thinking about a particular
transition that has been identified as a potential area for confusion and/or
distress for children if not handled correctly, and that is arriving and leaving
the day-care setting or school. The Ofsted report 'Early doors' (2005), which
focuses on the first hour in nurseries, had the following main findings:

1. In too many nurseries there are not enough staff on duty at the start
   of the day to offer good care for children; this was found consistently
   in one-fifth of the nurseries visited.
2. In a third of the nurseries visited the first hour or more of care lacked
   sufficient planning and organization to support the needs of all the
   children attending.
3. Some practice was unacceptable; in particular, security was weak,
   thereby allowing adults to enter the nursery unchallenged, and staff
   were not providing children with engaging activities.
4. The best nurseries plan carefully for the difficult transition from
   home to nursery and make sure that they have extra staff on hand to
   support both children and their parents at the start of what is, for
   many children, a very long day in the paid care of others.

Of course, it is perfectly possible to extrapolate these findings to consider how
such arrivals (and departures) are dealt with in school as well as nurseries,
especially with the 4-, 5- and 6-year-olds who are still very young and vulnerable to transitions. These times are so important, not least because they
often allow the informal sharing of information with parents, which can be so
important for the child. Unfortunately, within a busy classroom or day care
setting or when a practitioner has a number of children of varying ages in his
or her care, awareness of a child's individual ability to manage their ongoing
experiences may get lost, as might opportunities to talk to carers.

Of course, it is not just the transitions between home and day care or
school which need to be managed by the child, but also the many changes
that occur within a usual day. For example, practitioners can think about:

- the number of changes in adult care
- change from one activity to another
- from inside to outdoors
- from one room to another
- from one part of the building to another – (think of the child's
  understanding of space and size discussed in Chapter 6)

For some children, transitions can be potentially fearful. What seems everyday
to us may not be so to the child. Obviously the scale of the reaction will

depend on the context with some situations only causing mild anxiety while others may be genuinely fearful to the child – such as going into a large and echoing hall for a movement activity or for lunch. The other point is that infants and young children cannot explain why they may be anxious or fearful – they only know that they are and will respond accordingly. For example, a teacher noted that the children in her class (aged between 4 and 5 years) did not seem to use the book corner and, as the children seemed to enjoy stories and would take books and sit elsewhere, she wondered why. After observing and taking note of children's reactions, she told the children she was thinking about changing the book corner and what were their ideas. The children wanted to change a picture that was above the bookshelf – that of a clown – and she realised that many of the children were actually fearful of the picture and had simply 'voted with their feet'! It is up to us to carefully observe the child and notice the context, behaviour and/or appearance which may give clues as to how the child might be feeling. In addition, if the child's own internal perceptions are particularly idiosyncratic, for example a child who is very sensitive to noise, this may compound any environmental disharmony.

Instructions

Understanding what adults want is often difficult for young children, and instructions can be complex and confusing. As an example practitioners can think about a relatively simple instruction such as 'go and put your coat on' and identify what skills and abilities are involved. The sheer complexity of the integration between physical skill (for example, walk in the appropriate direction, accurately reach for the coat and lift it off the peg, put on the coat and begin to do up buttons or other fastenings), cognitive skills such as understanding the instruction (put the coat on ... what?, identifying your own peg/coat, dealing with sleeves, concepts of front and back, and so on), understanding 'mine' and 'yours' plus the self-confidence required to do the task and/or ask for help, is often illuminating. This helps to link behaviour with brain maturation, for example, the rate of myelination of axons (see Chapter 2) will influence the rate at which children can process instructions. Remember, the focus is on supporting the child's independance and ability to follow instructions rather than completion of the task.

Environmental provision

The environment is important and of course, adults are part and parcel of it. When thinking about environmental provision, consider:

- the range of activities provided with their various demands on skill and ability
- the way in which the room layout encourages independent access to resources
- the number of adults and children within the group
- noise levels – remember a child has no control over the volume in the classroom or day-care setting
- is there a 'quiet' corner/area?
- opportunities for rest, being alone and time to simply watch
- opportunities to 'snuggle' or hide, build dens
- availability of 'comfort' objects
- can children move around easily?
- do children have access to a drink at any time?
- is the area clean, fresh and pleasant?

Practitioners should then consider how they behave – for example:

- Are they people who 'like to get things done'?
- Do they prefer active or quiet children?
- Do they prefer noise or quiet in their own environment?
- What is their knowledge of child development?
- What is their reaction to strong emotions – distress, anger, joy?
- How do they talk to each other as well as the children?
- How do they meet and greet each other as well as children and carers?
- Is there room in the day for spontaneous activity?

Once they have gone through these questions, it is time to reflect on what support the children receive to deal with all the above and/or how much is 'taken for granted'. What is interesting is the discovery of high and often unrealistic expectations of behaviour in these very young children, accompanied by lack of insight into just how vulnerable they are and how many of the new skills and abilities these children possess and that they are still very early in their life-learning trajectory. To have high expectations of children per se is valuable as this promotes supporting children to do the best they can – but having high expectations that are inappropriate to the maturational level of the child is something else altogether. A 2000 report to the Select Committee on Education and Employment of the British Parliament by David and Claire Mills, devastatingly compared a 'Central European Model' of early education to that of Britain and the USA (Mills and Mills, 2000). The European model maintains that, of primary importance for children in the early years, is supporting their social/emotional growth – managing their emotions and promoting positive interactions with peers and adults. 'Formal' education was seen as not appropriate until around the age of 6–7 years. In comparison, in this country, pressures to introduce early literacy and numeracy is leading, in some cases, to children being forced to conform to styles of teaching and learning for which they are not developmentally ready in spite of the emphasis in government guidance on the use of play as the main medium for learning. On a more positive side, there are continuing initiatives to improve the care and learning needs of children from birth in day care. The UK government paper, *Every Child Matters* (DfES, 2003), is perhaps one of the most radical and far-reaching of these and indeed the introduction of an Early Years Foundation Stage Framework (DfES, 2006), combining development from birth to 5, is also part of a programme to support this age range. All the initiatives emphasize the role of the adult and the need for children to have safe, emotionally secure environments with opportunities for exploration, play and the presence of key workers. However, in reality the quality of day care/early education can be highly variable. Biddulph (2006) provides a passionate and well-researched account of the impact of long hours in day care on babies and very young children, and some school provision for 5- and 6-year-olds can remain very formal in style.

Learning from the child to support the child: the power of observation

I touched on the need for observation very briefly earlier but now want to emphasize how observation supports the care and learning needs of all children, whatever the context. In some situations, for example, social workers and health visitors, observations may indeed be 'one off's', but in these circumstances it is even more crucial for practitioners to be highly aware of typical development, the need to consider how the context may be influencing the child's behaviour and to pay particular attention to what may be the underlying 'communication'. In nursery and school settings, observations take on a different role in the sense that they are able to be carried out more frequently and, indeed, observations are meant to be part and parcel of everyday practice although time and staffing constraints can sometimes make this difficult. However, without observation, either planned or informal/spontaneous, overall planning would simply be based on what practitioners felt was important or fun or interesting (or all three!) but might not necessarily be meeting the needs of the children. Carrying out regular observations is important because it ensures that the child is put at the centre of day-to-day practice. In Elfer et al's (2003: 51) excellent book, they give a quote from Margaret Rustin: 'to be a good observer . . . requires a space in the mind where thoughts can begin to take shape and where confused experiences can be held in an inchoate form until their meaning becomes clearer. This kind of mental functioning requires a capacity to tolerate anxiety, uncertainty, discomfort, helplessness and a sense of bombardment'.

If we think about this quote carefully, it first becomes clear just how important it is that observations are done well, with focus and attention, and that time is taken to think about what has been seen and heard. This is because the assessments that are made to meet individual and/or group needs affect planning and/or decision making and have a very real and lasting impact on the well-being of the child. Observations are perhaps the most powerful of all the skills used when working with children because of the care, commitment and involvement needed when carrying them out. Second, the quote also emphasizes not only that carrying out observations is more than a 'task' but also that they can highlight the difficulties of practitioners when observing because of the wealth of information they see and the impact of the real child in front of them. In addition, as Elfer et al point out, practitioners can also not notice aspects of the child's behaviour because they may not want to see the difficulties a child may be having or acknowledge how they themselves might be feeling. Once something is noticed, then action is a requirement – and if resources are stretched and the child is difficult, it may be easier 'not to see'. To return to the example of the practitioner feeding three babies at once, what might an observer have noted in the reactions of the babies and, perhaps more importantly, what might they have interpreted from those reactions, which in turn might be influenced by how prepared an observer would be to notice something potentially distressing. This is why the emotional awareness of practitioners themselves is so important. However, honestly acknowledging that observing can bring up difficulties or mixed feelings can also be 'freeing' as practitioners recognize that it is the recognition of their own humanity, their feelings and the ability to deal with them that make them better practitioners. This leads me to consider the opportunities for carrying out peer observations, although this can seem very daunting in practice. Very few of us like to think we are under scrutiny and yet, without some means of reflecting on our practice, we may unconsciously be interacting with children in ways that may not be beneficial and we lose opportunities to improve both our practice and our relationships with the children whom we are supposed to care about. It is very hard, I know, but sometimes we have to set aside our own fears of failure and rejection – because, no matter how carefully observations of staff are introduced, these fears may still rear their heads – and recognise that these procedures are ultimately to help us help children.

Key workers/key persons: day-care settings

The Elfer et al (2003) book mentioned previously and the Goldschmied and Jackson (1999) book are both excellent texts to read about key workers/key persons as they not only set out the importance of such a role for infants and very young children, but also honestly acknowledge the difficulties in both implementation and the responses of staff to a more intimate approach to care. Goldschmied was the primary instigator of the key person approach, and the Elfer et al book is a means of moving the debate on. Goldschmied and Jackson (1999) recognized that the feelings of adults caring for children were often disregarded or 'actively discouraged' (a situation which can still exist) and the emotional needs of very young children were often not taken into account. Thinking has moved on and the realities of the importance of emotional well-being is now well documented (see references above and Chapter 5). The key person/key worker system (the terms seem to be inter-changeable) implies that for each child there is one person who takes a par-ticular interest in them. It does not mean one-to-one correspondence in day care as this would be impractical, but it does imply one adult taking a special interest in a small number of children. It is important that the role is well defined as a 'key person' as it is possible for a setting to say they have a key worker system but this simply means that one person is responsible for impersonal tasks while the comforting and care is still carried out by a range of people.

Goldschmied and Jackson (1999) movingly remind us that a young and almost totally dependent child is the only person in the nursery who does not understand why he is there. If, as practitioners, we see this system as sup-porting children finding their way through the plethora of experiences and giving them individual support, then it may make more sense than seeing it as some kind of 'imposed' system which is 'fashionable' for a time and has very little real purpose and meaning. Having such a system does not mean that the key person only works with that child, nor that they have to do so for the whole day – it means that there is someone who is consistently available for the child in times of need. In practice too, a key person can be off sick, go on holiday and so on, and many of the reservations about this system link with this, but children can tolerate a 'reserve' person who is also available to the child. The reality is, of course, that such a system places demands on individual staff and the setting as a whole, the risk of strong feelings in the practitioner for the child(ren) and the subsequent feelings of loss when the child moves on or leaves. However, it is possible to turn the situation around and acknowledge that in a group setting it is impossible for attention to be shared out equally like portions of a cake. Children will receive differing amounts of attention dependent not only on how the setting is organized but also on the nature of the child and of the adults in the group. Having a key person – and a reserve – assigned to a small group of children (or chosen naturally by them) – may go further in ensuring that individual children do receive attention more or less when they need it. For parents, too, the knowledge that there is a specific person with whom they can build a relationship may also be very helpful. The hard and committed work that the key person system entails does include fostering a sound relationship with parents and being seen as a partner in the care of the child – not a parental replacement. Elfer (personal communication) is currently (2005/06) carrying out further research on the role of key persons in the nursery and has examined the area in depth, including worker and parent reactions and worries.

A word for the teacher – in pre-school and school settings

Teachers are, of course, primarily 'educators' but their own involvement, attitudes and approach with very young pre-school and school children is clearly very important, as is their understanding of child development. Because of the changes in society, teachers are becoming more involved with the younger age ranges, that is, from 3 upwards, with a requirement for them to know about development from birth. The Primary National Strategy documentation[1] identifies practitioners as having to continuously develop their skills in the following areas:

- relationships both with children and adults
- understanding the individual and diverse ways that children learn and develop
- knowledge and understanding in order actively to support and extend children's learning in and across all areas and aspects of learning
- practice in meeting all children's needs, learning styles and interests
- work with parents, carers and the wider community
- work with other professionals within and beyond the setting

The paradox appears to be that while there is a very strong emphasis on knowledge and understanding of child development, the actual training of teachers, appears to be reducing the amount of time given to such study. In reality, the levels of this knowledge profoundly impact not only on styles of teaching but also on how the children will respond to the provision. Knowledge of early development is crucial for all but can be particularly helpful for teachers moving from other Key Stages.

Back to basics: some self-reflective questions for all practitioners:

The individual practitioner is responsible for his or her own feelings and level of knowledge about the child, children or family in their care, and it may be helpful to consider the following questions to help establish the level of individual understanding:

- What are my feelings *for* this child?
- What are my thoughts, feelings, beliefs *about* this child?
- What are my behaviours in response to this child's cues?
- What is my knowledge and understanding about behaviour?

In addition, we might ask ourselves:

- Do I have confidence in own knowledge and understanding?
- Do I have support and time to do my work?
- Can I receive additional training/support as necessary?

Finally, I found this gem on a website which pithily explains the role of the adult:

> (Almost) Everything I Need to Know About Being a Parent (or practitioner) in 25 Words or less
> - *Always*: be BIGGER, STRONGER, WISER, and KIND.
> - *Whenever possible*: follow your child's *need*.
> - *Whenever necessary*: take charge.
> (© Cooper, Hoffman, Marvin, and Powell, 1998,
circleofsecurity.org)

9 The final phase, conclusions and reflections on development

Coming to the end of this book's journey, it has probably become very obvious that the emphasis has been on the early months and years of life. This is no accident as, without doubt, most of the exciting, dynamic and monumental shifts in development take place in the pre-school years, providing the fundamental arsenal of skills and abilities for a child to use as they leave this phase and enter school and beyond. If you look at the summary in Table 9.1 of development between the ages of 5 and 8, it is as though development has reached a 'plateau', allowing a child to consolidate and improve on their previous abilities which now grow in complexity across the developmental spectrum. This plateau also means that the child is developmentally ready for the more formal demands of the school system in behaviour, physical dexterity and ability to abide by rules, to attend for longer periods, to relate to teachers and peers, and to cope with the various topics and varied styles of teaching. This 'readiness' is most obvious between 6 and 7 years for many children – something that many European countries have acknowledged for several years, with their later starting ages for formal schooling but something that the English Parliament still seems to ignore, as we saw in Chapter 8. Children are generally eager and ready to learn during this phase before the volcano that is puberty erupts!

If we look at the very first item in Table 9.1 – 'will enforce rules and can be critical of self and others' – we can discern that the child is now able to 'self-manage' their emotions, up to a point! They are also able to increasingly regulate and adapt their behaviour to different contexts/social situations. Neither of these would be possible without previously having learned via carers that emotions and behaviour can be controlled. From the infant whose heart rate and kicking rhythm can be modulated by the sound of mother's voice, the toddler whose rages and joys are tolerated and supported appropriately, comes the child who is able to self-regulate. Of course, the implication is that if the infant or young child does not receive appropriate love, care and attention, then the likelihood of dysfunction in one way or another is high. Sydsjo et al (2001) in a longitudinal study of a group of mothers with psychosocial problems, and their children and a group of mother and child pairs 'lacking in risk criteria', commented:

Table 9.1 5–8 years

Will enforce rules and can be critical of self and others. Gradually child can become quite serious and 8-year-olds are often very demanding of themselves and sometimes overconfident in what they can do	By 7 years, children are able to track across a whole page and able to track a full circle visually	Wrist bones are usually fully developed by age 6 allowing finer control over 'writing' tasks
By 7 years, seeks approval of peers as well as adults, can have strong friendships, and sometimes 'enemies'	After 5 years can usually sing a whole song in the same key	By 7 years, usually a 'mature' grasp for holding pencils, brushes and so on has developed Use of scissors becomes more skilful and can cut shapes easily
Generally cooperative. Team games with rules become increasingly popular but children often prefer same-sex playmates By 8 years, child can enjoy time alone as well as with friends, but peer pressure also becomes important and being part of a group is important too	Can kick a ball or write using preferred leg or hand (for example, right or left handed and 'footed'). Some children may do this much earlier but most are confident by around 6 years	Fine motor skills are improving and can include complex skills such as tying shoelaces
Around 5 years can confidently recognize categories of animals, objects, and so on	At 5 years can distinguish fantasy from reality but this may become blurred when under stress and new fears may develop because of their imaginations, for example, the dark By 8 years fears are replaced more by anxieties and worries rather than fears	Can understand concept of time better than when younger (by and from 5 years). Can understand days of the week and by 8 years can often tell time by the quarter hour
Play-based learning is still most appropriate, although most children can be ready for 'formal' learning by around 7 years (especially boys – girls may be ready earlier)	By 6 years can tell left from right (usually!) and by 7 years this has transferred to being able to understand opposites such as short–long, sharp–blunt, and so on	Attention span can still be short, but by 8 years can show good concentration, and is logical and thoughtful

By 6 onwards can begin to understand differences of opinion but sees the world very much in 'black and white' terms	Ability to deal with angry or jealous feelings gradually becomes greater – can still be physically expressed at around 5 years	Writing can still show word or letter reversals by around 6 years because of perceptual skills still not quite fully developed
		By 8 years can usually use both upper and lower case letters
Criticism or failure is hard to handle and needs sensitive adult support to help child deal with these feelings. The need to win, for example at card games and so on becoming less insistent over time	From 7 years likes projects, collecting and more complicated games. Can become very protective of own things	From about 6 years reads with understanding of vocabulary and 'proper' sentences. Some children may do this much earlier and others may take longer
Language is usually grammatically correct using past and future tenses and with growing vocabulary	Can get tired easily and may 'dawdle' and daydream Sleep needs are around 9–11 hours	

At 8 years of age, the index children, *especially the boys*, were found to display significantly more behavioural disturbances than the reference children. A significant correlation was also found in the index group, but not the reference group, between the quality of mother–infant interaction at birth and the extent of behavioural disturbance in children at 8 years of age.

(Sydsjo et al, 2001: 135, emphasis mine)

This is only one study, but it does two things. First, it suggests that we should take into account that boys appear to be less resilient to emotional distress than girls – even if the differences are slight. The boys in this study showed greater behavioural problems even though poor interaction patterns were similar between the mothers and their male or female children, that is, similar types of stressful interactions appeared to have greater impact on the boys. Other studies quoted by the researchers have had similar findings. Second, as the children were rated at birth, 6 months and 18 months, there was a clear picture of the type of relationship that existed between the mothers and their children. The strong links between poor interactions and the behaviour problems in the study group and the correspondingly low level of behaviour problems/more positive interactions in the control group does lend further support to the potentially lasting influence of early emotional experiences on behaviour, and thereby probably the ability to learn as well.

As time goes on, development continues to build on all that has gone before. Later, in adolescence, the individual's ability to travel through the maelstrom of feelings will depend in part on the pre-existing levels of self-esteem and relationships with parents and peers. The need for practitioners and indeed society as a whole to recognize that biology and physiology play a part in understanding behaviour is exampled by the growing numbers of research studies using brain imaging. Such studies have demonstrated that the difficulties many adolescents have regarding poor judgement, failure to see consequences and acting impulsively is not only due to hormonal changes but also to brain maturation, that is, 'undeveloped circuitry' and immature white matter and development in the prefrontal cortex – so involved in those 'executive functions' we met in Chapter 6. Once these areas are mature (late teens/early twenties) people themselves often notice a shift in the way they think and the decisions that they make – in other words, the processes of thinking itself become more 'mature' (Anderson, 2006).

In adulthood, we continue to carry with us the threads of our past, weaving them into our current experiences where they are reinforced or weakened. You may recall from Chapter 5, that emotional health also impacts on physical health. Biddulph (2006: 26) quotes from a large, longitudinal study and associated research which state:

> 91 per cent of those who did not have a close relationship with their mothers (by their own assessment) had been diagnosed with a serious medical illness in mid-life – double the rate of those who reported a warm relationship. Closeness to father, or the lack of it, predicted similar differences in health. Worst off in health terms were those who had been close to neither mother nor or father. Health conditions included heart disease, cancer, ulcers, alcoholism, hypertension and chronic asthma. Researcher Dr Norman Anderson, who reviewed these studies in 2003, was able to find over 20 similar studies, with 55,000 participants in total, all of which validated these findings.

Early emotional health matters throughout life for both body and mind. If you are someone who feels that we put aside our childhood as we mature, we only have to remember our reactions to rejection, to pain and loss, to the expectations we have of friends and partners, our ability to make friends and work relationships, our attitudes towards authority figures and our ability to self-motivate. None of these arise out of a vacuum – all have their roots in the ways in which all our developmental strands come together in our earliest years.

Development, therefore, is, a 'gestalt' composed of a number of elements or aspects (what you will) which come together in an integrated whole, resulting in a unique individual. As we have seen, all our thoughts, feelings and behaviours begin in the intricate connections between neurons arising from the information coming from within our bodies and all the sensory information from 'outside'. Our brains quietly and constantly second by second update and reorganize our understanding of the world in subtle, minute ways as we deal with day-to-day occurrences, and gradually, over time, our more general ideas, perceptions and knowledge can shift and change, dependent upon the relationship between experience, senses and the brain. We really are the sum of all our parts culminating in our own individual world and, because of common understandings about the minds of others and the physical properties of the environment, all these 'individual worlds' are able to connect. Without these connections we would not be able to interact or function.

To sum up, the cornerstones of human development occur within human species-specific timescales – the most rapid and fundamental, as we have seen, in the first 5 years, with the second major transition occurring at puberty. These transitions could be termed primary, secondary and tertiary maturation. The latter is the longest lasting and slowest, with potentially less integration between developmental domains than in childhood and adolescence as physical and biological changes occur broadly in line with the ageing process, while aspects of emotional and cognitive development may be more influenced by social, cultural and lifestyle opportunities, choices and pressures as well as life experience.

If we look at the progression of each developmental domain (emotional, social, physical, neurological, physiological, cognitive and communicative) compare them and link them together, a pattern emerges which is logical, highly integrated, sequential and hierarchical, spiralling in complexity but with each phase embedded in the one before. This pattern combined with the ongoing quality of emotional and social interaction with carers and opportunities for play and learning allows for the variability of infant and child behaviour and the variations seen in the manifestations of function and/or dysfunction. Seeing development in this integrated way also provides a logical framework for how later development reflects these early stages in spite of modifications through wider environmental experience, ongoing maturation and education, leading to a number of overall conclusions which the information in this book has aimed to express as follows.

Development is:

- set within a framework of emotional and social mutually influential interaction
- psychological, building on sensory information, movement, direct experience and accompanying feelings/emotion influencing the ability to learn

- following a trajectory which moves overall from simple to complex
- influenced by linear time as well as experience
- maturing, progressing at variable rates within and between individuals embedded in broad human species-specific timescales
- rooted in processes that are evolutionary adaptations for human beings but often shared in fundamental form by other species
- following similar processes in the way that information is organized – 'nature' often adapts rather than 'reinvents'
- encompassing a period of practice, discontinuity and/or regression prior to an observable shift in complexity

This leads to the following implications:

- First concepts, ideas and representations, together with first patterns of movement, communication and emotional experience do not disappear but are incorporated into biological and memory patterns built upon as the individual matures.
- Brain maturation in the lobes of the hemispheres occurs at different rates allowing for more resilience and flexibility to both experience and possible injury/trauma. It is easier for a child to learn than for an adult.
- All individuals, whether infant, toddler, child, adolescent or adult, will respond to their daily experiences in a behavioural style which reflects a dynamic interplay of the current maturational level of each specific developmental area, bound by the ongoing emotional state and influenced by the particular context.

This last point is particularly important for practitioners because, seeing the child 'holistically' as we saw in Chapter 8, does not mean seeing the child 'globally' but, realizing that the child is also the 'sum of all their parts' and that each area of development needs to be considered so that the relationship between them can be thought about and reflected upon. Sensitivity to noise, textures, responses to being in large or small spaces, trust and belief in adults, confidence or not in peers – all those can influence the child's attitudes and behaviour in many contexts, as will the child's ability to interpret adult behaviour and attitudes. For example, difficulty in communication may have a physical cause, may or may not be linked to a learning disability but, whatever the reason, it will have a 'knock on' effect not only on the child's ability to learn but also in the social and emotional realm as well. Alternatively, difficulty in communication could arise from problems in the child's social/emotional world. In either case, the child would not be well served if only the communication difficulty was seen as the area for intervention.

In infancy and childhood we are on a journey of discovery, where we learn to negotiate our way in our family and society, and we build up a picture of the person we think and feel we are. We ascribe a value to ourselves in relation to others. There are also children and adults who, in spite of very adverse circumstances, carry with them a positive sense of self, and it is in these early years that the foundation for this persona is laid – but it does not stop there. As adults, what seems to happen is that we can refine those early concepts. If we are imbued with a sense of failure and low self-esteem, we can seek to overcome it or at least replace the negativity of thoughts and beliefs by something more positive. If we know we are prone to certain behaviours, we can seek out possible causes and learn to adapt our lifestyles and ways of thinking. In other words, we can 'mature' and grow into a greater sense of peace within ourselves. The responsibility we have as adults is both to ourselves, to continue our journey and not see chronological age as being a 'full stop' to development and, at the same time, to carry the responsibility of how we behave to infants and young children who truly are in the formative years of their lives.

In the end, what I hope this book has emphasized, apart from the integrated nature of development, is that babies and children as they grow and develop need adults who care for and protect them, who will follow the child's lead but also know when to lead, who will talk to them and not leave them too much to their own devices, who will act responsibly and provide safe and secure boundaries, who will respect them but not give them choices beyond their understanding, and who will allow a child to explore and make mistakes but will also provide a safe haven. The developmental journey we all make should not take us too far too quickly, too soon and alone – it is for parents, carers and practitioners to travel alongside children, helping them discover the 'good road'.

Appendix: Detailed development charts giving shifts in development from 0 to 8 years

1 0–3 months

Open-mouthed vowel sounds – vocalization in response to speech. 'Newborns 1 to 5 days old have demonstrated an ability to discriminate differences in frequency' in speech	Limb position is usually flexed in both arms and legs plus presence of asymmetrical tonic reflex – if one arm outstretched, baby will lie with head turned towards outstretched arm	Will respond to familiar sounds by shifting eye gaze and head movements
Movements of arms and legs random at 1 month – gradually becomes more purposeful	Prefers lying on back	Follows object visually within a limited range
Levels of alleviation of distress – physical and psychological	First experiences of and reactions to the emotional quality of experience/environment	Visual interest for faces moves from periphery to centre and from mouth to eyes. For example, newborns up to 1 month show preference for schematic faces in the periphery – 1–2 months seem to 'pull faces together'.
First experiences of sensory integration 2 months colour discrimination	Very young infants are noted to have long periods of 'staring' – a period of 'sticky fixation'	Behaviour templates (reflexes) gradually subsumed into more proactive behaviours for example – startle reflex absent by 3–5 months and replaced by adult type 'startle'.

| Rapid brain growth especially in visual and auditory systems, especially at 8 weeks (visual system) | *Emergence* (from 3 months) of *open handed*, broadly directed reaching for objects and begins to 'bat' at objects. Note the 'fisted' position of the hands of new borns should diminish by 2 months | Establishment of physiological rhythms (sleeping, feeding, temperature control, heart rate) |

2 3–8/9 months

Increasing sociability and expression of feeling states through facial expression, bodily movements, vocalizations	Increasing curiosity allied with growing motor and visual coordination	Turns to familiar sounds *5-month-old babies* have shown a sensitivity to melodic contour and rhythmic changes. *6-month-old babies* have been successful in matching specific pitches	Shows signs of understanding words at 7–8 months	Shouts to get attention from 6 months
Expects mouth movements and sounds to synchronize	Ongoing brain maturation/ surge in synapse formation in some brain areas, for example, vision – 4 months appears to refine depth perception and binocular vision	Developing capacity to reach and grasp with hand tending to be shaped to object size by 9 months – coincides with disappearance of grasp reflex between 4 and 6 months (6–12 months for toes!)	Episode of 'compulsive reaching' between 6 and 9 months and child uses a 'raking' motion to bring objects into the hand – prior to the development of the pincer grasp	Emergence and development of selective attention with emergence at 3–4 months of controlled 'scanning'. Ability to more easily switch attention from one focus of interest to another emerges between 3 and 4 months and vision at 3 months also more acute

Greater upper body control – can hold head up when in prone position and by six months when in this position takes weight on the hands and is almost ready for crawling	Rhythmical kicking when supine and can begin to bear weight at around 3 months when held in standing position (emergence of first postural reflex)	General inhibition of early 'primitive' reflexes, for example asymmetrical tonic reflex diminishes between 3 and 4 months and usually gone by 6 months, rooting reflex usually diminished by 4 months	Rolling from lying on back begins to appear between 3 and 5 months	3–4 months emergence of laughter – often combined with rhythmic leg movements
Emergence of 'Landau' reflex' – baby extends head and limbs when held in 'ventral suspension' – one of the postural reflexes appearing around 3–5 months	4–6 months study suggests that infants appear to 'drop back' to featural processing both upright and inverted faces – 7 months integration of upright faces	Emergence and development of turn taking/ 'proto conversations' and cycles of activity	Specific emotions become clearer with joy differentiating from contentment and sadness and anger from general distress	Cooing and purposeful sounds emerge around 15/16 weeks

3   Shifts in skills and abilities 7/8–12 months

Refinement of facial recognition	Emergence of stranger anxiety and discrimination of attachments	Beginning of concept of object permanence
Ongoing brain maturation – evidence of ability to remember location of hidden objects	Earliest emergence of 'mark making' that is, through hand movements on tables with available resource, for example, food	Expansion of sensory world through greater mobility and introduction of new tastes, visual and hearing acuity

Able to localize source of sounds from behind	Refinement of vocal matching to home language – babbling becomes attuned to its rhythms. Some children may *understand* about 10–25 words and two-word 'couplets', for example, bye bye, pat hands, upsy daisy	Emergence and development of shared interaction/social referencing allied with possible basic understanding/linking of emotions and actions in others[1]
Emergence of declarative and imperative pointing – often synchronized with vocalizations which appear important for later development of speech	Imitation becomes more proactive and relates some gestures to appropriate context, for example raising arms to be picked up, waving when leaving or seeing others leave	Increasing sociability and expression of feeling states through facial expression, bodily movements, vocalizations
Can cross midline of body, that is, able to transfer objects from one hand to the other, and thumb/finger pincer grasp develops between 7 and 9 months Plays hand games such as 'pat a cake'	Increase in mobility – crawling, pulling to stand, first steps (for some) – combines with emergence of simple depth perception in most children by 12 months	'Parachute reflex' usually appears around 8–9 months and fully present by 12 months – the last 'postural reflex' to occur
Most babies will begin to use both eyes together and judge distances and grasp and throw objects with greater precision	Increasing curiosity allied with growing motor and visual coordination	Ability to 'creep', that is, as crawling but with trunk off the ground
Often able to sit from the standing position	Can begin to sit for long periods	May stand momentarily without support

4   12–24 months

Further emergence of mark-making – radials and circles using appropriate crayons, paints, sticks and so on	Ongoing brain maturation – 'wiring' of emotional areas and prefrontal cortex appears to be very active between 10/12 months and 18 months	Emergence of understanding of another's feelings and also begins to understand the apparent 'intentions' or goal-directed actions of another

Emotions are labile and powerful – beginning of emotional 'management' mediated by attitude, level of support, establishment of boundaries and understanding of carers	Emergence of growing independence – finds it difficult to be directed by adults!	Emergence of understanding of other's likes and dislikes
Great curiosity and exploration and emergence of learning 'schemas' such as trajectory (throwing), enveloping/enclosing (which links with establishing object permanence)	Emergence of ability to self-refer, for example pointing to identified parts of own body – towards the end of this age range most can identify 6–8 body parts	Imitation used as a means of communication between peers
Increasing mobility and range of movements with integration of movement in near and far space, for example, reach for objects reliably 1–1.5 years: movement to music through rocking, marching, rolling, and attending intently are more pronounced. Emergence of spontaneous song, continuing over the next year	Self-identification and understanding of a bodily self links with the use of name to help child to attend to what an adult is saying	Emergence of pretend and increase in imitative activities
Automation of parallel visual/motor co-ordination, for example, can begin to move around objects, move forwards purposefully and begin to clamber and climb. Can stoop to pick up an object without falling over by about 14 months and can also get up from a supine position by rolling over first and later will be able to lie, then sit and stand	Emergence of more complex emotions such as guilt and embarrassment – increasing awareness of restrictions on behaviour	Increase in fine motor control, development of mark-making and building/stacking – linked with motor maturation as a 15 month old can usually stack 2 bricks while an 18 month old can usually stack at least 4 bricks

Further development of verbal communication, first words emerging followed by rapid increase – understanding is usually greater than words spoken	Ability to throw overhand usually appears by around 18 months – with hand preference beginning to emerge at around 12 months	Independent walking usually develops between 11 and 15 months with hands held in 'high guard' position. Hands will gradually lower as walking becomes more confident

5 24–36/42 months

Seeks approval from adults and usually idolizes parents – but challenges!! Needs prompts to help child listen if busy doing something else	Ongoing brain maturation with over-proliferation of synapses – however 'organization' of language abilities is taking place. For example, child can look at picture and link the labelling that parents/carers are doing about the picture, simultaneously	Will respond to *simple*, that is, one-step requests and can gradually, over time, respond to two-step requests and hold in mind up to two concepts simultaneously, for example, bring me the round, blue ball
Aware of own gender	Increase in questioning about the world	Increasing but variable understanding of another's wishes, moods. Begins to be aware that desires/wants may not be immediately satisfied
Tests boundaries but begins to understand that actions have consequences	Will tell 'story' about and during drawing/painting activities	Toilet training usually under way during this period
Fine motor movements becoming more established	Greater confidence and variety in gross motor movements – walks with hands to sides and can run. Can also get up from the floor without using hands	Pretend play gradually extends into rich fantasy/role play
Emergence of drawing such as 'tadpole' figures	Some broad sense of time emerging such as today, tomorrow, yesterday – and the passing of time	Vocabulary continues to increase with much self talk and commentary on what child is doing – also begins recognition and imitation of popular tunes and nursery rhymes

Begins by *end* of this period to understand concept of me and mine but has difficulty with concept of sharing	By 3 years *may* find it easier to separate from parents and can also express a wide range of emotions	Finds it difficult to put feelings into words and needs supportive help from adults

6 36/42 months–5 years

By 5 years can begin to take turns and share but this is still rather 'shaky'! Ability to 'attend' is becoming more flexible as child can begin (between 4 and 5 years) to listen while still undertaking an activity	Increasing understanding of another's thoughts and beliefs – emergence of 'theory of mind.' Begins to be able to express feelings more easily over time and view themselves as having a body, mind and feelings	Can usually write recognizable letters from 4 years but often randomly scattered over page
Verbal communication is more sophisticated with use of past and future tenses and generally correct grammatical structure. Around 4 years can go through a brief period of repeating words or stuttering and some may have a 'lisp' with 'r', 'v' and 'th' often still difficult	Play-based learning is the most appropriate for all aspects of development in this age range	Reach and grasp becomes more typical of adult patterns Can use scissors for straight-line cutting from about 5 years
By 5 years, gross motor development is increasingly sophisticated with children being able to learn to swim, rollerskate, balance, climb, jump, kick and catch balls purposefully, ride bikes without stabilizers, throw and catch, and so on with conscious will but unconscious ability	Ongoing brain maturation – imagination is rich and drives much of play	Becoming steadily more independent but needs adult support
Becoming more serious and dependable	Using language to express feelings – can also now sing a whole song but pitch might be variable	Shows guilt over misbehaviour
Children need about 11–13 hours sleep	Wants to succeed, be 'best' (older age range)	Can usually (by 5) draw a person with a head, body, arms and legs

By 5 years can begin to tell long involved stories – with beginnings, middles and ends	By 5 years can usually change clothes with minimal help although children can and do vary	Brain spurt in frontal regions between the ages of 3 and 6 years

7 5–8 years

Will enforce rules and can be critical of self and others Gradually child can become quite serious and 8-year-olds are often very demanding of themselves and sometimes overconfident in what they can do	By 7 years children are able to track across a whole page and able to track visually a full circle	Wrist bones are usually fully developed by age 6 allowing finer control over 'writing' tasks
By 7 years seeks approval of peers as well as adults; can have strong friendships and sometimes 'enemies'	After 5 years can usually sing a whole song in the same key	Can understand concept of time better than when younger (by and from 5 years). Can understand days of the week and by 8 years can often tell time by the quarter hour
Generally cooperative and team games with rules become increasingly popular but children often prefer same-sex playmates. By 8 years, child can enjoy time alone as well as with friends but peer pressure also becomes important and being part of a group is important too	Sleep needs are around 9–11 hours	By 7 years usually a 'mature' grasp for holding pencils, brushes, and so on has developed. Use of scissors becomes more skilful and can cut shapes easily
Around 5 years can confidently recognize categories	At 5 years can distinguish fantasy from reality but this may become blurred when under stress and new fears may develop because of their imaginations, for example, the dark. By 8 years fears are replaced more by anxieties and worries rather than fears	Play based learning is still most appropriate although most children can be ready for 'formal' learning by around 7 years (especially boys – girls may be ready earlier)

Fine motor skills are improving and can include complex skills such as tying shoelaces	By 6 years can tell left from right (usually!) and by 7 years this has transferred to being able to understand opposites such as short-long, sharp-blunt, and so on	Attention span can still be short but by 8 years can show good concentration, and is logical and thoughtful
By 6 onwards can begin to understand differences of opinion but sees the world very much in 'black and white' terms	Ability to deal with angry or jealous feelings gradually becomes greater – can still be physically expressed at around 5 years	Writing can still show word or letter reversals by around 6 years because of perceptual skills still not quite fully developed. By 8 years can usually use both upper and lower case letters
Criticism or failure is hard to handle and needs sensitive adult support to help child deal with these feelings	Can get tired easily and may 'dawdle' and daydream	Need to win for example, at card games and so on becoming less insistent. From 7 years likes projects, collecting and more complicated games. Can become very protective of own things
From about 6 years reads with understanding of vocabulary and 'proper' sentences. Some children may do this much earlier and others may take longer	Can kick a ball or write using preferred leg or hand (for example right-or left-handed and 'footed'). Some children may do this much earlier but most are confident by around 6 years	

Glossary

Amygdala An almond shaped structure deep inside the temporal lobe and a few inches from either ear and plays a critical role in processing emotions. Has very strong links with memory and 'higher' regions in the brain

Auditory cortex This is concerned with processing sounds and is situated in the temporal lobe

Axon An extension of the brain cell (neuron) that carries messages to the next cell

Basal ganglia A group of nuclei situated in the mid brain and receives connections from wide ranging areas of the brain

Broca's area Very important in speech production and lies in the area of the left frontal cortex close to the temporal cortex

Cingulate cortex Situated in the middle of the brain and to a great extent, surrounds the corpus callosum. Different areas of this structure are connected with emotions, cognition and bodily functions such as heart rate and blood pressure thereby linking thoughts, feelings and bodily responses

Corpus callosum Is the 'large body' that connects the two halves of the brain and is both a bridge and a 'highway' for information

EEG Electroencephalograpahy is a measurement of the electrical activity in the brain

Epistemology A branch of philosophy that examines the nature and validity of knowledge and belief

Hippocampus It is situated in the medial (middle) of the temporal lobes. Strongly linked with memory and has strong connections to the amygdala

Homeostasis The tendency for the body to want to remain in psychological and physiological stability and much of our unconscious processing of information works towards keeping us in a 'stable' state – although what that is psychologically can vary from person to person.

Physiologically it is much clearer (e.g. think of blood pressure ranges, heart rate and human body temperature)

Hypothalamus It is about the size of an almond and is located just below the thalamus and just above the brain stem – it is involved with the production of hormones and is also involved with sleep cycles, temperature, hunger and thirst

Glia A type of cell that surrounds nerve cells and holds them in place. Glial cells also insulate nerve cells from each other

Gyrus (Gyri) The 'hill' on the outer surface of the brain made by the folding of the cortex

Kinetic Relating to movement

Lateral Geniculate Nucleus Is part of the thalamus and is the primary processor of information received from the retina

Limbic system Generally thought of as a group of interconnected structures associated with emotions, behaviour, sensory information

Myelin Fatty substance produced by glial cells in the brain

Myelination The process of producing insulating envelope of myelin that surrounds the core of a nerve fibre or axon and facilitates the transmission of nerve impulses

Morphogenetic Formation of a structure, in this context, how human bodies are 'put together'

Neuron A brain cell

Neurotransmitter(s) This is a chemical 'messenger' that carries information from one neuron to the next. Examples include dopamine and serotonin

Orbital frontal cortex The name is based on its location, which is the very front part of the brain resting on the orbits of the eyes. It is connected with sensory integration, decision making and planning and is still probably one of the least understood parts of the brain

Proprioceptive The sense of body position

Phonology How sounds are organised in natural speech

Phylogeny	The evolutionary interrelationship between species
Phylogenetic	Relating to evolutionary development (in this context, of humans)
Pituitary	It is about the size of a pea and is situated just at the base of the skull. It releases hormones particularly involved with homeostasis and is connected to the hypothalamus.
Reticular activating system	Situated in the brain stem, this is the name given to the structure involved in motivation and arousal in animals (and humans)
Retina	This is the layer of nerves lining the back of the eye
Somatosensory cortex	Area of the brain that deals with sensory information such as touch, pressure, heat etc. It lies next to the motor cortex. Both sit like a 'hair band' at the top of the brain
Superior Temporal Sulcus	Main landmark on the outside of the temporal cortex (of the brain)
Sulcus	A furrow on the brain's surface
Syntax	The exact structure of how we write what we write, e.g. where we place a noun or a verb
Thalamus	Sits deep within the brain, above the brain stem, and is the 'relay station' for all sensory information (apart from smell)
Wernicke's area	Very important for understanding spoken language. Strong connections to Broca's area and is situated in a part of the brain (left) called the Sylvian fissure where the temporal lobe and the parietal lobe meet

Notes

P.v

1. Robert Kall website: http://www.futurehealth.org/qbrain.htm

1 Introduction

1. This is, of course, why magicians are fascinating and why horror stories which show furniture moving, rooms changing shape and peoples' faces changing are so scary. They violate our 'safety' rules of the world we know.
2. The research underpinning these aspects and components will be highlighted as we go through the book.
3. It may well be that in humans, as in other animals, the environment/experience provides the necessary context for genetically programmed, species-specific behaviour to occur. For example, the female prairie vole only begins puberty once she has smelled the urine of an unfamiliar male.
4. The new Early Years Foundation Stage document has broad overlaps in the developmental phases, clearly indicating the wide variability of children achieving certain skills and abilities. However, this does not negate that there is still an expected phase of transition.
5. While these findings are based on Western children especially in the USA, nevertheless there is an inherent assumption made that while culture and social environment may well influence the type and style of progression, the core principle is that we do change and develop over time with broadly comparable shifts. Language development is a particularly robust example of a human species-specific timescale as many cultural studies have demonstrated similar achievements at similar times – including studies of deaf children who 'hand babble' at a similar time as hearing children begin to 'babble'.
6. Damasio does not give time frames as such in his work (Damasio et al, 2000) but these broadly correspond with Stern's identification of shifts and are put together by Fonagy and Target (2003).
7. Erikson's stages go across the life span into old age – ego integration versus despair.
8. This stage is followed by the pre-operational stage. Piaget's stages of cognitive development progess into early adolescence with his 'formal operational' stage at 12 years and over.

9. Schore integrates this period with the 'stages' of Margaret Mahler – the practising sub-phase – and also a substage of Piaget's sensorimotor development together with the emergence of a measurable assessment of attachment formation.

10. Such symbolic representation is supported by a parallel 'attainment of an experience dependent structural maturation of an orbitofrontal system' thereby linking brain maturation with a greater sophistication in the child's ability to 'represent'. Brain information is discussed in Chapter 2.

11. What this also highlights are the interesting similarities in timescale for the development of major shifts in skills and aptitudes to emerge which appear to be multiples of 9. For example, it takes about 8–9 months for the infant to reliably reach the stage of social referencing and shared attention and a further 8–9 months for self-recognition to emerge, that is, 16–18 months. Language is developing rapidly at around 27 months, fantasy play at 36 months, while a typically developing child achieves an understanding of 'false beliefs', that is, understanding that someone may believe something that one knows not to be true, usually around 4 years!

12. Both Tevarthen (2005) and Reddy (2005) suggest that 'self-conscious' emotions such as shyness and 'showing off' may appear in the first year.

13. The Early Years Foundation Stage Guidance is to be implemented in 2008.

2 Laying the foundations: brain works

1. The speed and diversity of brain research is ongoing; new discoveries and/or insights are being made all the time – this is one of the aspects that makes studying human development so exciting! However, I have tried to ensure that the research given is from as wide a base as possible.

2. A fascinating piece of information provided again by Changaux is that the human newborn meningeal (the coverings of the brain) system is remarkably similar to that of a humanoid ancestor who lived around 2–3 million years ago, while a later fossil, aged 2 million years, revealed a pattern similar to a 40-day-old infant-while homo erectus – about 1 million years – demonstrates a pattern similar to that of a modern 1-year-old child!

3. We get 23 chromosomes from each parent resulting in 23 *pairs*. Each human chromosome holds about 2.5 *feet* of DNA!

4. Our whole genetic make-up is based on four nitrogen bases in pair bonds together with strands of sugar and phosphates. The DNA structure itself is a 'right-handed' double helix. The base pairs form a ladder and stack one on top of another along the inside of the helix, of which the sugar and phosphates strands make up the 'sides' of the ladder and the 'rungs' make up the base pairs. These are Cytosine, Guanine, Adenine, and Thymine, which do not entirely intermix. Only Cytosine can attach with Guanine, and only Adenine

can attach to Thymine. The mathematician Ian Stewart (1998) reminds us that genes are only a part of the picture with physical, chemical and mathematical processes all combining to make human physiology work – let alone the influences of experience and so on.

5. I often imagine it as rather like old scrambled egg – the texture when it has been on a hot plate for hours!

6. 'Primitive' as in early in evolutionary terms – not in complexity.

7. I will refer to the brain cells as neurons from now on as this is the commonly used terminology and also to avoid confusion.

8. The problems experienced by those with damage to particular areas of the brain can illustrate what we have had to learn or have in place before we can smoothly achieve even such a simple task as 'working backwards'.

9. These three systems are the cortical white matter, the corpus callosum and the 'internal capsule', which links the cortex with the brain stem.

10. Researchers at Penn State University, USA, are currently (2006) collaborating to consider foetal brain and skull development and their relationship.

11. It is also important to point out that most of the research has been done on right-handed people as they comprise a high proportion of the population. Levitin (2006) points out that very recent research suggests that left-handed people may process information in the same way but perhaps not all the time.

12. One of the real problems in neuroscience is the complexity of the terminology and the fact that the same structures can have different names depending on the discipline of the author and, even more confusingly, similar or corresponding structures in animal and bird brains can also have different names!

13. The hypothalamus also plays a role in regulating the conversion of blood glucose to body fat, the timing of 24-hour biological rhythms, emotions and a part in sexual behaviour.

14. Apart from the books/articles referred to, the work of Professor Michael Lamb, Megan Gunnar and Margot Sunderland are all well worth exploring.

15. This emphasis on the processing of fear and anxiety is discussed in more detail in Chapter 5 on emotional well-being.

16. This is a complex and literally far reaching collection of neurons which extends from its base (which connects with the spinal cord) up into the midbrain.

17. The reticular system is said to be involved in arousal, attention, cardiac reflexes, motor functions, regulating awareness and relaying nerve signals to the cerebral cortex and sleep.

18. Enriched environments for rats actually means a replication in the laboratory of what many rats would consider as 'normal' with playmates, things to climb over, run around, feel and so on, that is, a rat-friendly environment!

19. Copyright 2002 Associated Press. All rights reserved.

20. There are also studies of patients who have congenital absence of limbs who nevertheless feel sensations in the absent body part. A study quoted by Gallese (2001) of fMRI imaging of a patient while experiencing sensation in a 'phantom' hand, showed activation in the premotor and posterior parietal cortex, providing further evidence of neural activity without actual limb activity.

21. Schore's work and ideas are based on an exhaustive review of a wide range of studies of which these findings are a summary.

22. Synaptic pruning is the 'cutting back' of connections between neurons, and myelination is the gradual covering of neural axons by a fatty sheath discussed later in this chapter.

23. Myelination is the process whereby the axons or 'senders' of information in the brain neurons are covered by a fatty sheath. See later in this chapter.

24. However, even here, while we have only one heart, it contains two halves each containing two connecting chambers of which each has a specific role.

25. This 'Yakovlevian torque' is more pronounced in males than females – and is found also in fossils and across several non-human species.

26. McManus's book *Right hand, Left hand* (2002) is a fascinating and detailed account of laterality and recommended for further reading.

27. Perhaps unsurprisingly *naming* smells and flavours appears to be the role of the left hemisphere.

28. The importance of the 'midline' is vital in foetal development where the developing cells are guided by a crucial protein 'Sonic hedgehog' (yes, really) which defines the midline so the cells go to the left or right. For example, we have a left and a right arm. Abnormalities closest to this midline produce devastating results, for example, 'Cyclops' where there is a single, malformed eye in the middle of the forehead.

29. This 'error pattern' appears to decrease between the ages of 4 and 6 and disappears by around age 10.

30. Baron-Cohen identifies six types of systems: technical, for example, tools; natural, for example, weather; abstract, for example, mathematics, grammar; social systems, for example, legal, politics; organizable, for example, collections; motor, for example, sports technique, music performance.

31. Some of this will find echoes with readers about some parts of early years provision as well as concerns being expressed currently at National Literacy and Numeracy Strategies being 'pushed down' into the pre-school years in spite of the emphasis on play and the constant hope that play as the key learning medium will be 'pushed up' into Key Stage 1 and ideally even Key Stage 2.

32. These are adapted from Balog (2006).

3 'A word of one's own': the body and the senses

1. The baby has had the experience of tasting the amniotic fluid.
2. There are four basic tastes: sweet, salt, sour and bitter – sweet is at the tip of the tongue and breast milk is very sweet. There is some suggestion that amniotic fluid and breast milk may have a similar taste.
3. Emergence of primitive reflexes is also listed as one of the later changes in dementia by the Alzheimer's Society: www.alzheimers.org.uk/Working_with_people_with_dementia/Primary_care/Dementia_diagnosis_and_management_in_primary_care/dementia.html
4. Adapted from Goddard (2005).
5. The pre-motor area guides movements via information from vision and other sensory feedback systems. The supplementary motor area appears to guide the planning and initiation of movements. The parietal lobe receives 'somatosensory, proprioreceptive, and visual inputs, then uses them to determine such things as the positions of the body and the target in space. It thereby produces internal models of the movement to be made, prior to the involvement of the premotor and motor cortices' (from 'The brain from top to bottom': http://www.thebrain mcgill.ca/flash/a/a_06/a_06_cr/a_06_cr_mou/a_06_cr_mou.html). The parietal lobe also integrates sensory information about the space around us, including knowing where we are in space and also how big or small we are in relation to other objects. For example, people with damage to the right posterior parietal lobe seem to suffer from disruptions in the sense of their own size.
6. This links with the study reported earlier in the mice whose whiskers were trimmed and the area in the cortex responsive to this information also changed.
7. The basal ganglia is a collection of nuclei deep within the cerebral cortex. Typically with anything to do with the brain, the different nuclei all have different names with different but complementary functions. One part of the basal ganglia – the substantia nigra – is particularly well known as it produces a neurotransmitter called dopamine and dysfunction here results in Parkinson's disease.
8. If any of you are familiar with the radio programme *'I am sorry, I haven't a clue'*, one of the games is for the panellists to start singing along with a record, the record stops, they keep singing and the idea is to see how closely they match when the music is brought back in. It is interesting just how close the panellists can be – even if they ostensibly 'can't sing'. It is the cerebellum at work!
9. It is well known that when we actively *think* about a particular action it becomes more difficult – such as when playing tennis or golf etc.
10. The face is the most pressure-sensitive part of the body, which is why we are so aware of a hair on our cheek for example.

11. Note yourself when you next reach for a cup or pen. Watch how your fingers automatically start to shape themselves to adapt to the object you want, and try not to do it. It is almost impossible.
12. This is the extrastriate body area located in the lateral occipitotemporal cortex.
13. A further example is given by Skoyles and Sagan (2002). They describe the case of a woman who had had two strokes and denied that her paralysed limbs were hers. Her most telling comment came when she was shown how her paralysed arm was merged with her shoulder. Her response was 'But my eyes and my feelings don't agree and I must believe my feelings. I know they (her arms) look like mine, but I can feel they are not and I can't believe my eyes'.
14. It has been illustrated that studies have demonstrated a period of 'brain reorganization' around puberty.
15. This is usually called 'motherese' or even 'parentese' but in much current literature it is referred to as Infant Directed Speech or IDS – see Chapter 4.
16. A fifth basic taste has been identified in Japanese psychophysics known as 'umami' which is associated with 'delicious' or 'savouriness' and refers to the taste sensations elicited by monosodium glutamate (Schiffman, 2001). Umami sounds rather like 'yummy' – so I remember this fifth taste as the 'yummy factor'. However, for me it would be elicited more by chocolate!
17. See Ramanchandran and Blakeslee (1999: 67).
18. I can remember people saying that infants were born 'blind' and I am not that old.
19. For the full schematic model of this developmental process see Atkinson (2000: 37).
20. This is known as the 'binding' problem or 'perceptual grouping', that is, how we see complete objects as complete, even when partly hidden, side view, and so on.
21. Linking again with aspects of hemispheric laterality.
22. The work of Paul Ekman is cited in many journal articles and texts because of his seminal work on facial expressions across cultures. His Pictures of Facial Affect-series are also used in many texts and were replicated in the above work by Calder et al.
23. Website for report: www.nature.com/nsu/nsu_pf/040322/040322–13.html
24. Peter Hobson (1997; 2002) includes some very interesting work on children with autism and face-processing.

4 Origins

1. This was a very simple set of questions relating to the basic principles of faith of the Catholic church.

2. As we say in Chapter 2, genes and experience intertwine and recent research is highlighting how experience 'switches' on various genetic behaviours. For example, there is research which has implications regarding the possibility that maternal parenting style can affect the activity of a child's genes.

3. Examples of 'final-state nativists' are Jerry Fodor and Elizabeth Spelke. The latter is particularly concerned with how infants understand objects.

4. It has to be said that while we have variations in our basic heart rate and breathing patterns, they nevertheless fall within a range of 'normal'.

5. Electro-encephelograph.

6. The different brain rhythms are categorized by their frequency range and these are: beta rhythms which are the fastest and signal an active cortex; alpha rhythms associated with a quiet, waking state; theta rhythms occur during some sleep stages and delta rhythms are the slowest and are a 'hallmark of deep sleep'. See also the stages of sleep in note 8.

7. At the time of revision of this chapter, there has also been discussion that lack of sleep is linked with altering hormonal levels in children, influencing dietary habits and linking with the trend towards obesity.

8. Sleep cycles are as follows (from the beginning of sleep – adults): Non-REM stage 1 – alpha rhythms, transitional, brief ('falling asleep'); non-REM stage 2 – slightly deeper and longer (up to around 15 minutes); activation of 'sleep spindles' seen; non-REM stage 3 – eye and body movements absent; slow delta rhythms; non-REM stage 4 – deepest stage of sleep, very slow delta rhythms. As the night progresses, stages 3 and 4 decrease in time and REM sleep increases, with the longest periods of REM sleep occurring in the last third of the night. However, there does seem to be a 'rule' that REM sleep is followed by at least 30 minutes of non-REM sleep before the next cycle of REM sleep can begin. This suggests that the brain activity during REM sleep may in itself require consolidating – to put it parochially, the brain needs a 'breather' after so much intense, self-generated activity.

9. Dahl (1996) goes on to say that by 2 years of age a typically developing child has spent almost 10,000 hours (nearly 14 months) asleep and approximately 7,500 hours (about ten months) awake. In addition, it is within these two years that the brain has reached 90 per cent of its adult size.

10. Difficulties in the disturbed child's sleep patterns is often a key concern for parents but often seems overlooked in the general assessment of the child's abilities, being seen perhaps more as a 'problem' in itself than a factor which is contributing to the ongoing difficulties of the condition itself.

11. People who are congenitally blind have 'auditory dreams' while those who become blind, gradually lose their ability for visual dreams over time.

12. That is, babbling to well-established rhythms of the home language.

13. Babies can also hear other voices but they will be much more muted than that of the mother – even though she too will be somewhat muted because of the barrier of skin and amniotic fluid.

14. When working with adopters, I have noted that even very early adoptions can still bring some problems and I have wondered about it. This may go some way to providing some understanding as to what the disruption in care might mean for the baby. The babies have been building on their initial knowledge of 'mother' at birth (for example, smell, sound).

15. This was shown in a clever experiment where samples of speech had the words 'filtered' so that only the sounds/tones remained. Adults were 'significantly better' at identifying the possible content of these sounds when they had been made in IDS rather than in adult directed speech.

16. I am using mother for clarity – but obviously includes all carers, importantly including fathers.

17. Agency is defined as 'the capacity of an entity to continually sense its environment, make decisions based on that sensory input, and to act out those decisions in its environment without (in general) requiring control by or permission from entities with which the entity is associated. The hallmarks of agency are reactivity (timely response to changes in the environment), goal-oriented (not simply responding to the environment according to a predetermined script), autonomy (having its own agenda), interactive (with its environment and other entities), flexibility, and adaptability'.

18. Which again ties in with the growing awareness of other's intentions, feelings, desires and a growing awareness of own body parts and self-recognition.

19. Theory of mind is also referred to in the literature by some as 'mentalizing'.

20. It is perhaps no coincidence that the ability to pick up small objects using finger and thumb also emerges around this time.

21. It may be useful to speculate what particular 'urge' is working in children with autism when they repeat an action such as spinning the wheels of a car over and over again. Of course, other facets of development are coming into play here, just as when children insist on the repetition of a story, without deviation, which provides a feeling of comfort and security in knowing what comes next.

22. Aspects of memory and types of memory occur in later chapters.

23. The leg or arm was loosely tied to the baby's leg or arm and then attached to the mobile.

5 Emotional and social well-being

1. http:www.geneticfutures.com/cracked/info/sheet2.asp
2. http:www.standards.dfes.gov.uk/primary/
3. Animals appear to be able to experience joy and grief, although some scientists would argue that our interpretation of their behaviours is too 'rich' and we are simply applying human emotions to animal behaviours inappropriately. However, anyone who has seen wildlife programmes either on

television, film or in reality would probably contest this assumption – as would anyone who has a pet!

4. Primary disgust items were those characterized by 'their ability to elicit fear of oral incorporation and their animal origin; and 'complex' disgusts consisted mainly of behaviours or activities that are considered to be socially or morally unacceptable. This latter ties in with the feeling of many researchers on emotions that 'shame' is 'disgust' turned towards the self.

5. In addition we have only three colour receptor cells in the retina and yet human beings are estimated to be able to discern 10 million shades of colour!

6. The PAG is associated with pain pathways and a role in defensive behaviour – as we know distress is 'painful' and we are born with a 'startle' reflex to sudden noises and so on.

7. This is true of babies too, as 'habituation' is one of the key ways in which researchers find out about what interests babies and what they notice. They present babies with various similar stimuli and then will introduce something different or unexpected. If the babies who have started to become blasé about what they are seeing, then become interested, this shows that they have noticed the change.

8. Disturbance in the cerebellum has been put forward as part of the aetiology for autism. This finding provides a further dimension in that the cerebellum may not only influence spatial processing, but also impact on how such sensory information may be experienced subjectively if this structure has a role in emotions.

9. Dr Beatrice Beebe is currently a professor at the New York State Psychiatric Institute. She has researched and written widely on attachment and emotions, also working directly with families.

10. Muir's research highlighted the importance of not just examining infant looking time (a standard method of measuring interest in infants) but also the emotional reaction. Looking times in these infants did not change across study groups and controls – what did change was their response.

11. The brain stem is fully functional at birth.

12. It is interesting that in times of stress, as adults, we turn to those whom we love and trust to support us and we do this to keep at bay the fear and anxiety we may be feeling.

13. Remember that basic reflexes appear to return in the order in which they were inhibited. There is not a 'straight' correspondence between how development occurs and the degeneration in Alzheimer's but there does seem to be a pattern.

14. www.medicalnewstoday.com. 31 July 2006.

15. PowerPoint presentation at Sunderland (UK) conference 2005 on effects of trauma on attachment.

16. They also emphasized that the overall behaviour of the child should be assessed so that differentiation between behaviours that seem 'autistic

specific' do not cloud the picture of the child's potential for forming attachments.

17. The Strange Situation is a process by which the quality of a child's attachment to its carers is assessed. It was devised by Bowlby's colleague, Mary Ainsworth.

18. The Adverse Childhood Experiences (ACE) Study is one of the largest investigations ever conducted on the links between childhood maltreatment and later-life health and well-being. As a collaboration between the Centers for Disease Control and Prevention and Kaiser Permanente's Health Appraisal Clinic in San Diego, Health Maintenance Organization (HMO) members undergoing a comprehensive physical examination provided detailed information about their childhood experience of abuse, neglect and family dysfunction (www.enotalone.come/article/7002).

19. This is not to say that there was no genuine want to give 'of itself' – at least I hope not – but there was always the undercurrent of wanting desperately to 'be good' to counteract how bad I thought I was.

20. This is especially interesting as the capacity to point usually arises between 8 and 12 months but the ability to point to oneself appears to link in with the self-recognition illustrated by knowing one's own image.

21. Such a strategy does not require a knowledge of language because animals can be observed carrying out a similar deceptive strategy – personal observation of family dog wanting to retrieve a favoured 'chew' from our other dog. The first dog barked and made a move as if going to the front door – the other dog dropped the chew and went to follow. The first dog immediately turned and grabbed the chew. Such occurrences also invite questioning as to how, without language, the young child or dog frames their strategy.

6 Learning and development

1. Like Locke, I have found the words 'affect' and 'emotion' to be used interchangeably in the literature, although 'affect' is the preferred term in psychoanalytic literature. Affect generally refers to the displays of feeling, while emotion is generally the subjective experience or labelling of the feeling. In this work, too, the words 'emotion' and 'affect' are sometimes used interchangeably!

2. Perhaps this is not surprising because, while Piaget did propose that 'all behaviour presupposes intelligence and motives in the form of emotions', he nevertheless portrayed the infant as the 'lone scientist' constructing a rather emotionless and asocial world (Kugiumutzakis, 1993), as mentioned in Chapter 4.

3. www.zdmu.ac.ir/learn/msc/ms03.htm

4. There is great controversy between researchers/theorists such as Daniel Stern and Colwyn Trevarthen re the nature of intersubjectivity. While both agree

that there is communication between carer and infant, Stern sees Tre-varthen's primary intersubjectivity as secondary subjectivity with the attri-butes that Trevarthen gives to infants from birth as not occurring until around 8–9 months old. Brief personal discussion with Trevarthen indicates that both are still confirmed in their views!

5.   Schore (1994: 92) also provides potential evidence for the 'cross fertilization' of cognition and affect as his 'practising period' 'overlaps with Piaget's 5th stage of sensorimotor intelligence which signals the cognitive ability to represent the self and external causation ... It is also the same developmental interval in which Bowlby's patterns of attachment behaviours can first be reliably observed and measured' and coincides with Mahler's timing for the 'psychological birth of the human infant'.

6.   This also links with the findings of the firing of 'mirror neurons' (see Chapter 2) which fired when a person or primate watched someone picking up an object but not if a mechanical device picked up the object. This again makes links with the growing 'me/you' process.

7.   Kinsbourne (2002) also discusses patients with transcortical lesions who repeat everything heard but without understanding – a finding, as he points out, notable in early autism.

8.   There is a very funny monologue by the American comedian Bob Newhart who, pretending to be returning a toupee, describes how he needs to buy a cheap replacement as his children love to watch the toupee going round and round in the washing machine! A rotation schema in action!

9.   With grateful thanks to Bedfordshire Educational Psychology and Learning Support Service.

10.   www.zdmu.ac.ir/learn/msc/ms03.htm

11.   Information put together by educational psychology colleagues and given as a presentation.

12.   With thanks to Les Staves, teacher and consultant working with children with profound special needs for this lovely phrase.

13.   This links with the 'chocolate conservation' task above, where children had a sense of correspondence when meaning was clear and obvious – and possibly edible or rewarding in some way!

7 Playing and imagining

1.   This very moving example was video-taped by my friend, colleague and international consultant on special needs, Flo Longhorn, and shown at a training session we were giving for special needs teachers. There was not a dry eye in the room.

8 The role of the adult: to understand the 'heart of the intended communication'

1. *Giving Children the Best Start in Life: Policy and Developments from Birth to the End of the Foundation Stage*. Crown Copyright 2006. This policy is built around the Children's Bill and Every Child Matters which encapsulates the current Labour government's ten-year plan for children's services.

Appendix   Detailed development charts

1. Barna and Legerestee (2005: 53–67).

Bibliography

Acredolo, L. and Goodwyn, S. (1988) Symbolic gesturing in normal infants, *Child Development*, 59: 450–66.

Adams, R.B. Jr and Kleck, R.E. (2003b) Perceived gaze direction and the processing of facial displays of emotion, *Psychological Science*, 14: 644–7.

Adams, R.B. Jr, Gordon, H., Baird, A.A., Ambady, N. and Kleck, R.E. (2003a) Effects of gaze on amygdala sensitivity to anger and fear faces, *Science*, 300: 1536.

Aguiar, A. and Baillargeon, R. (1999) 2.5-month-old infants' reasoning about when objects should and should not be occluded, *Cognitive Psychology*, 39: 116–57.

Ahnert, L., Gunnar, M., Lamb, M. and Barthel, M. (2004) Transition to child care: associations with infant-mother attachment, infant negative emotion and cortisol elevations, *Child Development*, 75(3): 639–50.

Allman, J. (2000) *Evolving Brains*. New York: Scientific American Library.

Anderson, V. (2006) What's the (grey) matter with teens? *Brain in the News*, Dana Foundation, November.

Armony, J.L. and LeDoux, J.E. (2000) How danger is encoded: toward a systems cellular, and computational understanding of cognitive–emotional interactions in fear, in M.S. Gazzaniga (ed.), *The New Cognitive Neurosciences*. Cambridge, MA: MIT Press.

Article ID cogp.1999.0717, available online at http://www.idealibrary.com.

Ashwin, C., Wheelwright, S. and Baron-Cohen, S. (2006) Finding a face in the crowd: testing the anger superiority effect in Asperger Syndrome, *Brain and Cognition*, 61: 78–95.

Associated Press (2003) *Noise Affects Brain Development*. 17 April. www.sciencemag.org.

Athey, C. (1990) *Extending Thought in Young Children: A Parent–Teacher Partnership*. London: Paul Chapman Publishing.

Atkinson, J. (1995) Infant eyes and infant brain: is newborn vision like 'blindsight'? in R. Gregory and P. Heard (eds) *The Artful Brain*. Oxford: Oxford University Press.

Atkinson, J., (2000) *The Developing Visual Brain*. Oxford: Oxford University Press.

Baddeley, A. (1994) *Human Memory Theory and Practice*. Hove: Lawrence Erlbaum Associates.

Baillargeon, R. (2002) The acquisition of physical knowledge in infancy, in U. Goswami (ed.) *Childhood Cognitive Development*. Oxford: Blackwell.

Balog, D. (ed.) (2006) *The Dana Source Book of Brain Science*, 4th edn. Washington: DC: Dana Press. On line version available at www.dana.org.

Bard, K.A. (1998) Social-experiential contributions to imitation and emotion in chimpanzees, in S. Braten (ed.) *Inter-subjective Communication and Emotion in Early Ontogeny*. Cambridge: Cambridge University Press.

Barkley, R.A. (1999) Attention-deficit hyperactivity disorder, in A. Damasio (ed.) *The Scientific American Book of the Brain*. Old Saybrook, CT: Lyons Press.

Barkow, J.H., Cosmides, L. and Tooby, J. (1995) *The Adapted Mind, Evolutionary Psychology and the Generation of Culture*. Oxford: Oxford University Press.

Barna, J. and Legerestee, M. (2005) 9 and 12 month old infants relate emotions to people's actions, *Cognition and Emotion*, 19(1): 53–67.

Baron-Cohen, S. (2002) The extreme male brain theory of autism, *Trends in Cognitive Science*, 6: 248–54.

Baron-Cohen, S. (2003) *The Essential Difference: The Truth about the Male and Female Brain*. New York: Basic Books.

Baron-Cohen, S. (2005) The empathizing system – a revision of the 1994 model of the mindreading system, in B. Ellis and D. Bjorklund (eds) *Origins of the Social Mind*. New York: Guilford Press.

Baron-Cohen, S., Tager-Flusberg, H. and Cohen, D.J. (eds) (2002) *Understanding Other Minds*, 2nd edn. Oxford: Oxford University Press.

Barrett, K.C. and Morgan, G.A. (1995) Continuities and discontinuities in mastery motivation during infancy and toddlerhood, in R.H. MacTurk and G.A. Morgan (eds) *Mastery Motivation: Origins, Conceptualisations and Applications*. Norwood, NJ: Ablex.

Bartzokis, G., Beckson, M., Lu, P.H., et al. (2001) Age related changes in frontal and temporal lobe volumes in men, *Archives of General Psychiatry*, 58: 461–4.

Bauer, P.J. (2002) Early memory development, in U. Goswami (ed.) *Childhood Cognitive Development*. Oxford: Blackwell.

Bauman, M.L., Kemper, T.L., (1994) Neuroanatomic Observations of the Brain in Autism in M.L. Bauman (ed.) *The Neurobiology of Autism*. Baltimore: John Hopkins University Press.

Bear, M.F., Connors, B.W. and Paradiso, M.A. (1996) *Neuroscience, Exploring the Brain*. Baltimore, MD: Williams and Wilkins.

Bednar, J.A. (2003) The role of internally generated neural activity in newborn and infant face preferences, in O. Pascalis and A. Slater (eds) *The Development of Face Processing in Infancy and Early Childhood*. New York: Nova Science.

Bell, S. (2006) Scale in children's experience with the environment, in C. Spencer and M. Blades (eds) *Children and Their Environments*. Cambridge: Cambridge University Press.

Belsky, J. and Nezworski, T. (eds) (1988) *Clinical Implications of Attachment*. Hillsdale, NJ: Lawrence Erlbaum Associates.

Benes, F.M., Turtle, M., Khan, Y. and Farol, P. (1994) Myelination of a key relay zone in the hippocampal formation occurs in the human brain during childhood, adolescence and adulthood, *Archives of General Psychiatry*, 51(6): 477–84.

Benoit, D. (1997) Mothers' representations of their infants assessed prenatally, stability and association with infants' attachment classifications, *Journal of Child Psychology and Psychiatry*, 38(3): 307–13.

Benoit, M., Dygai, I., Migneco, O., et al. (1999) Behavioural and psychological symptoms in Alzheimer's disease, *Dementia and Geriatric Cognitive Disorders*, 10: 511–17.

Berlin, L.J., Ziv, Y., Amaya-Jackson, L. and Greenberg, M.T. (2005) *Enhancing Early Attachments*. New York: Guilford Press.

Berthoz, A. (2000) *The Brain's Sense of Movement*. London: Harvard University Press.

Biddulph, S. (2006) *Raising Babies*. London: HarperCollins.

Birch, E.E. and O'Connor, A.R. (2001) Preterm birth and visual development, *Seminars in Neonatology*, 6: 487–97.

Blair, H.T., Huynh, V.K., Vaz, V., et al. (2005). Unilateral storage of fear memories by the amygdale, *Journal of Neuroscience*, 25(16): 4198–205.

Black, J.E. and Greenough, W.T. (1986) Induction of pattern in neural structure by experience: implications for cognitive development, in M.E. Lamb, A.L. Brown and B. Rogoff (eds), *Advances in Developmental Psychology*. Hillsdale, New Jersey: Lawrence Erlbaum Associates.

Blakemore, S.J. and Frith, U. (2005) *The Learning Brain*. Oxford: Blackwell.

Blakemore, S.J., Frith, C.D. and Wolpert., D.M. (1999) Spatio-temporal prediction modulates the perception of self-produced stimuli, *Journal of Cognitive Neuroscience*, 11: 551–9.

Blakemore, S.J., Wolpert, D.M. and Frith, C.D. (1998) Central cancellation of self-produced tickle sensation, *Nature Neuroscience*, 1: 653–40.

Borland, M., Laybourn, A., Hill, M. and Brown, J. (1998) *Middle Childhood, the Perspectives of Children and Parents*. London: Jessica Kingsley.

Bouchard, T. H, (1995) Longitudinal Studies of Personality and Intelligence in D. H. Saklofske and M. Zeidner(eds), *International Handbook of Personality and Intelligence*. New York: Plenum Press.

Bourgeois, J.-P. (2002) Synaptogenesis in the neocortex of the newborn: the ultimate frontier for individuation? in H. Lagercrantz, M. Hanson, P. Evrard and C. Rodeck (eds) *The Newborn Brain*. Cambridge: Cambridge University Press.

Bowlby, J. ([1969]1991a) *Attachment and Loss, Vol 1, Attachment*. London: Penguin.

Bowlby, J. ([1973]1991b) *Attachment and Loss, Vol 2, Separation*. London: Penguin.

Bowlby, J. ([1980]1991c) *Attachment and Loss, Vol 3, Loss*. London: Penguin.

Bowlby, J. (1988) *A Secure Base*. London: Routledge.

Bowlby, R. (2006) Attachment security and day care. Paper presented at WATch? (What About The Children?) conference, National Council for Voluntary Organisations, London.

Boysen, S.T. (1998) More is less: the elicitation of rule governed resource distribution in chimpanzees, in A. Russon, K.A. Bard and S.T. Parker (eds)

Reaching into Thought, the Minds of the Great Apes. Cambridge: Cambridge University Press.

Bradshaw, J.L. (2001a) Asymmetries in preparation for action in TRENDS, *Cognitive Sciences*, 5(5): 184–5.

Bradshaw, J.L. (2001b) *Developmental Disorders of the Frontostriatal System.* Hove: Psychology Press.

Brainard, M.S. and Doupe, A.J. (2000) Auditory feedback in learning and maintenance of vocal behaviour, *Nature Reviews, Neuroscience*, 1: 31–40.

Brazelton, T.B. and Sparrow, J.D. (2006) *Touchpoints*, 2nd edn. Cambridge, MA: Da Capo Press.

Brothers, L. (1997) *Friday's Footprints.* New York: Oxford University Press.

Brown, J.H., Johnson, M.H., Paterson, S.J., et al. (2003) Spatial representation and attention in toddlers with Williams syndrome and Down syndrome, *Neuropsychologia*, 41: 1037–46.

Bruce, T. (2005) *Learning through Play.* London: Hodder and Stoughton.

Bunge, S.A., Dudukovic, N., Thomason, M.E., Vaidya, C.J. and Gabrieli, J.D.E. (2002) Immature frontal lobe contributions to cognitive control in children, evidence from fMRI, *Neuron*, 33: 301–11.

Budiansky, S. (2003) *The Truth About Dogs.* BCA Books (www.bca.co.uk).

Burnham, D. (1993) Visual recognition of mother by young infants; facilitation by speech, *Perception*, 22: 1133–53.

Butterworth, B. (1999) *The Mathematical Brain.* London: Macmillan.

Cabeza, R. and Nyberg, L. (2000) Imaging cognition II: an empirical review of 275 PET and fMRI studies, *Journal of Cognitive Neuroscience*, 12(1): 1–47.

Calder, A.J., Rowland, D., Young, A.W., et al. (2000) Caricaturing facial expressions, *Cognition*, 76: 105–46.

Calder, A.J., Young, A.W., Perrett, D.I., Etcoff, N.L. and Rowland, D. (1996) Categorical perception of morphed facial expressions, *Visual Cognition*, 3(2): 81–117.

Capps, L., Sigman, M. and Mundy, P. (1994) Attachment security in children with autism, *Development and Psychopathology*, 6(2): 249–61.

Carey, D.P. (1996) Neurophysiology: 'Monkey see, monkey do' cells, *Journal of Current Biology*, 6(9): 1087–8.

Carlowe, J. (2002) Back to the beginning, *Observer Magazine*, 20 January.

Carter, R. (2000) *Mapping the Mind.* London: Phoenix.

Cashon, C.H. and Cohen, L.B. (2003) Construction, deconstruction and reconstruction of infant face perception, in O. Pascalis and A. Slater (eds) *The Development of Face Processing in Infancy and Early Childhood.* New York: Nova Science.

Cassidy, J. (1990) Theoretical and methodological considerations in the study of attachment and self in young children, in M.T. Greenberg, D. Cicchetti and E. Mark Cummings (eds) *Attachment in the Pre-School Years.* London: University of Chicago Press.

Cassidy, J. and Shaver, P.R. (1999) *Handbook of Attachment*. New York: Guilford Press.

Cavanagh, P. (2005) The artist as neuroscientist, *Nature*, 434: 301–7.

Changeux, J.-P. (2002) Reflections on the origins of the human brain, in H. Lagercrantz, M. Hanson, P. Evrard and C.H. Rodeck (eds) *The Newborn Brain*. Cambridge: Cambridge University Press.

Chomsky, N. (1980) *Rules and Representations*. New York: Columbia University Press and Oxford: Blackwell.

Cicchetti, D. and Toth, S.L. (eds) (1994) *Disorders and Dysfunctions of the Self: Rochester Symposium on Developmental Psychopathology*, Vol. 5. New York: University of Rochester Press.

Coldwell, J., Pike, A. and Dunn, J. (2005) Household chaos – links with parenting and child behaviour, *Journal of Child Psychology and Psychiatry*, April: 406–19.

Cole, J. (2001) Empathy needs a face, *Journal of Consciousness Studies*, 8(5–7): 51–69.

Corballis, M.C. (2002) *From Hand to Mouth: The Origins of Language*. Princeton, NJ: Princeton University Press.

Courchesne, E., Carper, R. and Akshoomoff, N. (2003) Evidence of brain overgrowth in the first year of life in autism, *Journal of the American Medical Association (JAMA)*, 290: 337–44.

Courchesne, E., Chisum, H. and Townsend, J (1994) Neural activity-dependent brain changes in development: implications for psychopathology, *Development and Psychopathology*, 6: 697–722.

Cox, M.V. and Howarth, C. (1989) The human figure drawings of normal children and those with severe learning difficulties, *British Journal of Developmental Psychobiology*, 7: 333–9.

Crittenden P.M. (1995) Attachment and risk for psychology: the early years, *Developmental and Behavioural Paediatrics*, 16(3): 512–16.

Crittenden, P.M. (1999) Danger and development: the organisation of self-protective strategies, *Monographs Society Research Child Development*, 64(3): 145–71.

Crittenden, P.M. and Claussen, A.H. (2000) *The Organization of Attachment Relationships, Maturation, Culture and Context*, Cambridge: Cambridge University Press.

Dahl, R.E. (1996) The regulation of sleep and arousal: development and psychopathology, *Development and Psychopathology*, 8: 3–27.

Dalton, P., Doolittle, N. and Breslin, P.A.S. (2002) Gender-specific induction of enhanced sensitivity to odours, *Nature Neuroscience*, 5(3): 199–202.

Damasio, A. (2000) *The Feeling of What Happens*. New York: Harcourt Brace.

Damasio, A. (2003) *Looking for Spinoza*. London: Heinemann.

Damasio, A. (ed.) (1999) *The Scientific American Book of the Brain*. Old Saybrook, CT: Lyons Press.

Damasio, A., Grabowski, T.J., Bechara, et al. (2000) Subcortical and cortical brain activity during the feeling of self-generated emotions, *Nature Neuroscience*, 3(10): 1049–56.

Das, A., Roy, A.B. and Das, P. (2000) Chaos in a three dimensional neural network, *Applied Mathematical Modelling*, 24: 511–22.

Dawson, G. and Fischer, K.W. (1994) *Human Behaviour and the Developing Brain*. New York: Guilford Press.

De Gelder, B., Pourtois, G., Vroomen, J. and Bachoud-Levi, A. (2000) Covert processing of faces in prosopagnosia is restricted to facial expressions, *Brain and Cognition*, 44: 425–44.

De Gelder, B. and Stekelenburg, J.J. (2004) Naso-temporal asymmetry of the N170 for processing faces in normal viewers but not in developmental proso-pagnosia, *Neuroscience Letters*, 376: 40–5.

De Waal, F. (2001) *The Ape and the Sushi Master*. London: Penguin.

De Haan, M., Johnson, M.H., Maurer, D. and Perrett, D.I. (2001) Recognition of individual faces and average face prototype by 1 and 3 month old infants, *Cognitive Development*, 16: 1–20.

De Wolff, M.A. and Van Ijzendoorn, M.H. (1997) Sensitivity and attachment: a meta-analysis on parental antecedents of infant attachment, *Journal of Child Development*, 68(4): 571–91.

Dehaene-Lambertz, G., Dehaene, S. and Hertz-Pannier, L. (2002) Functional neuroimaging of speech perception in infants, *Science*, 298: 2013–15.

DeLoache, J.S. (2002) Early development of the understanding and use of symbolic artefacts, in U. Goswami (ed.) *Childhood Cognitive Development*. Oxford: Blackwell.

Demetriou, A., Shayer, M. and Efklides, A. (1994) *Neo-Piagetian Theories of Cognitive Development*. London: Routledge.

DfES 2002 cited p6.

Department for Education and Skills (DfES) (2003) *Every Child Matters*. Green Paper. London: DfES.

Department for Education and Skills (DfES) (2006) *Early Years Foundation Stage*. Consultation document. London: DfES.

Department for Education and Skills and Qualifications and Curriculum Authority (DfES/QCA) (2000) *Curriculum Guidance for the Foundation Stage*. London: DfES.

Detlef, H. and Sultan, F. (2002) Cerebellar structure and function: making sense of parallel fibres, *Journal of Human Movement Science*, 21: 411–21.

Diamond, A. (2000) Close interrelation of motor development and cognitive development and of the cerebellum and pre-frontal cortex, *Child Development*, 71: 44–56.

Diamond, A. (2006) Bootstrapping conceptual deduction using physical connection: rethinking frontal cortex, *Trends in Cognitive Science*, 10(5): 212–18.

Diamond, A. and Doar, B. (1989) The performance of human infants on a measure of frontal cortex function, the delayed response task, *Developmental Psychobiology*, 22: 271–94.

Diamond, A. and Lee, E.Y. (2000) Inability of five-month old infants to retrieve a contiguous object. A failure of conceptual understand or of control of action? *Child Development*, 71: 1477–94.

Dienes, Z. (1999) Rule learning by seven-month old infants and neural networks, *Science*, 284: 875a.

Dominguez, A. (2002) Researchers watch as brain goes to work, *The Sentinel* (Milwaukee), 23 December.

Donaldson, M. (1978) *Children's Minds*. Sydney: Law Book Company.

Dudai, Y. (2000) The shaky trace, *Nature*, 406: 686–7.

Dudai, Y. (2002) Molecular bases of long-term memories: a question of persistence, *Cognitive Neuroscience*, 12: 211–16.

Dugatkin, L.A. (2002) Prancing primates, turtles with toys, *Cerebrum*, 4(3): 41–52.

Elfer, P., Goldschmied, E. and Selleck, D. (2003) *Key Persons in the Nursery*. London: David Fulton.

Elman, J., Bates, L., Johnson, E.A., et al. (1996) *Rethinking Innateness: A Connectionist Perspective on Development*. Cambridge, MA: MIT Press.

Erikson, E. (1950) *Childhood and Society*. New York: W.W. Norton.

Evans, S. (1987) Psychological risk of day care, *The Washington Post*, 7 November.

Everett, D.L. (2006) Don't count on it, *Scientific American Mind*, October /November: 75–7. http//ling.man.ac.uk/info/staff/DE/DEHome.html.

Farroni, T., Johnson, M.H., Menon, E., et al. (2005) Newborns' preference for face-relevant stimuli – effects of contrast polarity, *Proceedings of the National Academy of Sciences (PNAS)*, 102(47): 17245–50.

Ferrari, P.F., Kohler, E., Fogassi, L. and Gallese, V. (2000) The ability to follow eye gaze and its emergence during development in macaque monkeys, *Proceedings of the National Academy of Sciences (PNAS)*, 97(25): 13997–4002.

Filippi, C.G., Ulug, A.M., Deck, M.D., Zimmerman, R.D. and Heier, L.A. (2002) Developmental delay in children: assessment with proton MR spectroscopy, *American Journal of Neuroradiology*, 23(5): 882–8.

Fischer, K. (2005) Dynamics of cognitive and brain development and education. Paper presented to the launch meeting of the Centre for Neuroscience in Education, Cambridge, UK.

Fisher, E.S. (2006) Tangled webs, tracing the connections between genes and cognition, *Cognition*, 101(2): 270–97.

Fodor, J.A. (1983) *The Modularity of Mind*. Cambridge, MA: MIT Press.

Fonagy, P. and Target, M. (2003) *Psychoanalytic Theories, Perspectives from Developmental Psychopathology*. New York: Brunner-Routledge.

Fonagy, P., Steele, M., Steele, H., Higgitt, A. and Target, M. (1994) Theory and practice of resilience, *Journal of Child Psychology and Psychiatry*, 35: 231–57.

Fosse, R., Stickgold, R. and Hobson, J.A. (2001) Brain-mind states: reciprocal variation in thoughts and hallucinations, *Psychological Science*, 12(1): 30–6.

Fox, E., Russo, R. and Dutton, K. (2002) Attentional bias for threat: evidence for delayed disengagement from emotional faces, *Cognition and Emotion*, 16(3): 355–79.

Fox, N., Calkin, S.D. and Bell, M.A. (1994) *Neural Plasticity and Development in the*

First Two Years of Life: Evidence from Cognitive and Socioemotional Domains of Research. New York: Cambridge University Press.

Freudigman, K.A. and Thoman, E.B. (1993) Infant sleep during the first postnatal day: an opportunity for assessment of vulnerability, *Paediatrics*, 92(3): 373–9.

Frijda, N.H., Antony, S.R. and Bem, S. (eds) (2000) *Emotions and Beliefs.* Cambridge: Cambridge University Press.

Frith, U. and Hill, E. (2004) *Autism, Mind and Brain.* Oxford: Oxford University Press.

Galaburda, A.M. and Duchaine, B.C. (n.d.) *Developmental Disorders in Vision* (review article). www.faceblind.org/people/galaburda&duchaine03neur-olclinics.pdf (accessed 25 May 2007).

Gallese, V. (1999) From grasping to language; mirror neurons and the origin of social communication, in S. Sameroff, A. Kazniak and D. Chalmers (eds) *Towards a Science of Consciousness.* Cambridge, MA: MIT Press.

Gallese, V. (2001) The 'shared manifold' hypothesis – from mirror neurons to empathy, *Journal of Consciousness Studies*, 8(5–7): 33–50.

Gallese, V., Fadiga, L., Fogassi, L. and Rizzolatti, G. (1996) Action recognition in the premotor cortex, *Brain*, 119: 593–609.

Ganel, T. and Goodale, M. (2003) Visual control of action but not perception requires analytical processing of object shape, *Nature*, 426: 664–7.

Ganel, T., Goshen-Gottstein, Y. and Goodale, M. (2005) Interactions between the processing of gaze direction and facial expression, *Vision Research*, 45(9): 1191–200.

Garvey, C. (1991) *Play.* Glasgow: HarperCollins.

Gattis, M., Bekkering, H. and Wohlschlager, A. (2002) Goal-directed imitation, in A. Meltzoff and W. Prinz (eds) *The Imitative Mind.* Cambridge, Cambridge University Press.

Gazzaniga, M.S. (1999) The split brain revisited, in A. Damasio (ed.) *The Scientific American Book of the Brain.* Old Saybrook, CT: Globe Pequot Press.

Gergely, G. (2002) The development of understanding self and agency, in U. Goswami (ed.) *Handbook of Child Cognitive Development.* Oxford: Blackwell.

Gergely, G. and Watson, J.S. (1999) Infant's sensitivity to imperfect contingency in social interaction, in P. Rochat (ed.) *Early Social Cognition.* Hillsdale, NJ: Lawrence Erlbaum Associates.

Gerhardt, S. (2005) *Why Love Matters.* Hove: Routledge.

Ghim, H. and Eimas, P.D. (1988) Global and local processing by 3- and 4-month old infants, *Perception and Psychophysics*, 43: 165–71.

Giedd, J.N., Blumenthal, J., Jeffries, N.O., et al. (1999) Brain development during childhood and adolescence: a longitudinal MRI study, *Nature Neuroscience*, 2(10): 861–3.

Giles, J. (2004) Smiles reveal secrets to security cameras, *Nature*, 22 March.

Giving Children the Best Start in Life: Policy and Developments from Birth to the End of the Foundation Stage (2006). Crown copyright.

Glaser 2005 cited p113/116.

Goddard, S. (2005) *Reflexes, Learning and Behaviour*, 2nd edn. Eugene, OR: Fern Ridge Press.

Goldberg, E. (2001) *The Executive Brain*. Oxford: Oxford University Press.

Goldschmied, E. and Jackson, S. (1999) *People under Three*. New York: Routledge.

Gopnik, A. and Meltzoff, A. (1997) *Words, Thoughts and Theories*. Cambridge, MA: MIT Press.

Gopnik, A., Meltzoff, A. and Kuhl, P. (1999) *How Babies Think*. London: Weidenfeld and Nicolson.

Gottlieb, G. (1991) Experiential canalisation of behavioural development: theory, *Developmental Psychology*, 27: 4–13.

Grandin, T. and Johnson, C. (2005) *Animals in Translation*. London: Bloomsbury.

Graves, L., Pack, A. and Abel, T. (2001) Sleep and memory: a molecular perspective, *Trends in Neurosciences*, 24(4): 237–43.

Greenfield, S. (1997) *The Human Brain*. London: Weidenfeld and Nicolson.

Greenfield, S. (2000) *The Private Life of the Brain*. London: Penguin Press.

Greenspan, S.I. (1997) *Developmentally Based Psychotherapy*. Madison, CT: International Universities Press.

Greenspan, S.I. (2004) *The First Idea*. Cambridge, MA: DaCapo Press.

Grön, G., Wunderlich, A.P., Spitzer, M., Tomczak, R. and Riepe, M.W. (2000) Brain activation during human navigation: gender-different neural networks as substrate of performance, *Nature Neuroscience*, 3(4): 404–6.

Grossberg, S., Hopkins, B. and Johnson, S. (eds) (2001) *Annual Advances in Infancy Research*. Norwood, NJ: Ablex Press.

Grossman, K.E. and Grossman, K. (1995) Attachment quality as an organizer of emotional and behavioural responses in a longitudinal perspective, in C. Murray Parkes, J. Stevenson-Hinde and P. Maris (eds) *Attachment across the Life Cycle*. London: Routledge.

Gross-Tsur, V., Ben-Bashat, D., Shalev, R.S., Levav, M. and Ben Sira, L. (2006) Evidence of a developmental cerebello-cerebral disorder, *Neuropsychologia*, 44(12): 2569–72.

Güntürkün, O. (2003) Adult persistence of head-turning asymmetry, *Nature*, 421(6924): 711.

Gur, R.C. (2005) Brain maturation and its relevance to understanding criminal culpability of juveniles, *Current Psychiatry Reports*, 7(4): 292–6.

Hadders-Algra, M. and Forssberg, H. (2002) Development of motor functions in health and disease, in H. Lagercrantz, M. Hanson, P. Evrard and C.H. Rodeck (eds) *The Newborn Brain*. Cambridge: Cambridge University Press.

Hallett, M., Lebiedowska, M.K., Thomas, S.L., et al. (1993) Locomotion of autistic adults, *Archives of Neurology*, 50: 1304–8.

Harasty, J., Seldon, H.L., Chan, P., Halliday, G. and Harding, A. (2003) The left human speech-processing cortex is thinner but longer than the right, *Laterality: Asymmetries of Body, Brain, and Cognition*, 8(3): 247–60.

Hari, R. and Renvall, H. (2001) Impaired processing of rapid stimulus sequences in dyslexia, *Trends in Cognitive Sciences*, 5(12): 525–32.

Harris, P.L. (2000) *The Work of the Imagination*. Oxford: Blackwell.

Hashimoto, T., Tayama, M., Murahawa, K., Miyazaki, M., Harada, M. and Kuroda, Y. (1995) Development of the Brainstem and Cerebellum in Autistic Patients, *Journal of Autism and Development Disorders*, 25(1): 1–18.

Haxby, J.V., Hoffman, E.A. and Gobbini, M.I. (2002) Human neural systems for face recognition and social communication, *Biological Psychiatry*, 51(1): 59–67.

Hernandez-Reif, M., Field, T., Diego, M., Vera, Y. and Pickens, J. (2006) Happy faces are habituated more slowly by infants of depressed mothers, *Infant Behaviour and Development*, 29: 131–5.

Hobson, J.A. (2002) *Dreaming*. Oxford: Oxford University Press.

Hobson, J.A., Pace-Schott, E.F. and Stickgold, R. (2000) Dreaming and the brain, *Journal of Behavioural and Brain Sciences*, 23: 793–843.

Hobson, P. (1997) *Autism and the Development of Mind*. Hove: Psychology Press.

Hobson, P. (2002) *The Cradle of Thought*. London: Macmillan.

Hobson, R.P. and Lee, A. (1999) Imitation and identification in autism, *Journal of Child Psychology and Psychiatry*, 40(4): 649–59.

Hobson, R.P., Lee, A. and Brown, R. (1999) Autism and congenital blindness, *Journal of Autism and Developmental Disorders*, 29(1): 45–56.

Holland, P. (2003) *We Don't Play with Guns Here*. Maidenhead: Open University Press.

Hood, B. (2006) The intuitive magician: cerebrum. Paper presented at the Dana Forum on Brain Science, July.

Hood, B.M., Macrae, N., Cole-Davies, V. and Dias, M. (2003) Eye remember you: the effects of gaze direction on face recognition in children and adults, *Developmental Science*, 6(1): 69–73.

Hunnius, S., Geuze, R.H. and van Geert, P. (2006) Associations between the developmental trajectories of visual scanning and disengagement of attention in infants, *Infant Behaviour and Development*, 29: 108–25.

Hurst, V. and Joseph, J. (1998) *Supporting Early Learning*. Buckingham: Open University Press.

Huttenlocher, P.R. (1994) Synaptogenesis in the human cerebral cortex, in G. Dawson and K.W. Fischer (eds) *Human Behaviour and the Developing Brain*. New York: Guilford Press.

Iwaniuk, A.N., Nelson, J.E. and Pellis, S.M. (2001) Do big-brained animals play more? Comparative analyses of play and relative brain size in mammals, *Journal of Comparative Psychology*, 115: 29–41.

Izard, C.E. (1971) *The Face of Emotion*. New York: Appleton-Century-Crofts.

Jeannerod, M. (2004) Visual and action cues contribute to self–other distinction, *Nature Neuroscience*, 7(5): 422–3.

Johnson, M.A. and Farroni, T. (2003) Perceiving and acting on the eyes: the development and neural basis of eye gaze perception, in O. Pascalis and A.

Slater (eds) *The Development of Face Processing in Infancy and Early Childhood.* New York: Nova Science.

Johnson, M.H. (2001) Functional brain development in humans, *Nature Reviews Neuroscience,* 2(7): 475–83.

Johnson, S., Slaughter, V. and Carey, S. (1998) Whose gaze will infants follow? The elicitation of gaze-following in 12-month olds, *Developmental Science,* 1(2): 233–8.

Johnston, M.V. (1995) Neurotransmitters and vulnerability of the developing brain, *Brain and Development,* 17(5): 301–6.

Jones, T., Klintsova, A.Y., Kilman, V.L., Sirevaag, A.M. and Greenough, W.T. (1997) Induction of multiple synapses by experience in the visual cortex of adult rats, *Neurology of Learning and Memory,* 68: 13–20 (Article No. NL973774).

Juhasz, C., Chugani, H.T., Muzik, O. and Chugani, D.C. (2002) Hypotheses from functional neuroimaging studies, *International Review of Neurobiology,* 49: 37–55.

Kandel, E.R. (2006) Cerebrum. Paper presented at the Dana Forum on Brain Science, March.

Kandel, E.R., Schwartz, J.H. and Jessell, T.M. (2000) *Principles of Neural Science,* 3rd edn. New York: McGraw-Hill.

Kansaku, K., Yamaura, A. and Kitazawa, S. (2000) Sex differences in lateralization revealed in the posterior language areas, *Journal Cerebral Cortex,* 10(9): 866–72.

Kaplan-Solms, K. and Solms, M. (2000) *Clinical Studies in Neuro-psychoanalysis.* London: Karnac Books.

Karen, R. (1998) *Becoming Attached.* Oxford: Oxford University Press.

Keshavan, M.S., Genovese, C.R., Eddy, W.F. and Sweeney, J.A. (2001) Maturation of widely distributed brain function subserves cognitive development, *NeuroImage,* 13: 786–93.

Kinsbourne, M. (2002) The role of imitation in body ownership and mental growth, in A.N. Meltzoff and W. Prinz (eds) *The Imitative Mind.* Cambridge: Cambridge University Press.

Klin, A., Jones, W., Schultz, R. and Volkmar, F. (2004) The enactive mind, or from actions to cognition: lessons from autism, in U. Frith and E. Hill (eds) *Autism, Mind and Brain.* Oxford: Oxford University Press.

Kogan, N. and Carter, A.S. (1996) Mother–infant reengagement following the still face: the role of maternal emotional availability in infant affect regulation, *Journal of Infant Behaviour and Development,* 19: 359–70.

Kokkinaki, T. and Kugiumutzakis, G. (2000) Basic aspects of vocal imitation in infant–parent interaction during the first 6 months, *Journal of Reproductive and Infant Psychology,* 18(3): 173–87.

Kugiumutzakis, G. (1993) Intersubjective vocal imitation in early mother–infant interaction, in J. Nadel and L. Camaioni (eds) *New Perspectives in Early Communicative Development.* London: Routledge.

Labensohn, D., with Perkins, E. (1972) Look for these signs of speech and hearing problems. National Network of Child Care, FCC 565. www.canr.uconn.edu/ces/child/newsarticles/FCC565.html (accessed 28 May 2007).

Laureys, S., Peigneux, P., Phillips, C., et al. (2001) Experience-dependent changes in cerebral functional connectivity during human rapid-eye movement sleep, *Neuroscience*, 105(3): 521–5.

LeDoux, J. (1998) *The Emotional Brain*. London: Weidenfeld and Nicolson.

LeDoux, J. (2002) *The Synaptic Self.* New York: Viking Press.

LeGrand, R., Mondloch, C.J., Maurer, D. and Brent H.P. (2003) Expert face processing requires visual input to the right hemisphere during infancy, *Nature Neuroscience*, 6(10): 1108–12.

Lerner, R.M. (1998) Theories of Human Development: contemporary perspectives, in W. Damon and R.M. Lerner (eds) *Handbook of Child Psychology*, 1. USA: John Wiley & Sons Inc.

Leslie, A. (1987) Pretence and representation, the origins of 'theory of mind', *Psychological Review*, 94(4): 412–46.

Levitin, D.J. (2006) *This Is Your Brain on Music*. New York: Penguin.

Lewis, M., Allessandri, S. and Sullivan, M. (1990) Expectancy, loss of control and anger in young infants, *Developmental Psychology*, 25: 745–51.

Lewis, T.L. and Maurer, D. (2005) Multiple sensitive periods in human visual development. www.interscience.wiley.com.

Lewis-Williams and Pearce 2005 cited p.17.

Li, X.F., Stutzmann, G.E. and LeDoux, J. (1996) Convergent but temporally separated inputs to lateral amygdala neurons from the auditory thalamus and auditory cortex use different postsynaptic receptors, *Learning & Memory*, 3: 229–42.

Liben, L.S. (2002) Spatial development in childhood, in U. Goswami (ed.) *Childhood Cognitive Development*. Oxford: Blackwell.

Lillard, A. (2002) Pretend play and cognitive development, in U. Goswami (ed.) *Childhood Cognitive Development*. Oxford: Blackwell.

Lipton, J.S. and Spelke, E.S. (2003) Origins of number sense: large-number discrimination in human infants, *Psychological Science*, 14(5): 396–401.

Lis, S. (2000) Characteristics of attachment behaviour in institution-reared children, in P.M. Crittenden and A.H. Claussen (eds) *The Organization of Attachment Relationships, Maturation, Culture and Context*. Cambridge: Cambridge University Press.

Liu, J., Harris, A. and Kanwisher, N. (2002) Stages of processing in face perception, an MEG study, *Nature Neuroscience*, 5(9): 910–16.

Livesey, F.J. and Cepko, C.L. (2001) Vertebrate neural cell-fate determination: lessons from the retina, *Nature Reviews Neuroscience*, 2: 109–18.

Locke, J. (1995) *The Child's Path to Spoken Language*. Cambridge, MA: Harvard University Press.

Losonczy, M.E. and Brandt, L.J. (2002) Gender differences in emotional expression. Poster presentation at the World Association for Infant Mental Health's 8th World Congress, Amsterdam, July.

Luna, B., Thulborn, K.R., Munoz, D.P., et al. (2001) 786–93.

MacTurk R.H. and Morgan, J.A. (1995). *Advances in Applied Developmental Psychology: Mastery Motivation – Origins, Conceptualizations, and Applications.* Norwood, NJ: Ablex.

Main, M. and Solomon, J. (1990) Procedures for identifying infants as disorganized/disorientated during the Ainsworth Strange Situation in study of attachment and self in young children, in M.T. Greenberg, D. Cicchetti and E. Mark Cummings (eds) *Attachment in the Pre-School Years.* London: University of Chicago Press.

Maljkovic, V. and Martini, P. (2005) Short-term memory for scenes with affective content, *Journal of Vision,* 5: 215–29.

Mandler, J.M. (2000) *The Foundations of Mind.* New York: Oxford University Press.

Manning Morton, J. and Thorp, M. (2001) *Key Times – A Framework for Developing High Quality Provision for Children Under Three Years Old.* London: Camden Early Years Under Threes Development Group and the University of North London.

Markov, D. and Goldman, M. (2006) Normal sleep and circadian rhythms: neurobiologic mechanisms underlying sleep and wakefulness, *Psychiatric Clinics of North American,* 29(4): 841–53.

Martin, J.H. and Jessell, T.M. (2000) Development as a guide to the regional anatomy of the brain, *Principles of Neural Science,* 3rd edn. New York: McGraw-Hill.

Martin, K.C. and Kandel E.R. (1996) Cell adhesion molecules, CREB, and the formation of new synaptic connections, *Neuron,* 17(4): 567–70.

Marzillier, S.L. and Davey, G.C.L. (2004) The emotional profiling of disgust-eliciting stimuli: evidence for primary and complex disgust, *Cognition and Emotion,* 18(3): 313–36.

Maslow, A. H. (1943) A theory of human motivation *Psychological Review,* 50(4): 370–396.

Matsuzawa, T. (2004) Imitation in neonatal chimpanzees (*Pan troglodytes*), *Developmental Science,* 7(4): 437–42.

Matthews, J. (1999) *Helping Children to Draw and Paint in Early Childhood.* London: Hodder and Stoughton.

McGraw, M.B. ([1943]1989) *The Neuromuscular Maturation of the Human Infant.* Classics in Developmental Medicine Series, no.4. London: MacKeith Press.

McManus, C. (2002) *Right Hand, Left Hand.* London: Weidenfeld and Nicolson.

McNally, R.J. (1998) Information processing abnormalities in anxiety disorders: implications for cognitive neuroscience, *Cognition and Emotion,* 12(3): 479–95.

Meade, A. and Cubey, P. (1996) *Thinking Children.* New Zealand Council for Educational Research, PO Box 3237, Wellington, New Zealand.

Meltzoff, A. (1995) Understanding the intentions of others: re-enactment of intended acts by 18-month old children, *Developmental Psychology*, 31: 838–50.

Meltzoff, A. (2002a) Elements of a developmental theory of imitation, in A. Meltzoff and W. Prinz (eds) *The Imitative Mind*. Cambridge: Cambridge University Press.

Meltzoff, A.N. (1999) Origins of theory of mind, cognition, and communication, *Journal of Communication Disorders*, 32: 251–69.

Meltzoff, A.N. (2002b) Imitation as a mechanism of social cognition: origins of empathy, theory of mind and the representation of action, in U. Goswami (ed.) *Handbook of Childhood Cognitive Development*. Oxford: Blackwell.

Mills, D. and Mills, C. (2000) *Education and Employment – First Report*. Report to the Select Committee on Education and Employment, pp. 75–90. London: The Stationery Office.

Minard, K.L., Freudigman, K. and Thoman, E.B. (1999) Sleep rhythmicity in infants: index of stress or maturation, *Behavioural Processes*, 47: 189–203.

Mithen, S. (2006) *The Singing Neanderthals*. London: Weidenfeld and Nicolson.

Moore, M.S. (1990) Understanding children's drawings: developmental and emotional indicators in children human figure drawings, *Educational Therapy*, 3(2).

Morris, J.S., Frith, C.D., Perrett, D.I., et al. (1996) A differential neural response in the human amygdala to fearful and happy facial expressions, *Nature*, 383: 812–15.

Muir, D., Lee, K., Hains, C. and Hains, S. (2005) Infant perception and production of emotions during face to face interactions with live and 'virtual' adults, in N. Nadel and D. Muir (eds) *Emotional Development*. Oxford: Oxford University Press.

Muller, H.J., Elliott, M.A., Herrmann, C.S. and Mecklinger, A. (2001) Neural binding in space and time: an introduction, *Journal of Visual Cognition*, 8(3/4/5): 273–85.

Murray, L. and Trevarthen, C. (1985) Emotional regulation of interactions between two-month-olds and their mothers, in T.M. Field and N.A. Fox (eds) *Social Perception in Infants*. Norwood, NJ: Ablex.

Myowa-Yamakoshi, M., Tomonaga, M., Tanaka, M. and Nadel, J. (2002) Imitation and imitation recognition: functional use in pre-verbal infants and nonverbal children with autism, in A. Meltzoff and W. Prinz (eds) *The Imitative Mind*. Cambridge: Cambridge University Press.

Nadel, J. (2002) Imitation and imitation recognition. Functional use in pre-verbal infants and nonverbal children with autism, in A. Meltzoff and W. Prinz (eds) *The Imitative Mind*. Cambridge: Cambridge University Press.

Neuner, F. and Schweinberger, S.R. (2000) Neuropsychological impairment in the recognition of faces, voices and personal names, *Brain Cognition*, 44(3): 342–66.

Neven, R.S. (1997) *Emotional Milestones from Birth to Adulthood: A Psychodynamic Approach*. London: Jessica Kingsley.

Newberger, E.H. (1999) *The Men They Will Become*. Cambridge, MA: Perseus Books.

Newman, C., Atkinson, J. and Braddick, O. (2001) The development of reaching and looking preferences in infants to objects of different sizes, *Developmental Psychology*, 37: 1–12.

Nielsen, L. (2003) *Spatial Relations in Congenitally Blind Infants*. National Institute for Blind and Partially Sighted Children and Youth, Kystvejen 112, 4400 Kalundborg, Denmark.

Nishida, T. (2004) Lack of 'group play' in wild chimpanzees, *Pan Africa News*, 11(1).

Nix, R.L., Pinderhughes, E.E., Dodge, K.A., et al. (1997) Fear conditioning induces associative long term potentiation in the amygdala, *Nature*, 390: 604–7.

Nussbaum, M.C. (2001) *Upheavals of Thought – the Intelligence of Emotions*. Cambridge: Cambridge University Press.

Office for Standards in Education (Ofsted) (2005) Early Doors – the first hour in day nurseries, December. www.ofsted.gov.uk.

Orr, R. (2003) *My Right to Play*. Maidenhead: Open University Press.

Oster, H. (2005) The repertoire of infant facial expressions: an ontogenetic perspective, in J. Nadel and D. Muir (eds) *Emotional Development*. Oxford: Oxford University Press.

Ozonoff, A., Pennington, B.F. and Rogers, S. (1991) Executive function deficits in high-functioning autistic individuals: relationship to a theory of mind, *Journal of Child Psychology and Psychiatry*, 32: 1081–105.

Palmer, J.A. (ed.) (2003) *Fifty Modern Thinkers on Education: From Piaget to the Present*. London: Routledge.

Panksepp, J. (1998) *Affective Neuroscience*. Oxford: Oxford University Press.

Panksepp, J. and Panksepp, J.B. (2000) The seven sins of evolutionary psychology, *Evolution and Cognition*, 6(2): 108–30.

Panksepp, J. and Smith-Pasqualini, M. (2005) The search for the fundamental brain/mind sources of affective experience, in J. Nadel and D. Muir (eds) *Emotional Development*. Oxford: Oxford University Press.

Papousek, M. and Papousek, H. (1989) Forms and functions of vocal matching in interactions between mothers and their pre-canonical infants, *First Language*, 9: 137–58.

Pascalis, O. and Slater, A. (eds) (2003) *The Development of Face Processing in Infancy and Early Childhood*. New York: Nova Science.

Pascalis, O., de Schonen, S., Morton, J., Deruelle, C. and Fabre-Grenet (1995) Mother's face recognition by neonates: a replication and extension, *Infant Behaviour and Development*, 18: 79–85.

Paterson, S.J., Heim, S., Friedman, J., Choudhury, N. and Benasich, A.A. (2006) Development of structure and function in the infant brain: implications for cognition, language and social behaviour, *Neuroscience and Behavioural Reviews*, 30(8): 1087–105.

Patterson, K. and Lambon Ralph, M.A. (1999) Selective disorders of reading? *Journal of Current Opinion in Neurobiology*, 9: 235–9.

Paus, T., Zijdenbos, A., Worsley, K., et al. (1999) Structural maturation of neural pathways in children and adolescents: in vivo study, *Science*, 283: 1908–11.

Penn, A.A. and Shatz, C.J. (2002) Activity-dependent brain development, in H. Lagercrantz, M. Hanson, P. Evrard and C. Rodeck (eds) *The Newborn Brain*. Cambridge: Cambridge University Press.

Perner, J. and Lang, B. (1999) Development of theory of mind and cognitive control, *Trends in Cognitive Science*, 3: 337–44.

Perry, B.D. and Pollard, R. (1998) Homeostasis, stress, trauma and adaptation: a neurodevelopmental view of childhood trauma, *Child and Adolescent Psychiatric Clinics of North America*, 7(1): 33–51.

Phan, M.L., Pytte, C.L. and Vicario, D.S. (2006) Early auditory experience generates long-lasting memories that may subserve vocal learning in songbirds, *Proceedings of the National Academy of Sciences (PNAS)*, 103(4): 1088–93.

Phillips, K. and Cupchik, G.C. (2004) Scented memories of literature, *Memory*, 12(3): 366–75.

Piaget, J. ([1959]2002) *The Language and Thought of the Child*. London: Routledge Classics.

Pinel, J.P.J. and Edwards, M. (1998) *A Colourful Introduction to the Anatomy of the Human Brain*. Boston, MA: Allyn and Bacon.

Postal, K.S. (2005) The mirror sign delusional misidentification symptom, in T.E. Feinberg and J.P. Keenan (eds) *The Lost Self, Pathologies in Brain and Identity*. Oxford: Oxford University Press.

Quartz, S.R. and Sejnowski, T.J. (2002) *Liars, Lovers and Heroes*. New York: HarperCollins.

Quinn, P.C. (2002) Early categorization, a new synthesis, in U. Goswami (ed.) *Childhood Cognitive Development*. Oxford: Blackwell.

Ramachandran, V. (2003) *The Emerging Mind*. London: Profile Books.

Ramachandran, V.S. and Blakeslee, S. (1999) *Phantoms in the Brain*. London: Fourth Estate.

Rauch, S.L., Whalen, P.J., Shin, L.M., et al. (2000) Exaggerated amygdala response to marked facial stimuli in posttraumatic stress disorder: a functional MRI study, *Journal of Biological Psychiatry*, 47: 769–76.

Reddy, V. (2005) Feeling shy and showing off: self-conscious emotions must regulate self awareness, in J. Nadel and D. Muir (eds) *Emotional Development*. Oxford: Oxford University Press.

Reid, S. (1997) The development of autistic defences in an infant: the use of a single case study for research, *International Journal of Infant Observation*, 1(1): 51–79.

Repert, S.M. and Weaver, D.R. (2002) Coordination of circadian timing in mammals, *Nature*, 418: 935–41.

Richardson, K. and Sheldon, S. (eds) (1989) *Cognitive Development to Adolescence*. Hove: Lawrence Erlbaum.

Rizzolatti, G., Fadiga, L., Fogassi, L. and Gallese, V. (2002) From mirror neurons to imitation: facts and speculation, in A. Meltzoff and W. Prinz (eds) *The Imitative Mind*. Cambridge: Cambridge University Press.

Rizzolatti, G., Fadiga, L., Gallese, V. and Fogassi, L. (1996) Premotor cortex and the recognition of motor actions, *Cognitive Brain Research*, 3: 131–41.

Roberts, D. (ed.) (2002) *Signals and Perception*. Basingstoke: Palgrave Macmillan.

Roberts-Holmes, G. (2001) The whole family, *Co-ordinate* (journal of the National Early Years Network), 80, Spring.

Robinson, M. (1997) Pretend play, a study of the content and characteristics of pretend play in a group of pre-school children at a family centre. Unpublished master's dissertation, Tavistock and Portman NHS Trust.

Robinson, M. (2003) *From Birth to One*. Buckingham: Open University Press.

Russon, A.E., Bard, K.A. and Taylor Parker, S. (eds) (1998) *Reaching into Thought: The Minds of the Great Apes*. Cambridge: Cambridge University Press.

Rustin, M. (1989) Introduction, in L. Miller, Michael Rustin, Margaret Rustin and J. Shuttleworth (eds) *Closely Observed Infants*. London: Duckworth.

Rutherford, M.A. (2001) What's new in neuroimaging? Magnetic resonance imaging of the immature brain, *European Journal of Paediatric Neurology*, 6: 5–13.

Sadeh, A., Dark, I. and Vohr, B.R. (1996) Newborns' sleep–wake patterns: the role of maternal, delivery and infant factors, *Early Human Development*, 44: 113–26.

Salisbury, A.L., Hunsley, M.S. and Thoman, E.B. (1998) State organization in excessively crying infants, *Journal Infant Behaviour and Development*, 21: 667.

Sax, L. (2001) Reclaiming kindergarten: making kindergarten less harmful to boys, *Psychology of Men and Masculinity*, 2(1): 3–12.

Schiffman, H.R. (2001) *Sensation and Perception*, 5th edn. New York: John Wiley.

Schore, A. (1994) *Affect Regulation and the Origin of the Self*. Mahwah, NJ: Lawrence Erlbaum Associates.

Schore, A.N. (2001) The effects of a secure attachment relationship on right brain development, affect regulation, and infant mental health, *Infant Mental Health Journal*, 22: 7–66.

Schousboe, A. and Waagepetersen, H.S. (2002) Glial cell biology, in H. Lagercrantz, M. Hanson, P. Evrard and C.H. Rodeck (eds) *The Newborn Brain*. Cambridge: Cambridge University Press.

Scottish Executive (2005) *Birth to Three, Supporting our Youngest Children* (ISBN 1 84399 061 X). Edinburgh: Scottish Executive.

Shah, A. and Frith, U. (1993) Why do autistic individuals show superior performance on the block design task? *Journal of Child Psychology and Psychiatry*, 34(8): 1351–65.

Sheets-Johnstone, M. (1999) *The Primacy of Movement*. Amsterdam and Philadelphia, PA: John Benjamins.

Sherry, D.F. (2000) What sex differences in spatial ability tell us about the evolution of cognition, in M. Gazzanige (ed.) *The New Cognitive Neurosciences*, 2nd edn. Cambridge, MA: MIT Press.

Sigman, M. and Capps, L. (1997) *Children with Autism: A Developmental Perspective.* Cambridge, MA: Harvard University Press.

Singer, D.G. and Singer, J.L. (1992) *The House of Make Believe.* Cambridge, MA: Harvard University Press.

Sinha, P. (2000) The perception of gaze direction, *Perception,* 29: 1005–8.

Siraj-Blatchford, I. and Clarke, P. (2000) *Supporting Identity, Diversity and Language in the Early Years.* Buckingham: Open University Press.

Skoyles, J.R. and Sagan, D. (2002) *Up from Dragons – the Evolution of Human Intelligence.* London: McGraw-Hill.

Slotnick, B. (2001) Animal cognition and the rat olfactory system, *Trends in Cognitive Science,* 5(5): 216–22.

Smith, A. (2005) *The Brain's Behind It.* Norwalk, CT: Crown House.

Solms, M. and Turnbull, O. (2002) *The Brain and the Inner World.* London: Karnac Books.

Soussignan, R. and Schaal, B. (2005) Emotional processes in human newborns: a functionalist perspective, in J. Nadel and D. Muir (eds) *Emotional Development.* Oxford: Oxford University Press.

Sowell, E.R., Thompson, P.M., Mattson, S.N., et al. (2003) Regional brain shape abnormalities persist into adolescence after heavy prenatal alcohol exposure, *Cerebral Cortex,* 12(8): 857–65.

Sowell, E.R., Trauner, D.A., Gamst, A. and Jernigan, T.L. (2002) Development of cortical and subcortical brain structures in childhood and adolescence: a structural MRI study, *Developmental Medicine and Child Neurology,* 44: 4–16.

Spelke, E.S. and Newport, E. (1998) Nativism, empiricism, and the development of knowledge, in R. Lerner (ed.), *Handbook of Child Psychology,* 5th edn, Vol. 1, *Theoretical Models of Human Development.* New York: John Wiley.

Spencer, C. (2004) Place attachment, place identity and the development of the child's self-identity: searching the literature to develop a hypothesis, in S. Catling and F. Martin (eds) *Researching Primary Geography.* Special publication no.1, August, London Register of Research.

Spencer, J., O'Brien, J., Riggs, K., et al. (2000) Motion processing in autism: evidence for a dorsal stream deficiency, *NeuroReport,* 11(12): 2765–7.

Spiers, H.J., Burgess, N., Hartley, T., Vargha-Khadem, F. and O'Keefe, J. (2001) Bilateral hippocampal pathology impairs topographical and episodic memory but not visual pattern matching, *Hippocampus,* 11: 715–25.

Springer, S.P. and Deutsch, G. (1998) *Left Brain, Right Brain – Perspectives from Cognitive Neuroscience,* 5th edn., New York: Freeman.

Sroufe, L.A. (1995) *Emotional Development: The Organization of Emotional Life in the Early Years.* Cambridge and New York: Cambridge University Press.

Sroufe, L.A. (1997) Psychopathology as an outcome of development, *Development and Psychopathology,* (9): 251–68.

Stern, D. (1985) *The Interpersonal World of the Infant.* New York: Basic Books.

Stewart, I. (1998) *Life's Other Secret*. London: Penguin Books.

Strauss, M.M., Hyman, S.E. and Rosen, B.R. (1996) Response and habituation of the human amygdala during visual processing of facial expression, *Neuron*, 17: 875–87.

Sun, H.-J., Campos, J.L., Chan, G.S.W., Zhang, D.-H. and Lee, A.J. (2003) Multi-sensory integration in self-motion, *Journal of Vision*, 3(9): 36a. http://journalofvision.org/3/9/36 (accessed 31 May 2007).

Swanson, L.W. (2000) Cerebral hemisphere regulation of motivated behaviour, *Brain Research*, 886(1): 113–64.

Sydsjo, G., Wadsby, M. and Goran Svedin, C. (2001) Psychosocial risk mothers: early mother–child interaction and behavioural disturbances in children at 8 years of age, *Journal of Reproductive and Infant Psychology*, 19: 135–45.

Thatcher, R.W. (1994) Cyclic cortical reorganizations: origins of human cognitive development, in G. Dawson and K.W. Fischer (eds) *Human Behaviour and the Developing Brain*. New York: Guilford Press.

Thompson, P.M., Giedd, J.N., Woods, R.P., et al. (2000) Growth patterns in the developing brain detected by using continuum mechanical tensor maps, *Nature*, 4: 190–2.

Tomasello, M. (2001) *The Cultural Origins of Human Cognition*. Cambridge, MA: Harvard University Press.

Townsend, J. and Courchesne, E. (1994) Parietal damage and narrow 'spotlight' spatial attention, *Journal of Cognitive Neuroscience*, 6: 220–32.

Tremblay, H., Brun, P. and Nadel, P. (2005) Emotion sharing and emotion knowledge, in J. Nadel and D. Muir (eds) *Emotional Development*. Oxford: Oxford University Press.

Trevarthen, C. (1993) The self born in intersubjectivity: the psychology of an infant communicating, in U. Neisser (ed.) *The Perceived Self: Ecological and Interpersonal Sources of Self-Knowledge*. New York: Cambridge University Press.

Trevarthen, C. (1999) Musicality and the intrinsic motive pulse: evidence from human psychobiology and infant communication, *Musicae Scientiae*, special issue 1999–2000: 155–215.

Trevarthen, C. (2001) Intrinsic motives for companionship in understanding; their origin, development and significance for infant mental health, *Journal of Infant Mental Health*, 22(1–2): 95–131.

Trevarthen, C. (2005) Action and emotion in development of cultural intelligence: why infants have feelings like ours, in J. Nadel and D. Muir (eds) *Emotional Development*. Oxford: Oxford University Press.

Trevarthen, C., Aitken, K., Papoudi, D. and Robarts, J. (1999) *Children with Autism*. London: Jessica Kingsley.

Tronick, E., Als, H., Adamson, L., et al. (1978) The infant's response to entrapment between contradictory messages in face to face interaction, *Journal of the American Academy of Psychiatry*, 1: 1–13.

Umita, M.A., Kohler, E., Gallese, V., et al. (2001) I know what you are doing: a neurophysiological study, *Neuron*, 31: 155–65.

Uttal, D.H. (1996) Angles and distances: children's and adults' reconstructions and scaling of spatial configurations, *Child Development*, 67: 2763–79.

Valentin, D. and Abdi, H. (2003) Early face recognition: what can we learn from a myopic baby neural network? in O. Pascalis and A. Slater (eds) *The Development of Face Processing in Infancy and Early Childhood*. New York: Nova Science.

Valenza, E., Simion, F. and Umilta, C. (1994) Inhibition of return in newborns, *Infant Behaviour and Development*, 17: 293–302.

Vinden, P.G. and Astington, J.W. (2002) Culture and understanding other minds, in S. Baron-Cohen, H. Tager-Flusberg and D.J. Cohen (eds) *Understanding Other Minds*, 2nd edn., Oxford: Oxford University Press.

Vuilleumier, P., Armony, J., Driver J. and Dolan, R.J. (2001) Effects of attention and emotion on face processing in the human brain – an event-related MRI study, *Neuron*, 30(3): 829–41.

Vygotsky, L.S. (1962) *Thought and Language*. Cambridge, MA: MIT Press.

Vygotsky, L.S. (1981) The development of higher forms of attention in childhood, in J.V. Wertsch (ed.) *The Concept of Activity in Soviet Psychology*. Armonk, NY: M.E. Sharpe.

Walterfang, M. and Velakoulis, D. (2005) Cortical release signs in psychiatry, *Australian and New Zealand Journal of Psychiatry*, 39(5); 317–27.

Watts, A. (1997) *Zen and the Beat Way*. Audio cassette book.

Wellman, H.M. (2002) Understanding the psychological world: developing a theory of mind, in U. Goswami (ed.) *Handbook of Child Cognitive Development*. Oxford: Blackwell.

Whalen, P.J., Bush, G., McNally, R.J., et al.(1998) The emotional counting stroop paradigm: a functional magnetic resonance imaging probe of the anterior cingulate affective division, *Biological Psychiatry*, 44: 1219–28.

Whitehead, M. (2001) *Supporting Language and Literacy Development in the Early Years*. Buckingham: Open University Press.

Whiten, A. (2002) The imitator's representation of the imitated: ape and child, in F. De Waal (ed.) *The Ape and the Sushi Master*. London: Penguin.

Williams, J.H.G., Whiten, A., Suddendorf, T. and Perrett, D.I. (2001) Imitation, mirror neurons and autism, *Neuroscience and Biobehavioural Reviews*, 25: 287–95.

Winston, J.S., Strange, B.A., O'Doherty, J. and Dolan, R.J. (2002) Automatic and intentional brain responses during evaluation of trustworthiness of face, *Nature Neuroscience*, 5(3): 277–283.

Wolford, G., Miller, M.B. and Gazzaniga, M. (2000) The left hemisphere's role in hypothesis formation, *Journal of Neuroscience*, 20: RC64 (1–4). www.jneurosci.org.

Wolpert, D.M., Ghahramani, Z. and Randall Flanagan, J. (2001) Perspectives and problems in motor learning, *Trends in Cognitive Sciences*, 5(11): 487–93.

Wood, J.N. and Grafman, J. (2003) Human prefrontal cortex processing and representational perspectives, *Nature Reviews Neuroscience*, 4(2): 139–47.

Worthington, E.L, O'Connor, L.E., Berry, J.W., et al. (2005) Compassion and forgiveness, in P. Gilbert (ed.) *Compassion*. London: Routledge.

Wright, C.L., Martis, B., Shin, L.M., Fischer, H. and Rauch, S.L. (2002) Enhanced amygdala responses to emotional versus neutral schematic facial expressions, *NeuroReport*, 13: 785–90.

Yamada, H., Sadato, N., Konishi, Y., et al. (2000) A milestone for normal development of the infantile brain detected by functional MRI, *Neurology*, 55: 218–23.

Yin, R.K. (1969) Looking at upside-down faces, *Journal of Experimental Psychology*, 81(1): 141–5.

Zelazo, P.D., Mueller, U., Frye, D. and Marcovitch, S. (2003) The development of executive function in early childhood, *Monographs of the Society for Research in Child Development*, 68(3), serial no. 274.

Zimmer, C. (2003) How the mind reads other minds, *Science*, 300: 1079–80. www.sciencemag.org.

Index

FROM BIRTH TO ONE
THE YEAR OF OPPORTUNITY

Maria Robinson

The first year of life is the year of opportunity. It is when the foundations for our emotional and social well being together with our motivation and ability to learn begin to be laid down by an ongoing interplay of physical, neurological and psychological processes.

Maria Robinson draws upon up to date research to illuminate this process and highlights the importance of understanding the meaning and influence of adult interactions, reactions and behaviour towards their child and the child's impact on the adult. She indicates how the outcomes of early experience can influence the direction of future development so providing insight into the potential reasons for children's behavioural responses.

The powerful nature of working with babies and young children is addressed in a separate section which encourages practitioners to reflect on how personal attitudes, beliefs and values can influence professional practice.

This fascinating book is a valuable resource for all early years practitioners including teachers, social workers and health visitors who wish to understand behaviour within a context of early developmental processes.

Contents
Introduction – **Part one: Development in the first year** *– Making connections: a perspective on development – Setting the scene: parents and parenting – Starting out: from birth to three months – From smiling to waving: 3 months–7 months – Peek a boo and where are you?: 7 months–12 months – Unhappy babies –* **Part two: Reflections on professional practice and personal emotions** *– The personal in the professional – When dreams go awry – The year of opportunity – References – Index.*

208pp   0 335 20895 9 (Paperback)   0 335 20896 7 (Hardback)

YOUNG CHILDREN'S HEALTH AND WELL-BEING

Angela Underdown

The true wealth of a nation can be measured by the health of its youngest citizens and in the twenty-first century, children's health and well-being is largely determined by social, environmental and economic influences.

This book explores how factors such as parent-child relationships, family networks and social support, housing, poverty and the safety of the environment impact on children's early experiences and have consequences for their later health and well-being.

Topics include:

- Promoting infant mental health
- Family transitions
- Poverty, relative poverty and health inequalities
- Growth and nutrition
- Young children under stress
- Child public health
- Young children's involvement in health
- Research with young children and families

Underpinned by the United Nations Convention on the Rights of the Child and an ecological systems framework, this book takes difference and diversity into account to celebrate the rights of every individual child.

Young Children's Health and Well-Being is a comprehensive health text for students of early childhood. It is also important reading for student teachers, community practitioner nurses, social work students and others who work with young children and their families.

Contents: *Foreword – Acknowledgements – A note on the text – Young children's health and well-being in context – The transition to parenthood – Foundations for emotional and social well-being – Health inequalities in early childhood – Growth and nutrition – The impact of family change on children's health and well-being – Child public health – Children under stress – Children's involvement in health – Listening to young children – Glossary – References – Index.*

2006   216pp
978–0–335–21906-3 (Paperback)   978–0–335–21907–0 (Hardback)